SINGING AND
TEACHING SINGING

A Holistic Approach to Classical Voice

Second Edition

SINGING AND TEACHING SINGING

A Holistic Approach to Classical Voice

Second Edition

JANICE L. CHAPMAN, OAM, FGS

PLURAL
PUBLISHING
INC.

SAN DIEGO
OXFORD
BRISBANE

PLURAL PUBLISHING
INC.

5521 Ruffin Road
San Diego, CA 92123

e-mail: info@pluralpublishing.com
Web site: http://www.pluralpublishing.com

49 Bath Street
Abingdon, Oxfordshire OX14 1EA
United Kingdom

FSC
www.fsc.org
MIX
Paper from
responsible sources
FSC® C011935

Copyright © by Plural Publishing, Inc. 2012

Typeset in 11/13 Garamond by Flanagan's Publishing Services, Inc.
Printed in the United States of America by McNaughton and Gunn.

For permission to use material from this text, contact us by
Telephone: (866) 758-7251
Fax: (888) 758-7255
e-mail: permissions@pluralpublishing.com

Cover design for this second edition by Sam Grimmer.

*Every attempt has been made to contact the copyright holders for material
originally printed in another source. If any have been inadvertently over-
looked, the publishers will gladly make the necessary arrangements at the
first opportunity.*

Library of Congress Cataloging-in-Publication Data

Chapman, Janice L.
  Singing and teaching singing : a holistic approach to classical voice / Janice L.
Chapman. — 2nd ed.
      p. cm.
  Includes bibliographical references and index.
  ISBN-13: 978-1-59756-426-7 (alk. paper)
  ISBN-10: 1-59756-426-5 (alk. paper)
  1. Singing—Instruction and study. I. Title.
  MT820.C49 2010
  783—dc22
                                    2010044450

CONTENTS

FOREWORD TO THE FIRST EDITION

$\mathcal{J}$anice Chapman is not only a highly successful singing teacher, but more importantly an international role model for interdisciplinary open mindedness in vocal pedagogy. Throughout her career, she has combined a solid knowledge of traditional voice teaching with an active commitment to deepen her understanding of the voice. Over the last few decades, as physicians, scientists, speech-language pathologists, singing teachers, and acting teachers have collaborated in the evaluation of voice medicine and voice science as new specialties, our goal has always been to improve the care and training of our patients and students. Just as medicine has developed by integrating understanding and concepts from the voice studio, voice pedagogy has advanced by incorporating medical facts, scientific methodologies, and analytical rigor into traditional studio approaches. This book offers the insights of one experienced and successful teacher of singing and teacher of teachers. It is a fine example of progression from 18th century teaching tradition to pedagogical enlightenment of the 21st century. This process is defined by intellectual curiosity and interdisciplinary insights, superimposed on classical excellence and a willingness to change; and it represents the best of the present state of voice education and the hope of the future for teaching and learning.

Robert T. Sataloff, MD, DMA
Chairman, Board of Directors,
The Voice Foundation

PREFACE TO THE SECOND EDITION

The second edition of *Singing and Teaching Singing: A Holistic Approach to Classical Voice* gives me an opportunity to correct some misunderstandings about the application of the Accent Method to classical singing, and to refine and correct some things from the first edition which have come to light since publication.

Ron Morris and I have attempted to clarify the use of the Accent Method of breathing as a highly effective remedial and training technique appropriate for all singers and students. This valuable resource (in its gross form as a Speech and Language Therapy tool, where the belly wall moves athletically toward the spine on phonation, and out again on inhalation) has proved highly effective with singers, but the performer's body when trained, and functioning efficiently should not show gross belly wall activity. During remedial work and training, the vigorous movement of the tummy is used initially to ensure that the correct muscles are engaged in the correct order for supported airflow. When coordinated with the muscles used for supporting the classical voice, the movement of the belly wall both in and out is subtle and discreet. However, palpation may be needed to ensure that the muscle tone of the rectus abdominis is soft and not braced or rigid in singing. Research currently is underway to validate anecdotal evidence gathered so far.

I have included a description of the "ultimate tongue release" exercise, and also added in the "puffy cheeks" exercise, which I hope readers will enjoy and find useful. John Rubin has updated his chapter (Chapter 11) with news of some new research underway about the use of the transverse abdominis muscles in vocal support strategies. Marilyn McCarthy refined and updated Chapters 9 and 10.

Janice Chapman

ACKNOWLEDGMENTS

Grateful thanks to Ron Morris who inspired, propelled, and assisted the writing of this book and contributed to a number of chapters; my valued co-authors, Pamela Davis, Adrian Fourcin, Marilyn McCarthy, and John Rubin for their generosity and expertise; my chief illustrator Richard Webber for his wonderful anatomical drawings and cartoonist Simon Pearsall whose work speaks for itself; production assistance on the whole manuscript from Malte Ebach, Sam Grimmer, and Tony Gray; editorial expertise and encouragement from Noel McPherson, Angie Singh, Sandy Doyle, Lauren Duffy, and the team at Plural; general encouragement, reading and commenting by John Chapman, Gordon Stewart, Linnhe Robertson, Kristine Carroll-Porcyznski, Linda Hutchison, Ingrid Rugheimer, and Stephanie Martin; Ingrid and the late Gunnar Rugheimer for their long-term fostering of multidisciplinary voice work in the United Kingdom; to Colin McGee, Jacob Lieberman, and Meribeth Bunch Dayme for personal and professional input prior to writing; my students who took part in the surveys for Chapters 9 and 10; and to all my clients from whom I continue to learn.

CONTRIBUTING AUTHORS

PAMELA DAVIS, LACST, PhD
Kangaroo Valley, NSW, Australia
Chapter 12

ADRIAN FOURCIN, PhD
Emeritus Professor of Experimental Phonetics
University College London
Chapter 13

MARILYN McCARTHY, MEd (HRD); Grad Dip. Group Work., Dip T.
Chapters 9 and 10 and Appendix 2

RON MORRIS, BSpThy (Hons); MMusStud (Voice), MSPAA, MASA (CC)
Brisbane Speech and Hearing Clinic
Brisbane, Australia
Queensland Conservatorium of Music
Griffith University, Australia
Chapters 4, 5, 6, and 7

JOHN S. RUBIN, MD, FACS, FRCS
Consultant Otolaryngologist and Lead Clinician in Voice
Royal National Throat, Nose and Ear Hospital, London

Honorary Senior Lecturer, Institute of Laryngology and Otology,
University College London

Honorary Consultant Otolaryngologist
National Hospital for Neurology & Neurosurgery
London
Chapter 11

INTRODUCTION

$\mathcal{R}$ecently, while visiting Australia on a research project for Opera Australia and the University of Sydney, I met up with some of the singing teachers who had studied with me in the United Kingdom and in Australia in past years, some in private tuition, and some during workshops and training courses. A number of these teachers were achieving considerable success with their pupils and took the trouble to tell me that I was, in fact, the "vocal grandmother" of their students. As a real grandmother myself, I was delighted with the concept, in spite of feeling a bit ancient. This caucus of singing teachers were also asking me to write down my pedagogy—something I had sworn never to do. ("Yet another book on teaching singing!") But after much soul-searching I had to admit that, if only for them, it was important to explain, clarify, and in many ways, reiterate what I had been doing and learning in the studio for more than 25 years. I also had to acknowledge that my long experience in the introduction and development of the multidisciplinary approach to voice in the United Kingdom had given me a different perspective from that of many of my singing teacher colleagues. Also, I was often being asked to write by other members of the vocal professions such as speech and language therapists and physicians.

The Australian speech and language therapist Ron Morris, who is a singer, had studied with me in London for a short period. He also undertook Accent Method training, and was keen to return regularly to the United Kingdom for further tuition. I found out later that he had agreed to be "sent" by other Australian teachers to help me get started. We began an exploratory journey of working together to get the information out of my head and onto paper. We were able to meet for short dedicated periods of time, spread over about three years, and his enthusiasm, optimism, patience, and fortitude has made it possible for me, a reluctant writer, to begin this difficult and confronting task.

The way singing has been taught in past centuries has been passed down by word of mouth and in writings of the time. Much study has gone into the analysis of those writings in relation to what we now call Western Classical singing via the "bel canto" school of the Italians of the 16th, 17th, and 18th centuries, culminating in the work of Manuel Garcia whose early research and development of the mirror laryngoscope in the mid-19th century has paved the way for modern understanding of the vocal arts.

This empirical school of teaching voice has been highly successful, but it also has probably been relatively wasteful too. It has worked well for the few and badly for the many and I believe this is still true today. Who are "these few"? Perhaps they are those whose natural gifts are brought to the fore and developed by excellent teaching, or perhaps they are the highly gifted, intuitively talented ones who sing well regardless of the teaching they may be getting. These few represent only the very top of the vocal pyramid. But what about all those singers who make up its body? What about those of lesser natural talent who have much to offer as performers, or those who just want to be able to sing decently and pleasurably for a hobby, or those who love the voice as a musical instrument and wish to sing and to teach well? Even more importantly, what about those whose talents and gifts have been blocked or damaged? Have they not a right to a very good singing tuition?

Until the time of Manuel Garcia, the voice could not be "viewed" in situ and working. Not only was it invisible, but there are no nerve ends in the vocal folds themselves to give proprioceptive feedback. This has meant that vocal health at the level of the vibratory mechanism could only be monitored in other ways. Often the health of the actual vocal folds is only reflected in:

- The sounds the singer is making,
- The range they are able to comfortably sustain,
- The lack of pain or discomfort in the suspensory muscles that lie in the neck, and
- The ease with which they sing.

One of my American colleagues at a recent Symposium put it well: "If you can sing higher, lower, louder, softer, and longer then you probably have it right."

Until very recently, vocal instruction was based on a limited understanding of how the voice worked, conveyed through imagery which could be misleading, with the teacher often demonstrating and the student copying to the best of his or her ability. It was the way I was taught from the 1950s through to the 1980s, and the way I initially worked with my students when I began teaching in the mid-1970s. One of the main problems with this system, I believe, is with the singer's own aural perception of his or her sound. The conservatorium-type teaching model from the early days of classical tuition until the 19th century involved the student singer having daily tuition and not being permitted to practice alone. In this model, the power lay with the master teacher and not with the student. In many ways, until very recently, we have maintained this style of teaching singing but have lost one of its most important concepts. Namely, that the teacher supervises all practice. I think that this method in effect involved the training of the singer's ear to recog-

"A little louder please—Yes, your vibrato is healthy!" Copyright Simon Pearsall, 2005.

nize and accept those sounds that the teacher preferred rather than the ones that the singers themselves would find aurally acceptable. It also was a time for building trust between the teacher and the student, and ensuring a solid technique based on the structured vocalize systems of the period. Social and economic factors have long since precluded this teaching model. There also have been great changes in general educational thinking, where it is now expected that students take more responsibility for their own learning. The master teacher/apprentice model has had to be replaced with something akin to a weekly (one hour) session with the teacher, followed by individual unsupervised practice on a daily basis. Students do not have the opportunity and time to develop an understanding and acceptance of their own aural mismatch (see Chapter 13, Hearing and Singing). This leads to a number of common faults in singing that might be laid at the door of current methods.

The aural mismatch problems in part can be addressed by the use of high quality recording of lessons and practice. Provided the teacher is working correctly, students can build their own memory bank of sensations allied to their sounds rather than relying on their own ears during the actual singing. They then can take home the recording of their session and begin to take responsibility for this part of their vocal development. Regular lessons are essential, however, as nothing remains static. Goalposts shift regularly but not always predictably.

Teachers in the Garcian style also had control of the development of a basic vocal technique, using highly structured exercises and vocalize. I think that this may well be the component missing from a great many vocal studios today. Student singers, especially those within the tertiary/conservatoire system of training, are confronted with the demands of a college curriculum: classes, exams, scheduling, and pressure to learn masses of repertoire. At undergraduate level, daily practice of vocalize can be very valuable, and although I do employ them occasionally, especially for singers whose voice/mind/body synchronization is not well developed, over time I have evolved a different way of working, tailored to suit my students' needs and life styles. This pedagogy is the main subject of the book.

I firmly believe that building a sound basic vocal technique should be utmost in the singing teacher's mind, especially when dealing with young adult singers. The current tertiary system (music college, university, conservatoire) can work against this unless the teacher is particularly vigilant and actively prioritizes vocal development, helping students to **build their instrument while simultaneously learning to play it**.

While valuing the methods of the past, and respecting their validity, I have instinctively and deliberately adopted a more interventionist approach. For example, breathing and support, which would have developed over years, using the supervised vocalise and exercises is, in fact, fast tracked (see Chapter 4, Breathing and Support). Just as Garcia did, I firmly believe that the singer's body is as much his or her instrument as the larynx and pharynx, but we do not have the luxury of training only a few from the top of the pyramid for many hours a week each. We have to teach many more students and have had to find a methodology that can successfully be applied to them all. The myths and the imagery that were a central teaching technique for the old empirical way demand respect, but need translation and validation for current times and for the future.

The teaching of singing has changed significantly in the past 20 years as information from science, medicine, therapy, and other disciplines enables us to develop another methodology that can successfully teach what the old masters taught over many years to "the few." My own personal multidisciplinary education has been a central plank in my development as a teacher and in planning this book. I felt privileged to be able to invite authors from other disciplines in the voice world to contribute chapters. Ron Morris (speech and language therapist/audiologist, singer, and Accent Method teacher) has contributed greatly to the whole book, but in particular to the chapters on Breathing and Support (Chapter 4) and Articulation (Chapter 7). John Rubin (Consultant Otolaryngologist/ENT Surgeon and renowned Physician to the singing profession) has written Chapter 11, Vocal and Respiratory Anatomy and Physiology. Pamela Davis (Neuroscientist/speech and language therapist) contributed

Chapter 12, Voice and the Brain, making important connections between the emotional motor system and voice, and Adrian Fourcin (Emeritus Professor of Speech Sciences, University College, London) writes about Hearing and Singing (Chapter 13), which sheds much needed light on this topic. The teaching and learning partnership is the subject of Chapters 9 and 10 by the educational consultant/singer, Marilyn McCarthy. In these two chapters, The Singer's Journey: A Case Study and The H-Factor: Working Holistically Within the Teaching and Learning Partnership, Marilyn has introduced a fresh way of evaluating and describing these complex activities.

The language of the singing profession, in the past, has been creatively evolving but not always based on any physiological reality. Words to describe sound and its production have been passed on like a Chinese whisper: understood/misunderstood, passed on further, written down, reinterpreted, understood/misunderstood, and so on. With the scientific, anatomic, and multidisciplinary knowledge now at our disposal, I hope that the singing/teaching profession can agree to explore and use more common language so that our multidisciplinary colleagues can interact with us better in the future. There is still a great deal of confusion around singing and its science coming from different disciplines. The art of singing involves far more than just the craft, and this is an area where quantitative research and science may be limited. We need both accurate science and information as well as a holisitic appreciation of the art of singing and its practitioners.

Just as my teaching has evolved and changed continually over many years based on what I have been able to learn, borrow, appropriate, or rediscover, I also would expect other teachers to take, use, and modify creatively any ideas presented to them. This book aims to lay down the principles of my methodology as it stands at this point in time.

My own story (text in italics) is an integral part of the journey to my current philosophy and methodology, and is woven into the text from time to time. We also are making use of case studies (text in shaded boxes), throughout the book (disguised for the protection of identity, and with permission).

Singing is about making connections—the whole person and the voice, the singer and the audience, the audience and the singer, the singer and his or her musical colleagues, the singing world to the multidisciplinary voice world and vice versa, and, in a wider sense, singing has the capacity to join people and groups of people under the umbrella of shared musical and emotional experience. It's special indeed!

To my husband John,
sons Andy and Rod,
and singers everywhere.

Chapter 1

PEDAGOGICAL PHILOSOPHY

Everyone suddenly burst out singing;
And I was filled with such delight
As prisoned birds must find in freedom,
Winging wildly across the white
Orchards and dark-green fields; on-on-and out of sight.

Everyone's voice was suddenly lifted;
And beauty came like the setting sun:
My heart was shaken with tears; and horror
Drifted away . . . O, but Everyone
Was a bird; and the song was wordless; the singing
will never be done.

(Siegfried Sassoon "Everyone Sang," *Picture Show*, 1919)

ABOUT SINGING

What is singing? Simply put, it is emotional musical vocalization with or without text. At best, singing comes from feelings that communicate to other people's feelings. It has many forms and styles throughout the different cultures of the world.

People sing spontaneously as part of a group, for example, at football matches, in religious meetings, and in pubs. Singing is and should be a natural part of everyday life. It is an emotional expression of feelings that has the power to alter the mood of both the singer and the listener. Everyone is in essence a singer but in modern society we suffer from overcrowding, noise pollution, and emotional constipation. Instead of enjoying our own sounds, we are filling our ears with recorded music to try and blot out the surroundings. Until 50 years ago, people were still

1

singing in the workplace, the rhythmic impetus of the singing assisting the repetitive labor.

Babies sing before they speak. Their vocal mechanism is well developed and active in the womb and ready for making sound immediately after birth. The infant's early vocalization demanding food or attention soon is extended into a range of sounds like cooing and babbling and eventually copying the intonation patterns of the mother and immediate family. These vocal patterns are the precursor of singing, and some babies can sing recognizable tune fragments at a very early age (long before the development of language).

Singing is "primal," part of the fundamental heritage of the animal kingdom. Birds, primates, and sea mammals sing. Charles Darwin suggested that vocal communication evolved in humans from the need to attract a mate (see Chapter 12). Throughout the history of mankind, singing has been an integral part of all cultures. More recently, however, in western cultures it has sometimes become an elitist activity—for the "talented" rather than for the community. The tragic loss of much of the school-based singing during the past three decades has served to distance children from this vocal heritage.

I was in a supermarket the other day and a little boy of about three sang nonstop for the duration of his mother's shopping expedition. He went through his entire repertoire of nursery rhymes then extemporized further into a sort of vocal rhapsody. I was aware of his lovely little voice coming from different parts of the shop and I believe that this changed the atmosphere in the whole building for the duration of his concert. People seemed to be smiling more.

Many education systems have had to cut or downgrade music and singing from their curricula. Teacher training includes little or no singing and sometimes produces teachers who are too self-conscious to sing—even with children. The joy of making vocal sound for its own sake is in danger of becoming lost. We are *walking musical instruments* and singing is part of our birthright.

This book is about voice as used in a very strange and wonderful way, for the expression of classical music and opera, a field in which I have been involved for nearly all my life as a performer and for the past 30 years as a teacher and researcher.

PHILOSOPHY OF TEACHING

All good teaching has a philosophy that underpins its practice. This may be either conscious and systematic or unconscious and intuitive. Many teachers use an unconscious philosophy initially but over time and with experience this develops into a conscious and systematic method of working. This method is not static but ever developing and refining, so teachers themselves need to be ongoing learners.

After more than 30 years of teaching, I am able to share my current philosophy. My approach can be described under three main headings:

- Holistic
- Physiological
- Incremental

Because of the way in which this model developed over time and my experiences with different types of voice users, the model has proved appropriate for remedial work, the developing singer, and the ongoing development and maintenance of the technically able professional singer.

1. HOLISTIC

The *American and Heritage Dictionary* defines "holistic" as "emphasizing the importance of the whole and the interdependence of its parts." Alt. "emphasizing the organic or functional relation between parts and the whole."

I use the term holistic to mean that the act of singing involves the whole person (i.e., body, mind, spirit, emotion, and voice). Holistic singing has the potential to become great singing.

Regardless of the cultural or musical style, great singing reaches out to the audience on many levels. In some cultures, singing can even take the singers and listeners into "out of body" or trance-like states.

Holistic singing can be achieved when the performer is able to attain a state of unself-conscious focus. A number of complex factors can contribute to this "zone" but many performers have found it by accident. In this "zone," performers and listeners have a reciprocal empathy, wonderful moments in the concert hall, village hall, opera house, church, club, or indeed anywhere. Time stands still, critical faculties are suspended, and the experience imprints on the memory of those lucky enough to be there. Singers and audience are drawn into a web of shared concentration that is greater than any of its individual parts.

Early in my professional life, I managed to lose my ability to sing in this way, and I do believe that a deep yearning to reawaken this experience drove me to try and discover its nature. This has directed my journey for the past 30 years, a journey which I now recognize as being lifelong.

When very young, a connection between the audience and me seemed to exist, where I became a conduit for the music and drama to flow through me, the instrument, out into the environment. This occurred without much intellectual awareness, vocal technique, musical sophistication, or advanced training. I intuited that singing had to be innate, primitive, imaginative, or emotional in essence. In the 1980s, I was thinking around this subject and, while attending a music education conference with my husband in Innsbruck, heard a choir from Kenya. They sang and moved, and, although the music itself was unmemorable, the experience of seeing and hearing them became seminal. What came to me at that time was that the communication was primal and reached the audience of tired and grumpy music educators in a way that transcended all other factors. The singing was holistic, natural, earthed, emotionally connected, and intensely moving. The effect in the hall was riveting—a sort of umbrella of mass concentration and emotional response. This experience became pivotal in the direction my future vocal journey took.

At the present, I like to describe it in this way. Singing can be holistic and stem from a well-spring of complex interactions between body, mind, spirit, and imagination while in essence being deceptively simple. A singer is a walking musical instrument with all the complexities that implies.

I wrote a paper entitled "Primal Singing—Making Connections" (Chapman, 1990) where I argued that the singing voice emanates from a connection with the need to survive. This sound is called primal and cannot be achieved without the natural interaction of body, mind, and spirit. Oren Brown (1988) in *Discover Your Voice* said:

> When I hear great singing, it is as though I were listening to a marvelous animal. I believe this is why audiences are so deeply moved by great singing. At a subconscious level, empathy takes place when a singer shares his or her primal sound. (p. 4)

My Story

My own primal sound connections were strong enough to see me through my early years of development as a singer. I loved to sing, won competitions, and sang in the public arena with great pride and gusto most of the time. This was rather like a "child prodigy" who can do anything until they hit puberty and self-consciousness kicks in. For me, this self-doubt occurred and appeared to be provoked by my early years in the opera profession in the United Kingdom. I was in the fast track at the age of 26 (singing Donna Anna for Scottish Opera and The Countess for Sadlers' Wells Opera), naively Australian and psychologically out of my depth. It seemed that suddenly, instead of praise and encouragement from the critics, managements, audiences, and my colleagues, I began to get negative criticism. My confidence trickled away along with my intuitive vocal technique despite continuing to have regular singing lessons with an eminent teacher. With hindsight, I needed a much slower career path than the one I was on and a better psychological basis for my singing. I also would have bene-fited from a different style of vocal tuition, one that was probably not available at that time. I will spare readers the sordid details, but my singing "heaven" turned to singing "hell." The first thing to collapse was my breathing and support, which until that time had been adequate even though I did not know how it all worked. From this followed all sorts of vocal manifestations, including some psychosomatic ones like having a sore throat three days before every performance. This partic-ular problem was cured after a conversation that went something like this: Janice: "Oh God! I'm getting a sore throat and I've got a show in three days time." John (my husband): "Yes dear, you always get a sore throat three days before a show!"

After the first two years of professional life at the age of 28, my husband and I decided to start a family. I was thrilled to find myself pregnant and given a chance to escape temporarily from the pressures of the life I was leading into something more "normal." I found moth-erhood enormously fulfilling and John and I had our second child a couple of years later. I sang professionally throughout this period, including my second pregnancy at which time my body rediscovered its "support." The soprano solos in the "Verdi Requiem" while eight months pregnant was the clincher I think.

My career continued to lurch along for some years. Some of my work was good and some must have been fairly bad. I was in a state of confusion about my singing and in retrospect think that I may have been somewhat depressed. However, being a wife and the mother of two small boys meant that I had many other aspects of my life to enjoy while continuing to sing professionally and have singing les-sons and vocal repertoire coaching.

Eventually I had to face my problems and take responsibility for my own vocal condition. This moment in time is imprinted on my memory. I had taken on a few students and discovered that I was going to enjoy teaching. Being responsible for other people's vocal wel-fare meant that I had to deal with the vocal mysteries that I had not sorted out for myself. Once I started this dual process of teaching oth-ers to sing and singing myself, I had to ask myself the question: "Why on earth not apply myself properly to my own vocal welfare?" I had always hoped someone else would sort me out. The acceptance that I could and indeed must do it myself was the turning point. From the moment of this acceptance of "taking responsibility," doors to knowl-edge seemed to open miraculously!

As a wounded singer, I was intuitively drawn toward trying to help singers who were experiencing vocal difficulties. At the time I commenced teaching, there was an explosion in the information available from voice science and medicine, triggered in the main by the development of the fiberoptic endoscope and stroboscopic light source, which allowed the vocal tract and vocal folds to be viewed as though in real time. Through my involvement with the organization of the early multidisciplinary work in the United Kingdom, I was exposed to a broad range of information which made me aware that my teaching was being subtly influenced by my increasing ability to visualize the vocal machinery. This visualization became closely linked with auditory perception and tied into my own vocalization.

In the mid-1990s, I was fortunate enough to take part, both as a subject and as an investigator, in a research project on respiration in singing at the National Voice Centre, The University of Sydney entitled "Patterns of Breath Support in Projection of the Singing Voice" (Thorpe et al., 2000). This experience enhanced my ability to visualize the physiological functions of breathing and support that were affecting the singing voice and influenced both my singing and teaching. I learned a great deal including the fact that I really did not know very much, which paved the way for further learning.

I undertook an excellent vocal anatomy course run by Meribeth Bunch, and also had access to some anatomy wet-lab study days in Sydney and Melbourne. The handling of real body parts was enormously educative for me particularly in respect to weight, mass, and density.

Underpinning my work in the studio, now with singers of all levels, was a visualization of the way in which the machinery works in the torso and the organs of phonation, articulation, and resonance.

To illustrate this, it is valuable to look at a typical singer in crisis. When a singer's voice is not functioning well the person is often unhappy as a result. This state can spiral into a vocal decline. A dysfunctional voice leads to stress, which leads to extra effort especially in an inappropriate part of the vocal mechanism, which leads to less efficient vocalization, which leads to more dysfunction and more unhappiness— a vicious spiral that can continue to repeat itself and undermine the singer totally.

Barry: A Case Study

A 31-year-old professional baritone who had been singing principal roles with major companies for six years attended for a consultation. He had an exceptionally good voice, was a fine musician, had an engaging personality, and was a highly motivated achiever. After studying at one of the country's major music institutions, he was taken on by a big agency and offered engagements both in opera and concert repertoire at a very high level even though he was relatively inexperienced. The fact that he was very talented and a fine musician and linguist meant that he coped. After about five years, things started to go wrong. He was being criticized by conductors and repetiteurs, and as often can happen in these circumstances, the criticism was given in front of other singers and musicians. He found this very difficult to handle. His singing deteriorated and his confidence drained away. His agency sacked him suddenly, without any preparation or care—just told him that he was not performing up to standard and that he should seek another management.

Another agent who had seen his potential agreed to take him onto his books and he brought him to my studio for a consultation. I had seen him in an operatic role a couple of years earlier and had been impressed with his talent at that time, which was a good thing, because what presented when he sang to me was not recognizable. The voice production was wild, a mass of problems including a large unruly wobble and intonation variance. Not surprisingly, he was a desperately unhappy and demoralized person.

When I checked him over, I discovered that his breathing, posture, and in particular, support of his voice were at the root of the problem. We worked immediately in a technical manner to correct this. He had no engagements in the next few months, which gave us time to work technically. The training he had received, in my opinion, had made it almost inevitable that he would have come to grief at some stage. He had never been given any real insight into how to integrate his body under this wonderful big voice, and he himself admitted that he never knew what was going to come out of his mouth at any given time.

His vocal rehabilitation improved after about 18 months, but psychological and career damage can take longer to redress. It can be more like three to four years before a singer regains the position on the career ladder from which he or she has tumbled. Managements for whom he had worked before and during his crisis were understandably reluctant to take him back on until his vocal credibility was fully reestablished, and during that time he had to endure "confidence knocks" and live with them.

In my teaching, an early and very insistent observation was that postural alignment, breathing, and support were invariably inadequate, reversed, mysterious, or misunderstood. Many singers had no concept of how their postural alignment, support, or breath could affect their voice.

My work to that point on primal sound had given me insights into the underlying physiology of the breathing and support mechanism. When we make a primal sound, we do not take in a conscious breath but make an automatic and reflexive response in the torso (see Chapter 12, Voice and the Brain). I noticed that any form of overbreathing, for example, instructions from the teacher or coach to flare the ribs and hold, pull the abdomen in on inhalation, raise the upper chest wall in a militaristic posture, expand the waistband on inhalation, or to hold the ribs with the intercostal muscles, made it almost impossible to access primal sound. A reflexive diaphragmatic inhalation will invite air into the lowest part of the lungs, where they are largest, without causing inappropriate tension in the upper torso. Primal sound itself engages muscles in the abdominal girdle, which is defined in medical literature as being the muscles of active or forced expiration. If these muscles have been employed at the point of inhalation, the body can be in a state of confusion and tension. This topic is explored in detail in Chapter 4.

The discovery of this seemingly simple fact led me to develop my idea that teaching could be based in physiological reality rather than in the traditional empirical model of "teach how you were taught."

This brings us to the second aspect of my approach, namely, the understanding and use of the complex anatomy and physiology of the torso, larynx, and vocal tract when teaching.

2. PHYSIOLOGICAL

The *Oxford Pocket Dictionary* defines "physiological" as pertaining to "the science of functions and phenomena of living organisms and their parts."

I use physiological to mean teaching that is based on the laws of anatomy, muscular function, and the effects of muscular interactions. Physiological can also mean scientific, based in fact rather than myth.

Experience with the singer in crisis made it evident to me that technical interventions were a powerful tool to stop the descent of the negative spiral and reverse it. The psychological state of the singer in crisis cannot be ignored but intervention at a technical level leading to vocal improvement often assists the singer's sense of well-being as a starting point. If deep psychological issues are at the root of the crisis, they need to be addressed by appropriate professionals in tandem with the vocal rehabilitation.

Similarly, singers who have significant physical or physiological differences, for example, an excessively forward-set jaw (class 3 malocclusion), will possibly be using the tongue in a different way, which may affect vocal efficiency. This type of problem can be addressed by medical or therapy intervention.

The understanding of vocal anatomy and physiology is even more important when working with the developing singer, who often has to build his or her instrument simultaneously while learning how to play it. For example, a music student learning the clarinet arrives at college with an instrument one can see, touch, and manipulate. No one expects the student to build the clarinet first. A singer cannot see their voice, has only limited sensation of the instrument, and is strongly reliant on auditory perception, which must be educated over time. In the 21st century, I believe that a very important part of a singing teacher's duty is to inform students about their instrument and how it works.

Developing singers are better able to deal with demands of repertoire, examinations, auditions, and so forth during their early years, provided that sufficient time is taken to build the core components of their instrument at least to a functional level. These core components are primal sound, postural alignment, and breathing and support.

The physiological approach involves the study of the function of the larynx and the vocal tract and, in this respect, I was fortunate to be able to work with medical and scientific colleagues over many years and build up a knowledge base that continues to grow. For me, visualization of vocal activity is very much informed by my inner knowledge as a singer. My own vocal journey meant that I managed to get most aspects of singing wrong at various times in my life, and having to find my way back into good singing practices while visualizing the functioning of various parts of the vocal anatomy has, perhaps, been the major stamp on my teaching style. I am aware that it is individual to me, but the approach is certainly transferable to singers and teachers who are prepared to tackle the physiological approach.

Anatomy and physiology inform the core components (primal sound, postural alignment, breathing and support), phonation, resonance, articulation, and, indeed, the development of a full vocal technique. It is then possible for a singer to forget all about this technique and move forward into artistry and performance.

Some singers argue that, after a certain point, singing lessons are no longer necessary. In my opinion, this is a foolhardy concept—unsupervised singers very rarely maintain their level of technical prowess. There can be many reasons for this, but one of the most common relates to the fact that their instrument is invisible, and self-auditory perception can be so misleading. As a walking musical instrument, our ears are in the wrong place.

The singer who is using his or her own ears for feedback tends to develop vocal faults as a result (e.g., a depressed tongue root increases the sound of the lower harmonics within the singer's ears by damping the high frequencies, and can act like a comfort blanket). This feeds the singer's own ears but is experienced by the listeners as overly dark, muddy, and restricted in auditory radiance (i.e., doesn't carry through an orchestra). It also can have the effect of making all the vowels sound homogenized and unclear. Added to this is the physiological effect of the less efficient function of the vocal folds themselves, and the interference of the vocal constrictors and false vocal folds. Eventually, this can present as a muscle tension dysphonia, vocal fatigue, loss of range, and loss of vocal agility.

Singers who are successful often are away from home and their teachers for long periods of time. If they have been taught with a physiological model, they are much more likely to be able to self-correct as they understand the building blocks of their vocal technique. It is also easy for the teacher to diagnose problems from a distance. When both teacher and singer have a good working knowledge of the individual's vocal technique, phone calls or E-mails, although not a substitute for lessons, can be used in an emergency. In the future, I believe it will be possible for emergency singing lessons to be conducted on Skype or Ichat, although to date I have not had occasion to try it myself.

In my experience the best singers prioritize checkup lessons whenever possible. At these sessions, the teaching model is revisited automatically to prevent mannerisms and faults from impinging on their performance skills. The core components (primal sound, postural alignment, breathing and support) may or may not require much attention but they remain basic to the process. Following this, laryngeal, resonatory, and articulatory adjustments are made as required. Artistry and performance skills may be placed on hold during the lesson until the technical adjustments are complete, when it is then possible to revisit the holistic artist.

3. INCREMENTAL

Incremental is defined as "relating to the process of becoming greater."

I use incremental to mean that singing can be broken down into manageable components and that these components have a natural hierarchy of effect.

I believe in developing each component separately at first until there is some degree of unconscious muscle memory of that maneuver or posture. These individual components can be gradually developed until they have sufficient integrity, which allows them to begin to interact and interlock with each other.

My work with dysfunctional singers made me particularly aware that a singer can cope with only a limited number of changes or ideas at one time. A dysfunctional singer needs the experience of succeeding at a vocal task no matter how small. Working incrementally, allows this to occur naturally in the studio where the teacher can reinforce the changes with enthusiasm and positive encouragement.

I have found that this incremental approach also works extremely well for both developing and professional singers. Professional singers often drive the process by clearly stating what they want to achieve in the session.

We know that muscle memory takes a minimum of three to four weeks to change (Stemple et al., 1994), so it is confusing to add more components until the one under current study is at some level of subconscious control.

There appears to be a natural hierarchy that singers find easiest to manage. Primal sound raises the awareness of the true sound of the voice and is a good starting place, as it engages holistic bodily responses. It then is possible to move on to postural alignment, support, and breathing. These components form the core of the model, which can take many weeks to become integrated on a subconscious level. The length of time this integration takes depends on how kinesthetically aware the singer is and how well or badly his or her singing has functioned in the past.

When the large muscles of the torso that maintain postural alignment, support, and breathing are properly functioning, it is then much easier to gain fine control over the small muscles of the larynx, pharynx, and articulators. This means that, in this incremental model, we usually will prioritize the core components of primal sound, postural alignment, support, and breathing before attempting to change phonation, resonance, or articulation.

The incremental learning style also applies to the developing singer who is building his or her instrument as well as learning to use it simultaneously. The teaching of manageable components will be better retained by the student enabling one to develop a platform of skills in the least possible time.

By using physiological language that is unambiguous, it is possible to revisit the building blocks with more awareness and refinement regularly throughout the whole process of learning.

In addition to technical work, singers are encouraged to sing repertoire at every lesson, to experience the relevant change in their singing as a whole. This repertoire may be simple initially while the larger building blocks are being worked. Repertoire practice with the teacher present encourages awareness changes and the integration of singing in a different technical way.

I also have found that singers need to sing their music regularly for their own musical pleasure, regardless of their current technical ability. Reconnecting to the joy of singing is crucial for revisiting the holistic experience.

Valerie: A Case Study

A young soprano who came for a consultation had been studying with a well-known singer/teacher for two years. She was interested in many different styles of vocal music including jazz, folk, and pop/ballads but wanted to learn how to sing "classically." She was a good musician and had a lively intelligence. I asked her to sing classical repertoire initially, and found that she could hardly string two notes together. So I requested repertoire from other genres. To my surprise, her vocal abilities were manifestly present and her musical delivery free and unhampered (I would say "holistic"). So what had gone wrong? I asked her what her teacher had given her to sing during the two years of study and she replied that she had never been allowed to sing any songs at all because her /a/ vowel was not correct. "What did you do in your lessons?" I asked. She replied: "Just worked on my /a/ vowel." Even though this was probably an exaggeration, it was what she felt had happened. Working with this singer made me aware that I would need to be flexible as a teacher in order to help her. Although the core components were fundamental to this work, I felt that, for this student, it was a priority to put her back in touch with her talent for singing. I used her free singing in the other styles of music as a starting place, and as her confidence returned, was able to make small adjustments to her vocal setup to encourage a more classical sound. At the same time, we developed the core components that would underpin her singing in the long term. We worked together for about a year, during which time she "found" the voice she wanted using a combination of repertoire and exercises based on music she *could* sing.

My philosophy of teaching has been represented in various forms of a model, which has always contained the same components. The interactions and connections among the components have evolved over time. The linear model in its first form can be seen in Figure 1–1:

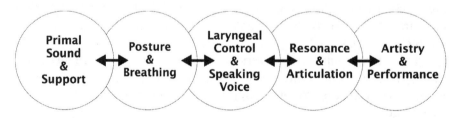

Figure 1–1. The Linear Model in its first form.

This representation certainly contained all the relevant information but did not truly reflect what was occurring in the studio. All the components were being visited again and again but at differing levels of depth and expertise.

This led me to try various other ways of describing what I was doing, all of which were unsatisfactory in some way. Finally, with the help of Ron Morris, I arrived at the model that I feel best reflects the process at this moment in time.

The Nucleus/Satellite Model

The components that were integral to the whole process, the large building blocks, need-ed to be central or core in the model. They needed to be in a position that allowed them to be revisited frequently and from any other component (Figure 1-2). These three blocks are:

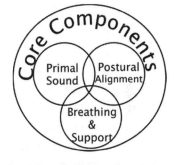

Figure 1-2. The Pedagogical Model Nucleus.

- Primal sound
- Postural alignment
- Breathing and support

These form the nucleus of the model. They also interact with each other directly.

The connections to the satellites arise from the whole nucleus rather than any of its three individual components. The satellites being:

- Phonation and speaking voice
- Resonance
- Articulation
- Artistry and performance

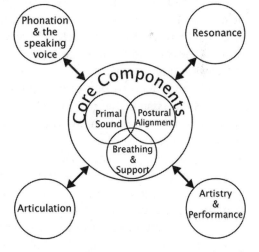

Figure 1-3. The core components and satellites.

Early on, movements among the satellites are best managed via the nucleus (Figure 1-3). Later, in the more advanced singer, these movements can directly occur. This provides us with the full model (Figure 1-4).

Although it is impossible to encapsulate any personal philosophy of teaching in any one model or even on paper, I feel that the nucleus/satellite model is a good schematic representation of how I work. It allows me to treat all the components holistically, physiologically, and incrementally.

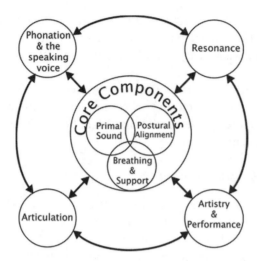

Figure 1–4. The Full Nucleus/Satellite Model.

I feel it is necessary to point out that this is a teaching model used for the development and rehabilitation of voices. Once a singer is fully functional, ("connected up"), he or she works most of the time in the "performance and artistry" satellite of this model.

My teaching model represents my current practices but I am aware of constant refinement and the potential for change. This equates to ongoing learning for the teacher. In my opinion, teaching is a creative process, never static, and must be fed constantly by the teacher/student interaction and growth.

Teachers need to be open to the continual growth of their knowledge base to ensure that their teaching remains creative. This can be difficult; it is part of our human condition that we like our "comfort zone" and the whole idea of constantly being open to change as pedagogues is very challenging. There is also the fact that, for many singing teachers, their teaching develops later in life out of their performance career. This can mean that they need to acquire different ways of learning at a later stage in life, which can in itself be problematic.

Being an ongoing learner as a singing teacher means receiving and working with new ideas, attending quality performances, interacting with student feedback, attending relevant multidisciplinary workshops and courses, taking an active interest in the work of other pedagogues, and reading, reading, reading. Wherever possible, it is of great value for the singing teacher to actually perform in front of the public. It is easy as a teacher to forget what it takes to perform, both the challenges and the rewards. The process of preparation in itself needs refreshing in the experience of the teacher. Some nonperforming singing teachers can have a rose-colored view of performance that focuses only on the pleasant aspects. Revisiting the performance process in all its complexity can be a strong reminder of how difficult it is to be a "walking musical instrument."

> **My teaching philosophy is holistic, physiological, and incremental. The teaching model provides a framework for working in components but these components must always be seen as part of the holistic singer. The singing teacher (and singer) must be ongoing learners. Subsequent chapters describe the model components in detail with supporting information in anatomy, physiology, learning, and perception.**

REFERENCES

Brown, O. L. (1998). *Discover your voice.* San Diego CA: Singular.

Chapman, J. L. (1990). Primal Singing—making connections. *Singing, 19,* 18-21.

Stemple, J. D., Lee, L., D'Amico, B., & Pickup, B. (1994). Efficacy of vocal function exercises as a method of improving voice production. *Journal of Voice, 8,* 1-8.

Thorpe, C. W., Cala, S. J., Chapman, J., & Davis, P. J. (2001). Patterns of breath support in projection of the singing voice. *Journal of Voice, 15,* 86-104.

Chapter 2

PRIMAL SOUND

The *Oxford Shorter Dictionary* defines primal as, "belonging to the first age or earliest stage: original; primitive, primeval."

In this chapter I use the term "emotional motor system," not as a neuroscientist would, but to describe the way emotional triggers can stimulate the commands to the brain to produce a holistic sound.

Human babies make primal sound as do primates and other mammals. Humans adults also use primal sounds such as crying, howling, wailing, laughing, groaning, calling, spontaneous joyful exclamations, grunts, the vocalized sigh and yawn, and the sound of agreement (MMM or uh-huh).

My awareness of primal sound was a starting point in the development of my own rationale about singing and forms a core component of the model. Primal sounds emanate from our human needs, have emotional triggers, and are part of a whole pattern of responses involving the body and mind in a holistic way. For example, when someone accidentally stamps on my foot, my response is a vocal "Aaaaagh." This response will not cause me to think about taking in a particular sort of breath or setting my vocal mechanism in a particular fashion. My cry of pain will come as part of a neurologic link to the vocal mechanism and includes a whole network of other stimuli in the body.

In an earlier conversation with Pamela Davis (Davis & Chapman, 1998), she suggested that, although we don't have research data on how singers' bodies respond in singing, we know from animal models that voice can only be evoked from groups of neurons in a brain structure called the periaqueductal gray, which is part of the emotional motor system. This is a primitive motor pathway that allows the animal to deal with and respond to the environment—whether danger or pleasure. When evoked, it organizes whole patterns of activity—many muscles of different body systems will be recruited, the cardiovascular system will be activated appropriately affecting heart rate and blood pressure, the hairs on the body may stand on end and the animal may sweat, move its body or breathe differently. If voice is evoked it also will be part of this whole body pattern with the appropriate muscles: abdominal, intercostals, diaphragm, larynx, pharynx, and mouth activated in an integrated manner (Davis & Chapman, 1998, p. 9).

Looking again at my yelp of pain, which is a primal sound, this would involve an unconscious diaphragmatic recoil breath, followed by enervation of the abdominal muscles to produce the air pressure appropriate to my yell or scream. The vocalization of the yell also occurs without conscious thought, with vocal fold closure and resonatory adjustments made automatically.

In singing of all varieties, I always want to hear and recognize this coordination, which is recruited from the emotional motor system. I am not using the term "emotional motor system" in the same way a neuroscientist would. In my pedagogy, the emotional motor system is used to describe the pathways in the singer's brain that organize whole patterns of activity, stimulated by emotional memory and imagination. The primal sound itself is not necessarily the end product in terms of vocal quality but it can be used as a means of "connecting up" the singer. The singer obtains an awareness of a more holistic experience when the emotional motor system is activated. This connection is trained and strengthened gradually over time so that the singer is able to call on the coordination from the emotional motor system at will. When fully connected up, the singer often has little conscious awareness of individual muscle systems or of particular vocal effort. They may comment, "But I don't feel as though I'm trying very hard—it's too easy!" yet it is clear to the teacher both visually and via palpation that all the appropriate muscle systems are activated. "I remember making those sounds. I used to do them as a child. I remember singing like that but I lost them once I started having singing lessons" is another common comment.

Matthew: A Case Study

Matthew enjoyed singing as a child treble in cathedral choir and sang in choirs at high school. He wanted to go to music college but his parents did not think it was an appropriate career move. He trained as a speech and language therapist but went back to singing in third year at training college aged 20 and started having singing lessons as a counter tenor. At 22 he started a course at a Conservatorium of Music as a first study singer full time, but found it very difficult. Unable to sing in tune, he felt he was getting nowhere. He withdrew from the course but continued singing in a cathedral choir and made a successful career as a speech and language therapist for the next 10 years. Matthew felt very inadequate and unhappy as a solo singer, but good enough for the alto line in a choir. He auditioned for the opera chorus (as a joke) and was offered a place. Starting lessons with another teacher alerted him to the fact that his voice was "big." He returned to the Conservatorium to do a degree in vocal performance which he passed.

As part of his special project study he came to London to have some lessons with me. My initial assessment was that the voice was produced without any actual physical support for the breath and with a locked abdominal wall. This created intonation and vocal facility problems. Initially much work was done on Accent Method breathing to facilitate the abdominal support system. The result of this was that an enormous voice appeared. It was a tenor larynx-type falsettist and operatic in timbre and size. Once the airflow/support/posture had been addressed (about six to eight months) and primal sound was accessed, the finessing of the voice took a further two years by which time the problems of tonal quality, dynamics, and intonation were all resolved. Particularly because this was a big voice (even though singing in the falsetto range) there was no way it could be a genuine musical instrument without the activation of the primal connections, in particular, the muscles of the torso.

PEDAGOGIC IMPLICATIONS OF PRIMAL SOUND

Using primal sound gives the singer access to the basic coordination available from the emotional motor system. With primal sound as our base, pedagogic instructions on breathing that contradict or countermand this basic connection, involving instead use of the conscious brain, for example, "Take a big breath," "Expand your rib cage and hold," "Fill your whole body with air," and so forth (in essence any type of overbreathing) will probably be counterproductive. The coordination from the emotional motor system synchronizes the muscles required for breathing to take in sufficient air for the task. This coordination is familiar within the muscle memory of the primal mechanisms as is the onset of phonation that follows. The neurologic network that is involved in making a primal sound recruits the exhalatory abdominal muscles at the onset of phonation. A baby seems to be able to cry for hours without suffering vocal fatigue, because its cries are vocally efficient, being produced with full body activation. It is using a primal sound with all the emotional motor system connections. A singer who is fully "connected up" can expect the same sort of vocal efficiency that the baby has.

Primal sound not only gives connection to the support system but also can be used to improve vocal efficiency. The work of Jo Estill, which uses a series of natural sounds to access different vocal qualities, has explored this very well. "Sob/cry," for example, lowers the larynx and closes the vocal folds efficiently, tilting the cricothyroid joint. Primal sound provides the singer with immediate connection to the support system and to phonation that is efficient and safe.

TRAINING ISSUES

This awakening of the emotional motor system then needs to be followed with systematic training to consolidate its use. The conscious brain is invited to oversee and assess the training process and to motivate the singer toward the discipline required to practice, but awareness of the holistic nature of singing should be constantly present during this training. The singer's body and voice may take many years to develop fully and there are few shortcuts. But when this training is based on primal sound with its connection to the emotional motor system the process can be quicker and less complicated. Just to tell a student to "sing with emotion" is not enough unless that student has had teaching which has been based on a correct physiologic model and been developed incrementally over time. Some examples of physiologically incorrect instructions about breathing that make it virtually impossible to access the connection would be: "Expand and raise your chest," "Flare your ribs and hold," "Fill every crevice of your body with air," "Engage your support as you inhale," "Pull your belly in as you breathe," and "Push your belly out as you sing."

EXERCISES

To get a singer to make a primal sound, it is necessary to allow their body to adopt a neutral "nonsinging" position as a starting point. I often have to say, "Don't consciously take a 'singing' breath, but allow your body to breathe naturally as though you were going to speak." This circumvents any incorrect breathing pattern as a starting point. Then I ask them to walk about easily and to suddenly call, "Hey" to me from the other end of the room. Often, it has to be louder than their first attempt.

I then ask them to place their hands firmly on the waistband of their skirt or trousers—between their lowest rib and the iliac crest (crest of the hip joint). They should cough to check the response under their hands. Following this, I ask them to make a more extended calling sound again and notice how their waistband expands at the onset of the sound. We follow this initial "Hey" sound with others such as monkey whooping noises, football terrace cheering, crying, chuckling, and so forth, then finally with the hummed affirmation sound of "HMM HMM," which is a gentler, modal register use of the same muscles. In my 30 or so years of teaching, I have found that even the most tense and unhappy singers can be encouraged to make this initial discovery. If it seems that the singer's posture is very lordotic (swaybacked), I may ask them to crouch over the piano or to stand in apelike posture. All singers can use this ape-like posture as it makes it easier to feel the activity in the abdominal and back muscles that is induced by the primal sound. It is important to stand with a neutral spine, bending the knees slightly, and then tilting forward from the hip without rounding the spine or changing the head position. Hands then can be easily placed on the waistband with fingers toward the back or the front for immediate manual feedback.

Singers who have been using rib-reserve or reverse abdominal breathing patterns for a long period may need intervention by a teacher of Accent Method breathing to reduce the holding patterns in the abdominal wall. They often are able to a make connection to their waistband muscle girdle but have great difficulty in releasing the tension for their next inhalation. Access to their next primal sound can be disturbed if they cannot release properly (see Chapter 4). It is at this point that I will either do this remedial breathing work myself within their lesson, or refer them to a speech therapist who will do it separately from their singing. A brief overview of Accent Method breathing is provided in Chapter 4.

At this earliest stage of using primal sound I also may suggest that a singer move one hand down to the lower abdominal/pubic synthesis muscle junction, three to eight centimeters above the pubic bone while maintaining the other hand firmly on the waistband. Making the primal noises again will alert the singer to the activity, which they can feel synchronized under both hands. As the muscles engage, they shorten and bunch up, and this can be felt as firmness followed by a release at the end of the phonation. However, if a singer has previously acquired poor posture or reversed support, he or she may not be able to access this lower abdominal muscle junction right away; I expect that this will develop over time (it may take as long as 6 months) with consistent exercise and postural realignment. If the problem does not resolve in this period, I sometimes ask the student to seek additional help from other professionals such as Pilates, Alexander, or Tai Chi teachers in tandem with their singing lessons.

The next stage of the training is to ask the singer to sing rather than call out the "Hey" on a reasonably high pitch. Then they can make a glide down and back up again from the note while maintaining their abdominal activity. I may ask them to sing a descending scale from this sound while maintaining their abdominal activity. Many students find this leap from noises into singing difficult, especially if they have been singing for some time without this connection. Once this is established with some degree of automaticity, the student is ready to move to the next stage.

The "Hey-Ha Exercise"

For a full description and notation of this exercise set, see Appendix 1.

This exercise can move from a primal sound exercise into one that extends breathing and support and is described again in Chapter 4.

Primal sound can easily be revisited during the whole of a singer's life if he or she feels any loss of that connection. Usually, singers who are well-connected (i.e., on a subconscious level) can access their primal sound by singing with emotion. Occasionally, the teacher will need to stimulate this by suggesting the use of an appropriate primal sound during the repertoire preparation stage.

> **The importance of primal sound cannot be overestimated. It helps the singer awaken the connections to his or her emotional motor system, which can be trained into appropriate abdominal support and natural breathing for singing. The interdependence of primal sound, posture, breathing, and support is at the core of the teaching model for a very good reason. It is the "human expression" in sound which truly communicates emotions and ideas to others. When fully developed and finessed from the emotional motor system, it can become holistic singing of the highest order across all styles of music.**

REFERENCE

Davis, P. J., & Chapman, J. (1998). Primal singing. *Australian Voice*, 4, 9–11.

Chapter 3

POSTURAL ALIGNMENT

$\mathcal{W}$hen a singer walks on stage, especially onto the concert platform, his posture gives an immediate and subtle message to the audience. An expectation of how he is going to perform is set up even before he opens his mouth to sing. Posture reflects confidence, self-image, and the general psychological state of the performer as well as his physiological condition, relevant to the task he is about to undertake. As soon as the singing begins, the audience will probably recognize, although subconsciously, whether its expectations are going to be fulfilled. In an opera house, there may be a similar expectation, although a singer's postural presence can be hidden or at least disguised by the costumes and the demands of the role being sung. However, unless an opera singer develops into a vocal athlete, he or she is unlikely to survive the rigors of the "heavy duty" vocal work required of them. A large part of vocal athleticism is based on a singer having excellent core stability and posture, and it is absolutely vital for vocal longevity (Figure 3–1).

During the past few decades there has been a valuable interaction between various physical disciplines and the training and maintenance of singers brought about by the multidisciplinary approach to voice. Sports science has contributed greatly to our potential for understanding the holistic nature of the singing machine. Great practitioners from other fields such as Moshe Feldenkrais, Frederick Alexander, Joseph Pilates, Ida Rolf, and many others have given singers and teachers the opportunity to make sense of our particular requirements for the efficient and long lasting use of the voice.

23

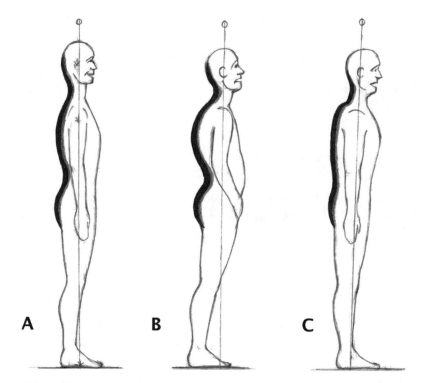

Figure 3–1. Examples of posture: **A.** Excellent. **B.** Lordotic. **C.** Militaristic or Overstraight. Copyright Richard Webber, 2005.

It must be said, however, that there is a huge variety of body and voice types among classical singers. Nor is there only one formula for producing successful singers when it comes to posture.

WHY DOES POSTURE MATTER?

VOCAL EFFICIENCY

The larynx is suspended in the neck. It is capable of movement in all six planes (up and down, side to side, and forward and back) and has the necessary muscle attachments to do this (see Chapter 11). The larynx houses the vocal folds, which need to be used efficiently. If the muscles that attach to the larynx are inappropriately tense, the actions of the vocal folds themselves may be affected. This freedom from tension is required in both the supra- and subglottal chambers as well as at the level of the vocal folds. The muscles that allow for this efficiency are all attached to other structures, which in themselves are affected by the basic posture of the singer.

RESONANCE

The vocal tract is unusual in that it has the potential for highly complex maneuvers. For classical singing, it is required to incorporate an amazing and extraordinary variety of changes to its shape and configuration at the same time as maintaining its particular timbre or quality. To do this efficiently, it must work from a resting position that is correctly aligned, which allows the larynx and pharynx to interact in the most efficient and free manner.

To test this, stand well, then sing a sustained note in the upper middle register of your voice using an "ŏ" (like in hot) vowel and slowly displace the neck and chin forward noticing how the sound changes. Resume your normal (good) postural alignment and you will notice that both the resonance and the efficiency of the vocal utterance are much better.

BREATHING AND SUPPORT

The muscles of the abdominal girdle have a dual role for singers. In the average population, they are predominately dealing with postural alignment and core stability, with only a limited amount of their work directed to managing breath. However, in classical singing with its particular breath compression requirement, the workload of the abdominal muscles needs to be shared differently. For these peculiar tasks, I have found it best for singers to develop posture, core stability, and breath management simultaneously, as each component has a "knock-on" effect on the others. When a singer has developed good postural alignment, it is easier to use the abdominal muscles for breath management. Likewise, when the breath is well supported it is easier to maintain the posture and core stability.

INDIVIDUAL PHYSICAL CHARACTERISTICS

Postural alignment interacts with the singer's own physical characteristics. The natural curves in the spine should be respected while small adjustments are being made over time, in order to bring about postural efficiency in each individual singer.

Attention also should be given to the relationship between the thorax and the hips. In some singers, the hips are forward (like a fashion model on the catwalk), which places the thorax too far back. The singing teacher needs to view the student in profile and gently adjust the positioning of the hips further back in relation to the thorax. This brings the body weight more over the balls of the feet rather than on the heels and gives the student an immediate feeling of buoyancy and readiness.

Jaw Jut

The jaw alignment is a good case in point. Ideally, the jaw should be relaxed and should hang freely from the temporomandibular joint but it sometimes has a natural "jut" that may need some patient correction in the classical singer. Singers with naturally large forward-set jaws may not always find it easy to attain this desired relaxed-jaw posture but can work toward it. Sometimes, the help of an orthodontist or osteopath is needed. An example of a large forward-set jaw being exquisitely managed is Dame Joan Sutherland, who can be seen on film to release her jaw into a loose "back and down" position as she moves into the upper range of her voice (Figure 3-2 and see Chapter 7).

"Street-Cred Slump"

Another physical characteristic that is counterproductive to good posture for classical singing is the "street-cred slump" adopted by many teenagers and young adults (Figure 3-3).

This style of posture can be corrected over time but requires much patience on the part of the teacher.

■ First, a change of self-awareness is required (aided by a video camera or set of mirrors).

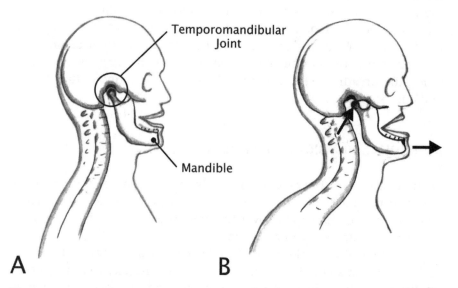

Figure 3–2. Jaw positions: **A** (position 1) and **B** (position 2). Side-on view showing the opening of the jaw into the two positions. Note how in position 2 the posture of the head and neck is distorted, closing down the pharyngeal space: the mandible (jaw) is slid forward in the temporomandibular joint. Copyright Richard Webber, 2005.

- Education about the reasons for appropriate posture should be offered.
- Gentle but constant reminders and manual adjustments need to be made by the teacher within the regular lessons.
- Assistance of alternative therapists should be sought if the problems are not resolving.

Militaristic Stance

Within the singing pedagogies, the term "noble posture" is often described as the desired state. I have used the term myself, but have found that, when this is taken to extremes, it can become counterproductive to singing well. My experience has been that, when militaristic posture is sought, aligned with rib-reserve or high-chest (clavicular) breathing, the whole body of the singer becomes rigid and unresponsive. This may be due to the pectoralis major and the trapezius muscles in particular becoming wrongly recruited as a postural device. Under these circumstances, they can act as an inhibitor of vocal function and dampen resonance (Figure 3-4).

Dynamic Posture

Bunch (quoting W J. Gould), points out that "posture is the dynamic interrelationship between muscular and skeletal tissues. The word dynamic is important because it implies an alignment that is stable rather than static and fixed and is a prelude to easy flowing movement." Bunch further goes on to point out that the body is aligned efficiently when a line can be drawn from the top of the head directly though the shoulders and knees to just in front of the ankle (see Figure 3-1).

Figure 3–3. The "Street-cred slump." Copyright Richard Webber, 2005.

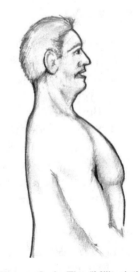

Figure 3–4. The "Militaristic or overly tense upper chest posture." Copyright Richard Webber, 2005.

I like to describe appropriate posture in two parts although both interlink.

Torso and Legs

- Shoulder girdle needs to be relaxed down.
- There should be no activity in the pectoralis major muscles. The upper rib cage is maintained in a comfortable setting (not military or pigeonlike) and could be described as "noble." This can be achieved by gentle activation of latissimus dorsi and serratus anterior muscles (singing teachers have referred to this as, "like having a small balloon under each armpit").
- The spine needs to feel elongated and not excessively lordotic (swayed). This can be achieved by releasing the knees, slightly tilting the pelvis up at the front and down at the back. (*Note:* This also helps to engage the lower abdominal and pelvic floor muscles in a posturally advantageous setting.)
- The back should feel wide.
- Buttocks should not be clenched.
- Knees should be soft and not braced back.
- The weight should not be back on the heels or fully forward on the front of the foot. Awareness of the heel and the ball of the foot in equal contact with the ground suggests that the body's weight is well distributed for singing.

Head and Neck

- The neck is free and allowed to lengthen forward and up.
- The ears are located over the shoulders.
- An imaginary 90-degree angle exists between the plane of the eyes and the neck (this encourages activity of the deep neck flexors).
- Sternocleidomastoid muscles should be inactive.
- Jaw should be relaxed and open backward and downward rather than jutting forward and out.
- Head balances and is free to move easily both up and down (tiny nods) and side to side, on the atlas and axis vertebrae (Figure 3–5).

Bodies vary enormously but I believe basic principles of posture and alignment transcend the body types. It is easier for a short-trunked, short-necked singer (often a soprano or tenor) to maintain physical integrity than it is for a willowy long-torsoed and long-necked singer (often a mezzo or bass). However, I have found that applying the same basic template and working with the principles outlined above can produce balanced equilibrium for all body types.

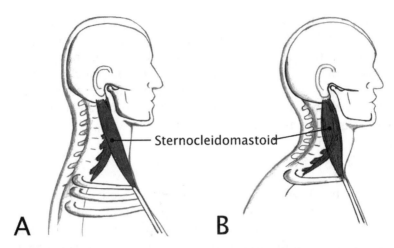

Figure 3–5. Head and neck position. **A.** Sternocleidomastoid relaxed. **B.** Sternocleidomastoid tensed. Copyright Richard Webber, 2005.

A QUESTION OF CORE STABILITY

Posture is important in many different forms of artistic expression but the rules for specific art forms differ according to their particular disciplines. Good core stability, that is, an underlying tonus in the abdominal and other torso muscles, is essential for the singer. Traditional classical dance training maintains a tight abdominal set to elevate the upper body, but this sort of postural alignment is counterproductive in the singer who needs flexibility in the abdominal wall in order to use the body's own elastic recoil action for breathing. Tonicity in the core stabilizers is crucial to the maintenance of high-energy singing tasks. Such systems as yoga, Pilates, and Tai Chi can assist in developing and maintaining core stability below the belt. In singers, this is very important as too much muscularity above the belt can interfere with the breath flow required for efficient vocalization. Singers need to have muscular tonus in the abdominal wall but the rectus abdominus muscles in particular should not be over-developed. The six-pack so desired by "gym junkies" is not useful for singers because it does not allow for the required flexibility in the abdominal wall.

SOME COMMON FAULTS IN POSTURE

Neck

Although this is a problem for many singers today because of lifestyle and peer-group pressure to "stand cool" (i.e., slouched), it is a particular problem for very tall singers who incline toward their smaller brethren in everyday life. This postural defect can encourage the head to protrude forward causing inappropriate tension in the vocal tract. Awareness-changing exercises can be used including Alexander technique lessons, Pilates, Tai Chi, and some forms of yoga. The singing teacher can achieve this change by means of gentle manipulation and correction as well as constant reminders and encouragement.

Shoulders

Tension in the shoulder girdle is counterproductive to good singing because of its effect on the larynx and pharynx. Overuse in everyday life of sternocleidomastoid and upper trapezius muscles can have a "knock-on" effect all the way to the vocal folds themselves. The normal daily life of city dwellers produces a resting tension in the shoulders that often is not recognized. The reasons for this may include carrying heavy bags on one shoulder (opera singers are often faced with lugging heavy operatic scores around), or one arm being strongly lateralized (right- or left-handed). Tension gets into the shoulders and posture suffers. The larynx has numerous attachments to the shoulder girdle and inappropriate tension in this region can lead to inefficiency and reduced function. I recommend busy singers to have regular sessions with a massage therapist (in the same way as athletes use this as a normal part of their training program). It also is useful to consult a physiotherapist or manual therapist should the problems not resolve. I strongly recommend the use of a wheeled carry-on bag for transporting heavy music much in the same way as instrumental musicians put their heavier instruments on wheels.

Lower Spine and Pelvis

When a singer habitually stands with a swayed back (lordosis), it may be due to overly tense psoas muscles. This pair of muscles lies deep in the body, with their origin at the last thoracic to fifth lumbar vertebrae, and inserting into the medial surface of the femur at the lesser trochanter (Figure 3–6).

When these muscles are habitually shortened, the control of breath often seems compromised. It can be argued that this may be because this lumbar area is where the crura of the diaphragm and all its attachments are housed. As the diaphragm acts as a braking system during phonation, it is important that the singer feels this lumbar area as being "open" and not shortened. Also in close proximity are the quadratus lumborum muscles, which are used in expiratory tasks, stabilizing the rib cage against the opposing forces of the abdominal muscles.

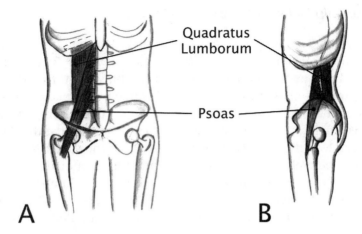

Figure 3–6. Diagram showing psoas and quadratus lumborum muscles. **A.** Ventral view. **B.** Lateral view. Copyright Richard Webber, 2005.

If a student singer appears to have this lordotic posture, it can be helpful to have a physiotherapist or osteopath check for psoas tension. A physiotherapist may be able to suggest suitable exercises to help correct this problem. My experience has been that the teacher has to actively encourage the student over a long period to achieve change in this area of the body. Releasing the knees often is a part of this change as this allows the hips also to release tension. Singers with this problem are often tightly locked at the hips. I check while they are singing, and have used the Alexander technique-inspired "wobble board," which resides under my piano, to address this problem on a regular basis. Singers who have been tight in the legs and pelvis love the freedom gained from singing while on the "wobble-board." Not only do they feel that their breathing is much better, but regular use of this board enables them to become used to singing and walking at the same time (quite a good idea if you want to work in an opera house).

A shortened psoas also can lead to the lordosis/kyphosis syndrome in other parts of the body, especially the cervical spine. This clearly has implications for the efficient function of the larynx and its housing in the neck (Figure 3–7).

Figure 3–7. Diagram showing tight and shortened psoas leading to lordotic spinal posture. Copyright Richard Webber, 2005.

Relationship Between Thorax and Pelvis

As singers' bodies vary greatly it is important to check that the alignment of the upper and lower parts of the torso is correctly maintained. As with the "slumped" posture, sometimes the hips are thrust into a forward setting in relation to the thorax. This needs to be adjusted so that the abdominal support is not compromised during singing and the in-breath is efficient. Care also should be taken to ensure that the thorax is not routinely carried too far forward (as though the singer is pleading), as this immediately misaligns the neck and puts additional strain on the lower back and pelvis. This question of thoracic and lumbar balance is addressed more fully in the recent publication, *What Every Singer Needs to Know About the Body* by Malde, Allen, and Zeller (2008).

Asymmetry

Asymmetry (e.g., one shoulder held higher than the other), or rotation of the neck are actually quite common (Figure 3–8). In the singer, asymmetry needs correction. The larynx prefers to align itself with the torso rather than the head, and asymmetric singers may be distorting their resonating tube as well as affecting laryngeal efficiency. Asymmetries can arise when a singer unconsciously tries to hear him- or herself better by bouncing the sound off one shoulder. Sometimes, a singer may use a hand cupped to the ear or bring a hand close to the mouth in an effort to bounce the sound off the fingernails. Likewise, asymmetries are brought about by singers

Figure 3–8. Asymmetric posture leading to distortion of laryngeal setting. Copyright Richard Webber, 2005.

habitually standing with their weight more on one leg, always holding a score in one particular hand, or always carrying a bag on the same shoulder and so forth. However, there also are asymmetries brought about by circumstances beyond the control of singer or teacher and which can come from childhood patterns as in the case study below.

Harry: A Case Study

Harry was a tall, slim 25-year-old tenor with a lovely, light lyric voice, who had come from abroad to study. Although he often produced sounds of great beauty and clarity, he could not access the top of his range with any degree of reliability, the tone was scratchy, and he experienced yodeling from time to time. I had begun working on the fundamental aspects of posture, breathing, support, and phonation when I noticed that as he sang up a scale his larynx was rising obliquely toward his left ear away from the midline. This immediately started to ring bells in my memory. I had had many clients who had been through the English cathedral boy chorister process and had ended up with deviated larynges. I asked Harry if he had sung as a child chorister, and he replied that from the age of 8 to 14 he had been singing regularly, first as a treble then later as an alto. I then asked him to describe his stance and posture in the choir stall as he remembered it. The stalls were cramped, so his body was facing to the front but the conductor was at a 45-degree angle to his right. From his description and demonstration, it was possible to observe that his head and neck were rotated toward the conductor while his pelvis and torso were facing front.

The osteopath Jacob Lieberman, who has great experience in the field of vocal function and health, was able to use manual techniques to redress residual muscle tensions in Harry's neck This allowed the vocal and postural adjustments I was making during his singing lessons to take effect more quickly and permanently. After 2 years, he was able to sing at the top of his range with confidence and no yodeling.

Jacob and I were commissioned to write this case study for a Choral Directors' journal. I quote from Jacob's explanation:

Anatomically, the larynx is not attached to the spinal column, but is suspended between the skull and the sternum through a complicated network of muscles. From above, the suspension is via three groups of muscles, and from below by one group of muscles which attaches it to sternum and clavicle. Interestingly enough, from clinical observation in working with singers, it emerges that, if muscles that suspend the larynx from above are relaxed, rotation of the head doesn't affect the position of the larynx until the rotation is extreme. In other words, there is a flexibility of the superior suspensory system. However, the attachment of the larynx from below is different. Because the larynx via the cricoid cartilage is attached to the trachea, the structure of the inferior suspensory muscles cause the whole of the voice box to move with the torso when the head and pelvis are fixed in the midline. It should be borne in mind that the development of the spine is not complete until after puberty, and postural patterns set in childhood can dictate the formation of spinal curves (scoliosis). Scoliosis is accompanied by the rotation of the torso, and can result in laryngeal asymmetry and its related problems. It is accepted that asymmetry of the larynx in adults may have a number of contributing factors: for example, habitual carrying of a heavy bag on one and the same shoulder, or twisted posture during other activities and sports. The adult singer can be effectively treated with skilled manual therapy and voice tuition, but correction does not just involve merrily rotating the head to the opposite side. It requires a detailed study of the spine as a whole and the laryngeal musculature. New muscular habits need to be learned, aiming towards more symmetrical posture both of spine and larynx. (Chapman & Lieberman, 1998, pp. 2–3)

REMEDIES AND THERAPIES

I find the underlying premises of the Alexander technique are the best we have although I am not a trained Alexander teacher myself. As a singing teacher, I am much more interventionist than an Alexander technique teacher would be in my approach to a singer's body. I also have found it valuable to use selected techniques gained from different therapies in related fields—Estill Voicecraft, Pilates, Feldenkrais, physiotherapy, osteopathy, speech therapy, manual therapy—in fact, anything short of magic, to which I do not subscribe. Although many of these techniques and therapies can help singers change their awareness, the actual changes in muscle memory can take much longer to achieve.

A STRATEGY TOWARD ATTAINING A GOOD SINGING POSTURE

1. Pilates roll-down: With feet at hip-width apart, and knees slightly bent, roll down to the floor then gradually unroll the spine bringing the head up last.
2. Reach up to the ceiling with the arms fully extended and the head/neck posture maintained, then drop the arms to resting position while maintaining the spinal/rib setting.
3. Repeat steps 1 and 2.
4. Finally roll down again, come back up noticing that while the upper chest feels open, it is not artificially elevated. The spine feels long and the back wide. The knees remain soft and the buttocks unclenched.
5. Remain in this position and practice some diaphragmatic breathing.

PEDAGOGICAL IMPLICATIONS

At the start of their training, students come in all shapes and sizes and with a wide variety of postural patterns. At the other end of the time spectrum, what becomes clear is that singers of all types who maintain successful careers over a long period of time, from the tiniest "early music" soprano to the Wagnerian heroic baritone, have the "look" of the singer about them. The operatic world perhaps shows us this at its most extreme. It is interesting to stand near the stage door at the Royal Opera House, Covent Garden, or the Metropolitan Opera in New York and observe the different people as they come and go. After a while, it is possible to pick out the singers from the others (stage hands, ballet dancers, wardrobe staff, orchestra, administration, etc.). The "look" of opera singers transcends actual body size and is produced by this line of work, that is, it usually includes strong backs, straight necks, tree-trunk-like torsos, and so forth. The fact that the soloists are able to maintain a "full frontal" contact with the audience means that they probably have an extroverted personality, although this is by no means always the case.

Teachers of young and developing singers need to work holistically on a week-by-week basis to bring about a confident but natural posture in their students. This postural alignment should become an unconscious part of their vocal technique and carry over into everyday life.

Whatever a student's age or level of attainment, I feel that it is the singing teacher's duty to raise the issue of postural alignment from the outset. The very act of singing classically produces a potential for postural distortion. As the larynx itself is not attached to a fixed surface but is suspended in the neck, it requires well-balanced muscles as a basis from which to operate. For classical sound, the vertical larynx position needs to be relatively deep to maximize resonance potential. The postural setting of the head, neck, and shoulder girdle are crucial for the exquisite management of the tiny internal structures within the vocal mechanism. Thus, developing singers need constant monitoring and adjustments to their posture as their vocal techniques grow. This discipline is applicable to all types of classical singer, but especially important for those voices that have the potential to sing the bigger heavier roles in opera. In working with these bigger voices, my experience has been that the heavier workload on the larynx itself imposes a postural imperative on the supporting structures of the whole instrument.

Ideally, the modern-day vocal studio should be equipped with video equipment that can give a singer a side and back view of his or her posture. Where this is not possible, the use of multiple mirrors can achieve the same result. Singing teachers must regularly view their students from various angles. It is impossible to adequately monitor the student if the teacher is sitting at the piano for the entire lesson. The profile view is especially important for identifying deviations in jaw and neck posture while the view from the back helps identify shoulder asymmetries and overall alignment.

My work on developing diaphragmatic breathing and abdominal support dovetails with the postural adjustments as each feeds the other: the greater the flexible strength in the muscles of the torso, the less there will be inappropriate pressure at the level of the larynx itself. I use an analogue-type comparison in lessons (i.e., "How hard are you working with your support muscles on a scale of 1 to 10?" "How much voice are you using on a scale of 1 to 10?"). Quite often, the ratio will be reported as "3 in the body and 8 in the voice" so I might ask the student to reverse the numbers to 8 in the body and 3 in the voice. The results are quite often revelatory. As the singer's technique and muscle tonus improve, these ratios change and refine, until there need be fewer interventions. During the time this development process is underway, attention needs to be drawn to postural alignment. The use of some of the complementary therapy systems (Pilates exercises, Alexander technique, and Feldenkrais interventions) can bring about the required change. More recently, I have had personal experience with manual therapy offered by both osteopaths and physiotherapists and also have undergone massage therapy. All these complementary systems have much to offer singers in development, awareness, and remediation in their progress toward the attainment and maintenance of an appropriately singer-type posture.

PERFORMANCE, ARTISTRY, AND POSTURAL INTEGRITY

No matter how high up the performance ladder singers rise, they need to pay constant attention to their general postural alignment. The stresses of maintaining a professional career with its travel and rehearsal schedules can gradually erode the singer's posture and over time this can result in vocal problems. This very gradual and subtle decline is one of the main reasons that the elite singer still needs to check in regularly with a trusted pedagogue.

THE DEMANDS OF ROLES AND PRODUCTIONS

Young singers starting their training might ask, "But how does Desdemona sing when required to hang her head off the end of the bed?" This is a good question, and an experienced pedagogue might answer: "Once a singer's mechanical function is established and they are fully trained, it should be possible for them to sing in any number of amazing physical contortions."

Today, operatic producers, often uncluttered with any vocal knowledge, ask singers to perform feats of potential vocal suicide. Some roles in themselves, unless approached with care, are potentially damaging, for example, the hunched Rigoletto, Olympia the doll in *The Tales of Hoffman*, and wheelchair-bound Harry in *The Silver Tassie*. Managing these demands really comes down to the singers having their own physiological knowledge base. With this as an underpinning, they often can perform daring and demanding physical feats without vocal compromise. Alternatively, they could put up a good reality-based argument against some of the more whimsical suggestions of stage directors.

THE RAKED STAGE

One of the biggest challenges opera singers have to deal with is the raked stage. Most rehearsal time is spent on a flat surface and the rake only available to the cast and chorus in the final few days before the performances start. It is not at all surprising that vocal problems can result. Remember that the larynx itself is housed within the neck, not fixed to any structure. When the scaffolding (i.e., the extrinsic musculature) is changed, which occurs on a raked stage, there are compensatory mechanisms which may change the larynx setting. The singer must be even more aware of the desired postural alignment for singing and strive to overcome the effects of the stage raking with adjustments to knees, pelvis, and back (Figure 3–9). Similar postural challenges occur when singers are required to wear high heels, for example. Should they have to cope with high heels and a raked stage at the same time, the problems are further exacerbated. The raked stage can be particularly disadvantageous for members of an operatic chorus who may spend many hours with their spine and legs thrown out of alignment and with limited opportunities to relieve this posture. Principal singers often have the luxury of moving around more, giving their legs and back some relief. They also may be politically in a position to complain, whereas chorus members may have a more difficult time. Ultimately, everyone involved in the production wants the performances to be the best possible, but singers on the way up the ladder do not always have much attention paid to their suggestions.

Exercises to destress the body at the end of each day are advisable: for example, the Alexander technique semisupine position, or Pilates roll-downs and stretches are only two of many possible techniques.

Figure 3–9. Raked Stage with high heels. **A.** Uncorrected. **B.** Corrected. Copyright Richard Webber, 2005.

COSTUMES

Operatic costumes can be a source of difficulty for the singer and involve postural compromise. These can include:

- Heavy hats and wigs
- Head gear and masks, which also can restrict hearing
- Heavy costumes
- Corsets and restrictive garments.

There is no one way of dealing with these difficulties, but when a singer has a fully developed and strong vocal technique, which includes a well-honed postural integrity, he or she is much more likely to be flexible in dealing with the demands of the profession.

> **The large muscles of the torso take the workload and create an environment in which the small discrete muscle systems of the larynx, the resonating system, and articulators are free to function without inappropriate tension. Ideal posture for singers is a crucial part of getting the breathing and support, phonation, resonance, and articulation systems to work efficiently.**

REFERENCES

Bunch, M., (1995). *Dynamics of the singing voice* (p. 25). Wien, Germany: Springer-Verlag.

Chapman, J., & Lieberman, J. (1998). Posture and voice: Safeguarding children's future singing. *Mastersinger, 30*, 2–3.

Malde, M., Allen, M .J., & Zeller, K .A. (2009). *What every singer needs to know about the body.* San Diego, CA: Plural.

Chapter 4

BREATHING AND SUPPORT

Janice Chapman and Ron Morris

This is an area of vocal pedagogy that has always occupied the singing world. Great controversy still exists over the issues around breathing and support, and students invariably find this the most difficult area of their training. They receive all sorts of different advice such as, on inhalation, "Fill every crevice of your body with air," "Raise the chest and pull your abdomen in as you inhale," "Use your intercostals," "Flare your ribs and hold," "Breathe into your buttocks"; on supporting the voice, "Push your belly wall down and out while singing," "Maintain a flared rib cage during singing," and even full denial of the importance of breathing and support such as "Don't worry about it, it will take care of itself," and (to a first-year singer in a music college) "We don't do breathing until the third year, dear." Sometimes the imagery used can be couched in nonphysiologic terms but have at its root, something that has worked for the teacher during his or her own singing. A good example is, "Sing from your 'little Mary,' dear" (Figure 4–1), which was passed on to me by a student as something said by a previous teacher but which meant nothing until the physiology of the lower abdominal muscles had been experienced and understood by the student under my tuition. "Oh, now I understand what she meant!" she exclaimed.

Many of these types of comments, which so confuse students today, can be traced back to the writings of the past. These writings have sometimes been wrongly interpreted and passed on like the Chinese whisper.

Figure 4–1. *"Sing from your 'Little Mary,' Dear."* Copyright Simon Pearsall, 2005.

Many of these developed from what teachers and singers described from their own sensations, but were not based on physiologic function.

Francesco Lamperti (1813–1892) was very influential in the history of vocal study for his description of the *lutte vocale* (vocal struggle), which is synonymous with the *appoggio* technique which already existed in an exercise that the famous castrato Farinelli allegedly had learned from Porpora a hundred years earlier.

Here is a translation of Lamperti's description:

> To sustain a given note, the air should be expelled slowly; to attain this end, the respiratory (inspiratory) muscles, by continuing their action, strive to retain the air in the lungs, and oppose their action to that of the expiratory muscles, which is called the *lutte vocale* or vocal struggle. On the retention of this equilibrium depends the just emission of the voice and by means of it alone can true expression be given to the sound produced. (as quoted in Sataloff, 1998)

I would suggest that, during the last 50 years, much confusion has been created in the application of the term "appoggio" that is synchronous with *lutte vocale*. Pedagogues have misused the idea of appoggio by interpreting the interaction of inspiratory and expiratory muscles in a way which has not accounted for the interdependence of the abdominal girdle, diaphragm, and rib cage. By describing this vocal struggle as being driven by an expansion of ribs/flanks on inspiration, which then continues during phonation, singers have been subjected to an unnatural form of breath management that, in my experience, often leads to a "locking" of the airflow. This flank area of the body is in actuality part of the **expiratory** muscle system. Some of the expiratory muscles, in being applied inappropriately during the in-breath, become tense and rigid during singing and can no longer perform their appropriate expiratory functions.

Diaphragmatic/belly-release inhalation or *Singers Please Loosen Abdominal Tension*, hereafter referred to as SPLAT, on the other hand, does not recruit any expiratory muscles during the in-breath, but relies on a flexible abdominal wall, which allows the diaphragm to descend quickly, fully, and efficiently. The timing of the activation of the expiratory abdominal girdle muscles is *with the onset* of phonation or just prior to it, as demonstrated so clearly in the making of a *primal sound*, which is always preceded by a "normal" or SPLAT inhalation in everyday life.

The timing issue related to breathing and support is a crucial one. According to Hixon, "they (the inspiratory muscles) actually continue their activity into the early part of expiration, with the force they exert gradually decreasing and acting as a releasing brake against the lung recoil forces" (Hixon, 1987, p. 19). He also states that, even in quiet breathing, the inspiratory muscle forces switch off from their braking function at about the second "second" of the expiratory cycle. As classically trained singers, we exploit this physiological fact by recruiting the abdominal girdle muscles (expiratory) immediately, increasing the intrathoracic pressure, which helps maintain the action of the diaphragm working as a brake for longer during the sung phrase. This could be a realistic physiologic explanation of Lamperti's *lutte vocale*.

In my pedagogy, the SPLAT in-breath is followed just prior to phonation by free but subtle movement of the belly wall toward the spine, which brings about the activation of the abdominal girdle and lower abdominal pubic synthesis (LAPS). This raises the intra-abdominal pressure and the intrathoracic pressure and is synchronized with the impulse to sing. This gives the singer the ability to use the compressed air with complete control. It is as though the singer has both accelerator (anterior abdominal wall and LAPS) and brakes (abdominal girdle sides and back and consequently the diaphragm) under the same foot. In an experienced well-trained singer, the movement of the abdominal wall can be discrete and subtle; however, it always remains flexible and moves toward the spine throughout the phrase. This is necessary in order for breath to flow. If the abdominal wall becomes braced or locked, breath flow becomes inadequate and vocal production will be compromised.

In singers who need to project their voices unamplified over large orchestras and in large venues, these breathing and supporting mechanisms need to be trained to a high standard of efficiency, strength, and endurance. But the baseline in this training is always going to be, "not to depart from the natural functioning of the respiratory system."

NATURALNESS OF THE BREATH

The first step in breathing easily and freely is attaining proper alignment of the body (see Chapter 3). Without such alignment, the breathing mechanism has to cope rather than respond. Many of the muscles used in supporting the air also have postural responsibilities. Therefore, it is very important to stand well. The principles adhered to by both the Alexander technique and Feldenkrais method offer good guidelines for singing. Some forms of Pilates teaching are very useful in the development of core stability, especially with the work related to the transverse abdominis muscles, although some singers have found the "dance-based" work controversial. I have personally explored Tai Chi and Pilates, attending regular classes over some years, and have found both these systems highly beneficial for the training of a singer's body with respect to efficiency and strength. Modifications may need to be applied for specific types of singing tasks, but the principles remain similar: core stability, balance, endurance, flexibility, and "earthedness." In both these classes, I have felt myself on the point of vocalizing (how embarrassing for them if I did), purely because the singer in me recognizes the "feel" of the body's alignment in preparation to sing.

Inhalation (breathing in) commonly has been the prime focus of many breathing exercises, but for singers the out-breath is of more importance. When working on breathing and support with students, I prefer to focus first on the out-breath. Initially, I encourage the student to breathe out maximally without loss of postural alignment. Following this, the in-breath will be a reflex action rather than something conscious and complicated.

To test this, stand well. Breathe out through pursed lips—as though through a drinking straw to the end of available breath without losing posture. Hold this position for a couple of seconds while noticing where the tension is in the body, that is, check with hands on waistband, xiphoid area (apex of sternum and ribs), and the lower abdominal/pubic synthesis (LAPS). Then release all tension and notice how the air is drawn into the lungs automatically. The reason for this is that the diaphragm is free to contract and descend quickly creating a vacuum in the lungs. When the diaphragm descends, there is an automatic expansion of the lower ribs as the diaphragm is attached to them. In some young singers who have not been involved in aerobic/sporting activity, their usual rib expansion may be more limited and need some training. However, under no circumstances should the ribs be consciously expanded and "held" during singing. Be aware of maintaining postural alignment during this release. (i.e., if postural alignment is lost this rapid diaphragmatic descent is less efficient). This is the basis of the SPLAT-breath (Figure 4–2).

You will have noticed that on exhalation the waistband muscles increase in bulk as they contract ("fire up") in order to compress the air

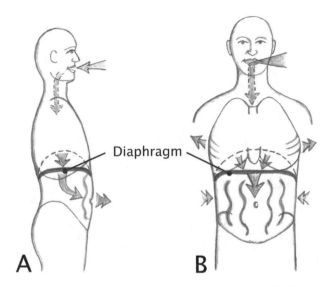

Figure 4–2. Direction of movement of rib cage, diaphragm, and abdominal wall on inhalation. **A.** Lateral view. **B.** Ventral view. Copyright Richard Webber, 2005.

before expelling it from the lungs. You also will feel muscular activation at the xiphoid and lower abdominal/pubic synthesis (LAPS). At inhalation, with the release of tension, these muscle junctions return to their neutral positions. Working in synthesis with this apparent increase in girth of the waistband during singing will be a decrease in rib expansion. (i.e., the ribs are not "held" expanded at any time but are free to move according to lung content). This does not mean that the ribs collapse, but rather that they are maintained both as part of posture and because the abdominal girdle muscles appear to be exerting a secondary control over them via the diaphragm. This physiology is highly complex and, to my knowledge, has not been adequately researched with respect to singing. On exhalation, the abdominal muscles will "bulk up" and the rib cage will be free to decrease in girth as the air is used up (Figure 4-3). The rib cage does not collapse but slowly reduces in girth as lung volumes decrease.

STABILIZING THE TORSO

Some of the muscles that attach to the upper rib cage such as the latissimus dorsi and the serratus anterior can be incorporated to act as postural stabilizers throughout the breath cycle. Vocal pedagogues sometimes suggest to students that they imagine they have a balloon under each armpit and gently squeeze. This would engage these postural stabilizers.

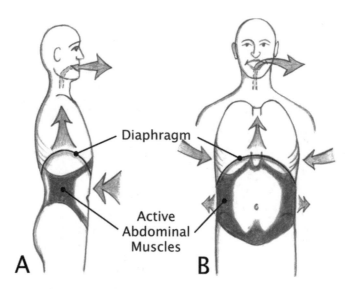

Figure 4–3. Direction of movement of rib cage, diaphragm, and abdominal wall on exhalation. **A.** Lateral view. **B.** Ventral view. Copyright Richard Webber, 2005.

This is a prime example where imagery would have been used in past pedagogic models to engage a physiologic response. I feel that this is appropriate use of imagery in that it can induce a correct physiologic response in the student's body. However, unless the teacher understands the reason why such a device works, there can be a danger of misapplication. For example, overactivation in this area also could engage pectoralis major, upper trapezius, and sternocleidomastoid muscles, which would not be appropriate for this type of singing (although in rock, belting, and pop they may be employed deliberately). For classical sound, this would not be advantageous as sternocleidomastoid, upper trapezius, and pectoralis major muscles may act both to dampen the sound and cause laryngeal constriction by false vocal fold activation. The teacher needs to be able to differentiate between these muscle groups. The sound of false vocal fold activity sometimes can be heard in the speaking voice quality of professional weightlifters who have hugely developed upper-chest musculature.

ACTIVE MUSCLE JUNCTIONS

Coordinated thoracic and abdominal systems are needed to ensure adequate air pressure for all types of singing. To support sound, we contract a large area of the abdominal musculature or wall. Figure 4–4 shows a large diamond-shaped area where support can be recognized in well-

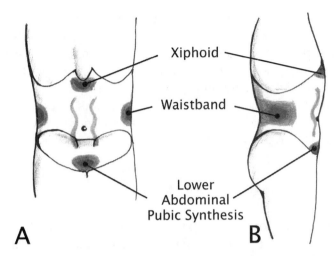

Xiphoid

Waistband

Lower
Abdominal
Pubic Synthesis

A

B

Figure 4–4. Active muscle junctions. **A.** Ventral view. **B.** Lateral view. Copyright Richard Webber, 2005.

trained singers. This diamond comprises four main areas where support can be felt with the singer's own hands.

1. The xiphoid region (where the ribs come together at the front just below the sternum).
2. The lower abdominal/pubic synthesis (LAPS—the junction 3 to 6 centimeters above the pubic bone).
3. The sides of the waistband (hands on hips with thumbs to the back).
4. The back of the waistband, which is an important power source during phonation. (Thumbs pointing forward on the waistband with fingers spread to the back. This can be best felt initially in a slightly crouched position.)

The interaction between postural alignment, breathing, and support is not yet fully understood. The muscles of active expiration also have significant postural functions. We can increase awareness of some of their expiratory functions by changing posture. For example, crouching in a monkey-type position will make the waistband activity more obvious and allow direct palpation of the muscles in the back of the waistband. Conversely, standing with a lordotic posture (swayed back) will reduce these sensations greatly. It appears that the postural functions of the muscles are engaged in a crouched position due to the shift in the center of gravity in the body. When expiratory demands are added, the movement of these muscles is greater and more obvious to palpation. It may be argued that the more efficient use of these muscles in a crouched position is related to the fact that man became fully upright relatively recently in his evolution. The interactions between the respiratory system and primal sound probably evolved during this period of less-upright posture. It is not suggested that a crouched posture would be suitable for classical voice performance, but rather that it is a means to an end in finding and training the primal support system for the voice or for correcting misaligned postures in students at the development and correction stage of their training. Posture in performance should be appropriately upright or "noble."

MUSCLES OF "FORCED EXPIRATION"

Muscles of "forced" or "active" expiration (as used in laughing, sneezing, calling, coughing, etc.) are the transverse abdominis, internal obliques, and external obliques. The rectus abdominis is cited in some literature as contributing to expiration, but in my experience as a singer and singing teacher, I have increasingly found that deactivation of this "six-pack" is essential in freeing up the supported airstream and the voice itself. Indeed, I forbid students to do stomach crunchers and to lift weights, which would strengthen this pair of muscles. The upper epigastric area of the abdomen should feel like unset jelly during phonation and inspiration, except for a connection point at the topmost border where the ribs join to the sternum and the diaphragm itself is anchored (the xiphoid process). In this area, specifically, there will be palpable muscle activation, but this should not compromise the inward movement of the belly wall during phonation (Figure 4–5).

IMPORTANT THINGS TO REMEMBER

1. The length and flexibility of the spine should appear unaffected by the act of breathing for singing in the upright position. Although there are small changes in spinal length during the breath cycle, this should not affect the postural alignment of the singer.
2. The abdominal wall around the area of the umblicus must remain flexible to allow:
   a. the belly button to move naturally toward the spine during singing.
   b. The belly button to move outward on the intake of breath.
3. The upper airway must remain free of tension on the intake of air.
4. The shoulders and upper chest should remain serene during inhalation. Any tensing or lifting of the shoulder girdle should be avoided.

Reestablishing this natural setting for respiration in students can take time, especially when they have been taught any form of overbreathing or reverse abdominal breathing.

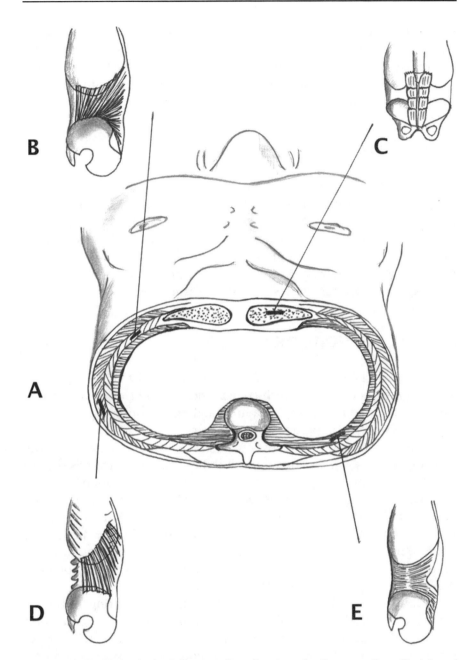

Figure 4–5. Abdominal girdle muscles showing: **A.** Cross-section. **B.** Internal oblique muscles. **C.** Rectus abdominis. **D.** External oblique muscles. **E.** Transverse abdominis. Copyright Richard Webber, 2005.

I personally attended a course in Accent Method in the 1990s and initially felt that it might have benefit in the studio. Not until I began to use it in my own singing did I realize the impact it could have. I then tested it with students, and since that time, I have been an advocate for the use of Accent Method for singers. In keeping with my own pedagogical model, I have modified Accent Method to incorporate its abdominodiaphragmatic breathing and airflow into the supported primal sound that forms the basis of my teaching. This then flows into my classical singing pedagogy.

ACCENT METHOD

Accent Method breathing normally is taught by speech and language therapists as part of the treatment for a person with a disordered voice. My Australian colleague Ron Morris is both a speech and language therapist/audiologist, and a singer who studies with me, and has studied the Accent Method with Sara and Dinah Harris, contributors to the *Voice Clinic Handbook* (Harris et al., 1998). In the next section, Morris describes the Accent Method for singers from this perspective.

ACCENT METHOD FOR SINGERS

Accent Method breathing was developed in the 1930s by Professor Svend Smith, who was a Danish speech therapist and voice researcher. He was interested in developing a holistic training approach for speech-disordered patients, in particular, stammerers. The use of Accent Method breathing was transferred early on to voice-disordered patients. The basis of Smith's work was breathing and these breathing exercises were "transferred from expiration at rest to expiration for phonation" (Thyme-Frøkjaer, 2001). These exercises were then followed by voice exercises that mirrored the natural prosody of speech. Accent Method has been widely used by speech and language therapists in Europe and in the United Kingdom but is almost unknown in the United States or Australia. In the United Kingdom, groups of singing teachers also have recognized the benefits and advantages of the method.

The fundamental principles of Accent Method; "that during the breathing cycle contraction of the diaphragm alternates with the contraction of the abdominal muscles" (Thyme-Frøjkaer, 2001) are absolutely correct for singing as well as for speech. Some modification to the exercises, however, greatly enhances their efficacy for training the dual functions of breathing and support in singers.

THE BREATH CYCLE

Inspiration occurs when additional space is created in the thoracic cavity which allows the lungs to expand and fill with air. This expansion is controlled by the primary and secondary muscles of inspiration.

The diaphragm and intercostal muscles are the primary muscles for taking in a breath, with the diaphragm by far the most important. The absolute action and function of the diaphragm is still undergoing research but we now know that, on inspiration, the diaphragm contracts downward and slightly outward causing flaring of the lower ribs and some distension of the abdomen. This creates a large amount of additional space in the thoracic cavity allowing a deep, free in-breath. The intercostal muscles appear to stabilize the rib cage to prevent its collapse when the pressure in the thoracic cavity drops as the diaphragm descends.

The secondary muscles of inspiration are those that surround the rib cage and include: the neck, shoulder, chest, and arm muscles. They can be used to gain some expansion in the upper chest but as their primary functions are in posture and movement the internal thoracic space gained is small. This upper chest breathing is inefficient and, to use, it activation of a number of these secondary muscles is required. These increases in tension can have a direct, negative impact on the efficiency of laryngeal function and resonance, thus affecting vocal tone and quality. The effects of these muscles on breathing can be seen in forced inspiration, when the person is under stress or fighting for air. The use of this upper-chest type of breathing is not recommended for classical singing.

Expiration can be either passive or active. In passive expiration, air is expelled from the lungs by simple elastic recoil of the system. The diaphragm ceases to contract and slowly returns to its resting position. Similarly, the intercostal muscles relax and some changes in the chest wall may occur. This serves to allow the air to flow out slowly and gently. Expiration in this passive way occurs at rest—sleep is an ideal time to observe passive expiration. During passive breathing, expiration can be observed to take about twice as long as inspiration.

Active expiration requires the use of the abdominal muscles to take control of the outgoing airstream. Blowing, speech, and singing all require active expiration. This type of expiration can be slowed very significantly and can take 20 to 30 times longer than the type of inspiration that occurs in singing.

The muscles that form the abdominal wall are the primary muscles of expiration, consisting of the external and internal obliques, the rectus abdominis, and the transverse abdominis. These muscles act directly to change intra-abdominal pressure, which controls the outward flow of air.

The secondary muscles consist of the internal intercostals and the transverse thoracic muscles. For many years, the intercostal muscles were thought to play a major role in most types of respiration but more recent research suggests their role is one of stabilizing the chest wall (Rubin, 1998). Indeed, they appear to act as "brakes" when the lungs are at maximum capacity. Hixon (1987) also suggests that the muscles of the rib cage are more active during expiration when the lungs are quite full with air. The muscles of the rib cage seem to play an important role in maintaining the correct breath pressure to ensure a steady vocal tone.

These rib cage muscles (predominantly the intercostals) probably act as an inhalatory balance to the expiratory force of the abdominals when lung volumes are large, such as at the beginning of a sung phrase.

In speech and singing, when expiration is active and the intra-abdominal pressure controls the outward flow of air for phonation, some interaction of the inspiratory and expiratory muscles is required. All the muscles of respiration are striated muscles and thus most are under voluntary control. The diaphragm is an exception to this rule as in some instances it does not appear to be controlled voluntarily (e.g., in sleep) and the intercostal muscles work only when involved in the cycle of respiration. Supported respiration, which is used to some extent in speech, but is vital for singing, requires an opposition of the primary muscles of inspiration and expiration so that a steady stream of air at the necessary pressure is provided. It is this interaction between inspiration and expiration that that has led to the development of various breathing techniques for singing such as "rib reserve breathing," which are not physiologically correct in their basis. In some vocal pedagogies, the inter-costal muscles are referred to as being the main breath control system when, in fact, they are not under conscious control and are always breath-dependent in their activity. The intercostal muscles are well provided with pressure receptors that help maintain the correct intrathoracic pressure for singing even though they are not under direct voluntary control. In other words, intercostal activity is driven by changes in breath pressure in the thoracic cavity rather than by conscious control. The abdominal muscles, however, are fully under voluntary/conscious control.

The development of an appropriate breath management system for singers must focus on:

- Voluntary control of breathing so that the singer can use sup-ported breath flow at will. Once this is motor-learned it becomes unconscious, and driven by the music/text.
- Efficient and flexible use of the respiratory physiology.
- Maintenance of good postural alignment.
- The natural functions and actions of both the inspiratory and expiratory muscles.
- Training of respiratory muscles in terms of strength, coordina-tion, and endurance.

Because of its focus on abdominodiaphragmatic breathing, volun-tary control of respiration, and repetitive rhythmic exercises, Accent Method breathing fulfills these requirements well. The use of the repet-itive exercises, first with fricatives and later with consonant-vowel babble, ensures a high breath flow and gradual strengthening of the respiratory muscles. The use of rhythm also encourages the development of flexi-bility and coordination.

TEACHING ACCENT METHOD TO SINGERS

Accent Method breathing for singers can be taught either individually or in groups. Group instruction is quite appropriate for singers who do not have a vocal or respiratory pathology, as the method aims to develop and strengthen breathing and support from a position of essentially normal (if not well-used) function. Singers with vocal pathologies or grossly distorted respiratory patterns should be seen individually for Accent Method instruction. Initially, it may be even more appropriate for these singers to be seen by a speech and language therapist rather than the singing teacher.

At first, Accent classes for singers focus on the development of awareness of the abdominal muscles and their uses in breathing but over time issues of support also are addressed.

Classes commence on the floor so that correct tidal breathing can be established. This ensures that the correct muscles are being used for both inspiration and expiration. Singers are then encouraged to "waste" the air. In this step, the air is expelled from the body as quickly as possible using maximal abdominal movement. This is done on the voiceless and voiced fricatives; sh /ʃ/, s /s/, f /f/, th /θ/, zh /ʒ/, z /z/, v /v/, w /w/, voiced th /ð/, and a breathy French "oo" /y/. These exercises are repeated in the side-lying position where SPLAT (see below) can be taught easily. Once this is established, the student is placed into a sitting position and all of the above steps are repeated. Each session ends with the students checking that waistband muscles are becoming active with the vigorous abdominal movements.

Over the course of lessons (usually 6 for individuals or 10 to 12 for groups) the normal pattern of accent lessons continue with students taught the rhythmic patterns from the first accent bounce (/ʃ-ʃ/) through Largo and Andante to Allegro (see the Accent Method of Thyme-Frøkjaer & Frøkjaer-Jensen, 2001). In the early stages, very vigorous abdominal movements are encouraged so that access to the waistband is obtained. The violence/excursion of the tummy movement is lessened as the complexity of the rhythmic patterns increases but for singers monitoring at the navel, epigastrium, and waistband is maintained.

As a general rule more time is spent on the fricative sounds in all the patterns as these encourage supported airflow more so than simply vowels alone. The transition from a fricative into a vowel which is usually covered quickly in traditional Accent Method instruction is given greater emphasis at all pattern levels. This serves to encourage similar degrees of abdominal support in the vowel as in the fricatives. Once this release onto vowels is well established, the consonant and vowel babble exercises and word and phrase exercises can commence.

Arm and body movements are also expanded on and singers are strongly encouraged to maintain upper body posture during these activities.

Particular care also is taken that the SPLAT breath does not alter the "noble" body posture in either seated or standing positions.

Swaying forward and back from foot to foot is used from early in the instruction period. The side-by-side skater position is used but the upper body posture and spine remain the same (long and noble). Arm movements from the shoulder also are used to ensure that the abdominal muscles can maintain their respiratory functions when additional postural work is called for; this exercise is made more difficult when marching or stepping out is added.

Specific standing work has been added to ensure that the upper body posture remains unchanged despite respiratory demands. Students stand with arms level with the shoulders, elbows are bent, and then the arms are gently brought forward so the fingers touch. This provides a good upper body posture and breathing exercises then are done to ensure that appropriate respiration is occurring beneath this posture.

CARRYING ACCENT METHOD INTO SINGING

Once release onto vowels is well established at the Largo level, carry-over into singing work should be commenced. This consists of glides and sirens using rolled "rr" and the voiced fricatives moving into simple scalar exercises. Additional exercises that promote connection such as the "Hey-Ha" scale or a triplet driven "Zeh, Zeh-eh-eh" can be given.

At this point, the singer can begin to use more subtle abdominal movements; however, it is important to ensure that the abdominal wall continues to move toward the spine throughout the "out" breath and that the front of the tummy, particularly the epigastric area, remains flexible and not braced or tense. In the studio, it has been observed that, when a singer is emotionally stressed, the solar plexis (epigastric area) sometimes becomes locked in a holding pattern, which reduces airflow. Teachers and students should be aware and monitor this potential problem.

Janice Chapman now continues:

FROM ACCENT METHOD INTO SUPPORTED SINGING

For singers who do not have severe breathing/support/posture problems, but whose breathing style for singing may need to be changed, I, (J.C.), use a sequence of simplified Accent Method exercises that lead quickly into the location and recognition of abdominal support centers as described previously. This sequence is as follows:

1. The singer lies semisupine with maximum connection of the back to the floor, and allows breath to ebb and flow as though during

sleep (i.e., belly wall will rise on inhalation and relax toward the floor on exhalation) (Figure 4–6A).

2. More active and energized use of the same tidal belly wall movement (up on inhalation and down toward the floor on expiration) with the use of breathy tone and fricative consonants, rhythmically using an up beat and a main (down) beat as follows: ss-SS /s/, sh-SH /ʃ/, zh-ZH /ʒ/, zz-ZZ /z/, ff-FF /f/, vv-VV /v/, th-TH (voiceless and voiced) /θ,ð/, whoo-WHOO /wu/

3. These sounds are repeated until an element of boredom sets in. This is usually when the conscious control gives way to the subconscious.

4. This exercise then is repeated lying on the side with the hand on the belly wall. Singers notice that they need to be a little more proactive with the belly wall in this position (Figure 4–6B).

5. The standing version of this exercise is with student and teacher paired like skaters, one foot ahead of the other, preferably in front of a mirror. They place their hands so that contact is maintained with the back of the hand on each other's belly wall. Then a gently forward and backward rocking movement is added, raising the front toe and then the back heel in turn. This rocking movement coordinates with the movement of the belly wall, that is, belly out as the body moves forward, and belly back as the body moves back, but not disturbing the general posture. The upbeat and main beat fricatives/ vowels sequence is used to gain access to the voicing (Figure 4–6C).

This step may not be used until the previous four steps are well established and easy for the student. The singer then places his or her own hands in turn on the muscle support junctions as described and repeats exercise 4, noticing the muscle activation, which occurs naturally following an Accent Method (or SPLAT) in-breath (Figures 4–6 D–F).

DEGREES OF SPLAT

SPLAT is an onomatopoeic word that I began using in the studio as a quick reminder to singers to release abdominal tension at the end of a sung phrase. Subsequently one of my colleagues, Dinah Harris suggested that SPLAT was an acronym for *Singers Please Loosen Abdominal Tension*, which gave it more gravitas. This word seems to have caught on among singers and singing teachers. As my pedagogy has evolved, we are now using "semi-SPLAT" (during which the LAPS remain partially engaged) and "demi-semi-SPLAT"—even quicker! The advantages of the SPLAT (or diaphragmatic) in-breath are:

■ The air is taken into the lowest and largest part of the lungs (i.e., the bottom of the pear shape).

A

B

C

D

Figure 4–6. A. Accent Method—Supine position. **B.** Accent Method—Side position. **C.** Accent Method—Side-by-side standing position. **D.** Xiphoid muscle junction. *(contin-*

56

E F

Figure 4–6. *(continued)* **E.** Waistband muscle junction. **F.** Lower abdominal pubic synthesis muscle junction.

- The intake is very quick, especially for semi and demi-semi-SPLAT.
- The air intake is efficient.
- The air intake is noiseless (i.e., no audible gasping).
- The singer's body is immediately ready to automatically reconnect to the necessary support for the next phrase.
- The singer's shoulders can remain inactive and down.
- Upper chest tension is kept to a minimum.

When a singer comes for a vocal consultation, I may recommend an initial course of Accent Method training prior to commencement of vocal lessons. Once this course of training is underway or completed and we commence vocal lessons, I extend their Accent Method training into supported vocalization as discussed above. However, the residual postural problems, which may have become entrenched because of the poor breathing patterns, can take many more weeks to remediate. There is always an ongoing monitoring of breathing, support, and postural alignment thereafter.

Use of primal sounds to awaken abdominal muscle awareness is appropriate at this stage. Calling, moaning, laughing, strong sounds of agreement (Mmm, mmm, etc.) These then can be extended in duration and finally turned into singing sounds.

Once there is a comfortable recognition of the muscles that engage under primal sound and an acceptance of their function during singing, scales on lip trills, rolled "rr" and semivoiced fricatives can follow.

ROLE OF THE LAPS

The role of the lower abdominal/pubic synthesis junction (LAPS) in both postural and respiratory function needs to be addressed. I believe that, in a well-trained and experienced singer, the LAPS maintain a tonicity throughout the whole breath cycle (i.e., never fully releasing as in Accent Method breathing) but partially releasing for the in-breath, especially when a fast intake of air is needed (e.g., Handelian fioratura). Once the support junctions are able to react on an instinctive level, and the basic abdominal movement is easy and natural, then what I would describe as the "semi-SPLAT" version can be introduced. Once semi-SPLAT is achievable, it becomes the default position for the in-breath for most repertoire singing. Much research will be required before this interaction between muscle tone for posture and movement overlaid with muscle action for the specific singing tasks is evaluated and understood. Research currently is underway using ultrasound to differentiate the abdominal girdle muscles in action (see Chapter 11, Vocal and Respiratory Anatomy and Physiology).

As a singer myself, I am aware that this area of my own body is very strong, but in experienced singers, this strength often is not recognized and is taken for granted. As a teacher, when I work with young, inexperienced, or poorly trained singers, the absence of this muscle tone and the resultant effect on the voice itself is quite amazing. Anecdotal studio-based statements are not good enough in this day and age, but money is unlikely to be allocated for quantitative research into this sort of work in the near future. At this time, qualitative studies are more likely to be possible.

THE COLLAR CONNECTION

Once the abdominal muscles are supporting the out-breath, and the posture is good, it will be easy to see a natural expansion occurring at the base of the singer's throat that coordinates with phonation. The singers themselves may have no awareness of this, except that their voicing feels more efficient and easy. Conscious awareness can be gained either by looking in a mirror, or by placing a hand on the base of the throat with fingers lightly spread like a necklace. This could be identified as "open throat" or in the Estill model "Sob," but it also is evidence of good subglottal air pressure and activation of the sternothyroid strap muscles, which are the true depressors of the larynx. The collar connection is an interaction of muscle and breath which can be described for students as being the "top of the support system" as it only can be achieved with good supported airflow, good posture, and an absence of upper-chest muscular tension. The collar connection also is a resonance phenomenon and is dealt with in more detail in following chapters.

NOTES ON SUPPORT

For most people, the muscles of active abdominal support engage naturally under emotional utterances. A singer can use his or her hands, his or her teacher's, or a partner's hands to reinforce the subjective experience of using the system. The muscles should engage at, or just in advance of, the actual voicing, and never during the inhalatory cycle. Prephonatory tuning (imagining the pitch, dynamic, and color of the sound) engages the appropriate support fractionally ahead of the sound production (i.e., with the imagination). This should occur without conscious control, but where singers have been using other systems (such as rib reserve, rib flaring, or reverse abdominal holding), some retraining is needed.

This active abdominal support as described should be used as a continuum throughout the vocal phrase, and should not "pump" with the music or text. The use of an extended rolled "rr" or sung fricative when practicing a phrase should give the singer's body the experience of this continuous flow of subglottal air pressure.

THE TIME FACTOR IN TRAINING

The teaching of breathing and support in a young undergraduate singer who begins with nothing in place can be relatively easy. A gradual process of assimilation, combining constant affirmation to practice good postural alignment, use of physiologically correct inhalation and exhalation, and encouragement to find and maintain the emotionally connected primal sound base can take between 1 and 2 years of normal weekly lessons. However, some students are much quicker and some much slower depending on their kinesthetic awareness, motivation, and psychological state. Where permitted and appropriate, one of the best ways to shorten the learning process and teach a student's body to be suitably active is for the teacher and student to use their hands like a manual therapist. The student can feel appropriate muscle activity when the teacher demonstrates (student's hands on teacher's body) and the teacher can check for appropriate muscle activity when the student sings, (teacher's hands on student's body).

Remedialization for singers who have been taught other methods of breath management can be fast or slow depending on many factors such as how long they have been singing, their psychological state enabling change to take place, trust in the teacher, motivation, and willingness to work hard. Changes to muscle memory can involve many interdependent systems within the body and these systems all need to interact. I sometimes feel that a singer needs to have 75% of the pieces of their jigsaw puzzle more or less in position before the last 25% falls into place making the whole picture. During the process of making changes, singers often get a "flash" of what the holistic end product is going to be. This is very valuable as these flashes present as phrases or even multiple phrases where they suddenly feel everything is easy and flowing and they are able to be musicians again. Many of the problems that a singer experiences at a vocal level in essence, are support issues, and it is the intervention at this level, which can produce the "flash." It may take another 6 months or more and interventions on other levels for this holistic integration to become automatic.

Regardless of whether one is working in a developmental or remedial mode, it takes time for the student's body to motor-learn new muscular patterns. In particular, changes to the breathing and support system move from gross movements through to finer and more subtle ones, and this may take anything from 6 weeks to 6 months. Repetitive daily practice is the only way to integrate and refine these new movements. Unfortunately when well connected up, the singer may have very little kinesthetic awareness of the support system underneath their sound (i.e., it feels suspiciously natural). The best way to check that the support is appropriately active is by palpation by student or teacher.

PEDAGOGICAL IMPLICATIONS

The core of the teaching model consists of primal sound, postural alignment, and breathing and support. All three of these components are of vital importance and should be addressed before other aspects of voice production (see Chapter 1, Figure 1–3.)

The demands of the classical singing style on the whole body of the singer make it imperative to address the issues of primal sound, postural alignment, and breathing and support in a way that allows these three core components to be constantly visited and adjusted. As each component improves, other vocal functions can change. In my experience, poor posture has a huge effect on vocal function not only because of the housing of the larynx in the neck, but also because of the need for core stability within the torso for the demands of balanced airflow tasks such as classical singing. There is a sort of chicken and egg scenario in many singers, where poor posture is both caused and made worse by poor vocal habits and vice versa. Addressing all three core components, both separately and interactively, is vital in these cases.

BACK TO NATURE

When a singer has established and developed the breathing and support system under his or her singing, it can end up in performance feeling like he or she is not doing anything. This is because the muscles are connected to the emotional motor system and consequently working on "autopilot." Once a singer's muscle systems are trained athletically for the task of singing classically, he or she can work without conscious control during performance conditions. Ideally, a singer should take a breath at the start of an opera or concert, and not be actively aware of any aspects of breathing and support throughout the performance. The opera and concert singer needs his or her full attention for artistry and performance and only when problems occur is there any need at all for awareness of the mechanics of breathing and support. Then, there can be a quick mental checklist available for reference if necessary.

> **The most affirming thing about this system of breathing and support is that a performing singer who is able to use emotional imagination and stimulus (which is part of one's artistry) will constantly be reconnecting to the breathing and support machinery in an unconscious way. Active abdominal support (athletic in its nature) is required for classical singing. When this has been entrained in the body, it is awakened and reinforced by the emotional stimulus of performing. Herein lies the "back to nature" element; singing from the emotions in a way that has the power to move the audience while contributing to the integrity of the instrument.**

REFERENCES

Harris, T., Harris, S., Rubin, J. S., & Howard, D. M. (1998). *The voice clinic handbook*. London, UK: Whurr.

Hixon, T. J. (1987). *Respiratory function in speech and song*. Boston, MA: College-Hill Press.

Rubin, J., in Harris et al. (1998). *The voice clinic handbook*. London, UK: Whurr.

Sataloff, R. T. (1998). *Vocal health and pedagogy*. San Diego CA: Singular.

Thyme-Frøkjaer, K., & Frøkjaer-Jenson, B. (2001). *The accent method: A rational voice therapy in theory and practice*. Bicester, UK: Speechmark.

Chapter 5

PHONATION AND THE SPEAKING VOICE

Janice Chapman and Ron Morris

Phonation — "the production or utterance of vocal sound"

(Shorter Oxford Dictionary)

As in any other musical instrument, there must be a source of the vibrations required to make sound, and for the voice, this is the vocal folds (or cords), situated within the larynx. The vocal folds are like two tiny muscular shelves that close, meeting in the middle to create sound, and opening to take in air. The pure sound produced at the level of the vocal folds is like a buzz. You can get an idea of this sound by stretching the neck of a partially filled balloon and hearing the sound of the escaping air. The more stretched the balloon the higher the pitch.

A variety of sounds is possible within the larynx itself. These are made by the gradations of vocal fold thickness and mass, stretch, tension, and air pressure. The vocal folds come together in response to the impulse to make sound. The mechanism for this is extremely complex and is discussed in Chapter 12.

Pitch differentiation is made by changing the length and mass of the vocal folds and/or adjusting breath pressure. Low pitches typically are made with short, thick vocal folds and high pitches with longer, thinner vocal folds. Ideally, there is a constant, subconscious adjustment of the vocal muscles and breath pressure, allowing the pitch to change easily and rapidly.

ACTIONS OF THE VOCAL FOLDS

Appropriate phonation relies on three components (Thyme-Frøjkaer & Frøjkaer-Jensen, 2001):

- Muscular activity to bring the vocal folds to the midline
- Onset of airflow
- Coordination between muscle and breath.

In the prephonatory phase, the glottis (the space between the vocal folds) narrows to 2 to 3 millimeters and then air begins to flow through the glottis as exhalation occurs. There is an increase in the pressure of air below the glottis (this is sub glottal air pressure), which increases the speed at which the air moves past the vocal folds. Negative pressure develops in the lungs and this draws the vocal folds together (Bernoulli effect). Complete adduction, that is, closure of the vocal folds, is then accomplished by the intrinsic laryngeal muscles (see Chapter 11). The timing of the muscle movement and the breath flow is vital to develop an appropriate onset of phonation for the task in hand.

If the airflow occurs before the glottis is closed, a breathy onset (sounding like an /h/) will occur. If the closure is complete before the airflow commences, a glottal attack (sounding like a small click) will result as the air forces the vocal folds apart. If used with too hard an attack, this can be seen as a vocal fault. However, a light glottal stroke can be used effectively in the correction of vocal fold closure deficiency. The glottal attack also needs to be developed technically for the purposes of language and artistry. Explained and monitored carefully, it can be a very useful vocal tool.

Coordinated action of muscle and breath leads to a simultaneous onset, which is efficient and usually the most appropriate for classical singing. The Estill figures for vocal onset are an excellent teaching aid (Appendix 1).

Research into vocal fold vibration continues but we now acknowledge that the myoelastic/aerodynamic theory of voice production as the most valid. Interaction among physicists, voice scientists, anatomists, and voice users has developed and shaped this rather complicated theory that explains the muscle/breath balance within the larynx. A full description can be found in works by Hirano and Titze, but for our purposes, a simple 10-step view will suffice (Figure 5–1).

1. Air pressure builds up below the closed vocal folds.
2. The folds begin to separate from the bottom with the mucous membrane being driven up toward the top of the fold (this wavelike movement can be seen on stroboscopy).
3. The upper borders of the folds are blown apart and the air flows through the glottis.

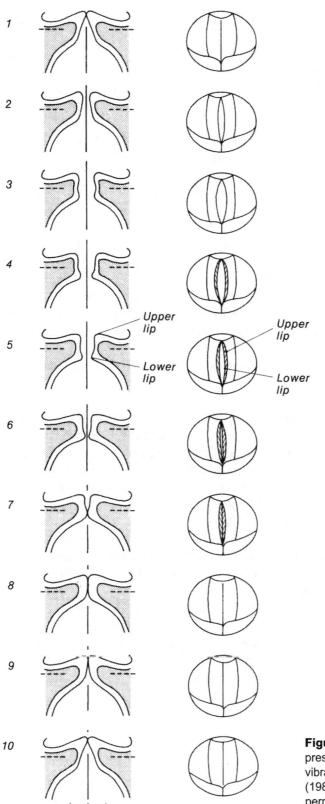

Figure 5–1. Schematic presentation of vocal fold vibration. From Hirano (1981), reproduced with permission of Springer-Verlag.

4. The lower borders of the vocal folds are sucked together by a combination of changes in air pressure and the elastic recoil of the system.
5. The movement accelerates and the lower or inferior borders of the vocal folds approximate.
6. This movement continues.
7. The lower borders of the folds close again and airflow ceases.
8. This closure continues vertically up the vocal fold
9. The entire vocal fold is closed.
10. Subglottal air pressure continues to increase to commence the cycle again.

In head voice or falsetto, the waveform is different in that the whole mass of the vocal fold is not engaged in the action. Because only part of the mass of the vocal fold is used, the vertical excursion of the wave is smaller and simpler in its movement. This results in the closed phase (i.e., the time which the vocal folds are approximated) being shorter, and in some cases, the vocal folds do not actually meet at all (i.e., unsupported falsetto).

In classical style singing there are three basic types of valving the voice:

1. *Breathy*—incomplete closure of the vocal fold edges with air escaping through the glottis. This can be a glottal chink, where the posterior one third of the folds remain open during phonation; an hourglass configuration (a vocal fold pathology or muscle tension dysphonia may be the underlying cause); and general laxity of tonus in the vocal fold musculature (hypovalving).
2. *Balanced*—this is described in Johann Sundberg's book, *Science of the Singing Voice* as "flow phonation," and is the most desirable condition for classical voice production. Vocal fold closure and subglottal air pressure are balanced to create full closure with appropriate valving for the vocal tasks.
3. *Hyperadducted*—described as "pressed phonation." Vocal folds are pressed too tightly together to allow easy phonation. This often is caused by insufficient subglottal airflow, and resulting muscle tension in the neck and articulatory system. Sound quality is "pressed," tight and small in tone, and singers using this type of quality often suffer from hoarseness, vocal fatigue, and even vocal pathologies.

EFFORT LEVELS

A very valuable concept, highlighted by Jo Estill in her Voicecraft system, has been the recognition of effort levels within the various components of voicing. I use this concept in teaching but prefer to call it "energy" to help students identify and quantify effort in terms of where it is and how much they are using in singing. Initially, most students locate energy at the level of the voice in general, with very little energy located in the body. In my pedagogy, a balance of energy is required. Over time, it is possible to use this concept of effort/energy toward finer and finer discriminations within the vocal tract.

VIBRATO

Vibrato is intrinsic to the singing instrument and should feel natural to the singer. It can be described as an oscillation of intensity and pitch perceived as a fuller quality of sound. It creates the illusion of true pitch and can deviate as much as a semitone and still be perceived by the listener as acceptable. A healthy vibrato is regular and consistent around the pitch, and is the product of a well-coordinated, balanced vocal production (therefore, it is gained rather than taught). Once breathing, support, and postural alignment are well established, vibrato usually will appear as a natural phenomenon.

Most studies look at vibrato as a function of the larynx. However, viewed holistically, the entire singing machine contributes to it. Vibrato arises from sympathetic oscillations in the larynx and pharynx. Its extent and intensity is dependent on a number of factors such as airflow, emotional connection, and voice training. When a sung sound has no vibrato, it is like a siren or sine wave and often is unpleasant to listen to (oops! Kettle's boiled!). In the singing voice, "straight" tone often is produced by excessive tension of throat and facial muscles that ultimately may diminish the efficiency and health of the voice. Sometimes straight tone is chosen by the singer for artistic reasons, and in some schools of early music singing, a straight tone is preferred. If breathing and support are well-trained, the use of a straight tone for artistic effect is not necessarily vocally unhealthy. In my experience, the straight tone preferred by some choral conductors can, however, produce vocal difficulties especially if the singing is not supported by good breath and posture.

FALSE VOCAL FOLDS (VENTRICULAR FOLDS)

The false vocal folds, which lie above the true folds, are a secondary valving in everyday life, to help in tasks of heavy lifting, swallowing, coughing, and grunting. They also have a role in protecting the true vocal folds. However, when a singer has inadequate vocal technique, these folds can become partially active during phonation and create an effortful sound that often has a component of white noise in it. This type of inappropriate valving can be heard in the speaking voices of professional weightlifters, for example. The cause in singers often can be traced to inadequate airflow, effortful phonation habits, tongue root and jaw tension, and reversed abdominal support (i.e., with the belly pressed down and out during voicing).

Because of the effects the false vocal folds can have on classical singing, I advise students to refrain from using heavy weights in the gym especially if hypervalving is involved. There also are concerns if their weight training leads to muscular imbalances especially around the shoulders and chest. Singers who wish to take up a gym program must ensure that their exercises are designed to give a balanced body shape and never involve a weight they cannot lift without constantly exhaling. Good personal trainers and Pilates teachers stipulate a free out-breath for all resistance activities.

THE INTERACTION OF PHONATION AND THE CORE COMPONENTS OF THE PEDAGOGICAL MODEL

The vocal folds and their housing, the larynx, are suspended in the neck. Therefore, the integrity of the spinal posture is crucial to maintaining the setting and flexibility of the vocal machinery. When alignment and breath support are inadequate, this mechanism almost inevitably will be compromised.

When working with singers who present with problems at the level of the vocal folds, I work first with the core components of the model (i.e., breathing and support, postural alignment, and primal sound). Quite often, phonation problems are a result of inadequacies in other parts of the mechanism. If these more fundamental problems in the vocal system are not dealt with, the phonation problems will tend to recur. For example, pressed phonation, which may be due to a recalcitrant tongue root and jaw tension, will not be fully eradicated until the deficiencies in support/posture/breathing have been addressed.

In some cases, however, corrections to phonation do have to be introduced during the development of the core components as the efficiency of the valving directly affects the subglottal air pressure. This is particularly important when there is evidence of air escape through the glottis.

It may be difficult for the teacher to differentiate between the sound of escaping air, and the white noise that is generated when the false vocal folds are too active. An exercise that can provide a remedy for both these problems at the same time is to use a soft glottal stroke onset and immediately go into a "suppressed giggle" for the vowel. The soft glottal stroke will close the vocal folds while the suppressed giggle encourages false vocal fold retraction. This maneuver cannot be accomplished successfully without good abdominal support.

THE YOUNG AND DEVELOPING SINGER

The phonatory mechanism of the voice strengthens over time with good use and habits. Until children reach puberty, their larynges are small and set high in the neck. There is a gradual descent of the larynx from about one year of age but adult laryngeal position is not reached until after puberty. The main sexual hormones (estrogen in women and testosterone in men) flood the young person's system causing considerable growth in the vocal organ, especially in boys. Until this growth spurt is complete, the voice will be relatively unstable in its behavior and capability. It is best not to assign a "fach" (classification of voice type) to young voices while physical development is still underway. Singing within a small comfortable range is to be encouraged should the adolescent wish to keep singing throughout this mutational period (see Cooksey, 1992).

Vocal exercises for the young or developing singer need to be chosen carefully. Research into human exercise physiology tells us that exercises using heavy resistance build strength but not endurance, whereas exercises that are repeated can build both strength and endurance. Singers need to build both strength and endurance with the additional burden of flexibility.

I believe that, in classical singing, the appropriate gross muscle systems in the torso should provide the required strength and endurance, allowing the smaller discrete laryngeal maneuvers, which demand both precision and flexibility, to function free of inappropriate tension.

Exercises for young singers to develop the strength and endurance within the torso are best introduced with repetition at a moderate level of muscular activity. Development at the level of the vocal folds can then follow naturally, but I have found that using the secondary valving of a rolled "rr," the lip trill, or voiced fricative ensures that the laryngeal function is healthily maintained (see Appendix 1, Exercises rolled "rr").

REGISTERS

Until recently, it was accepted by the scientific community that there are two principal physiologic registers in the voice, that is, where there is a clear and demonstrable difference in the way the vocal machinery functions as evidenced by videostroboscopy. This is evident in the vocal fold mass, length, tension, and waveform (Baken in Sataloff, 1998; see also chapter 11). These often are referred to as "modal and loft," "heavy and light mechanism," or "thick and thin folds."

More recent thinking as described by Nathalie Henrich (2006) defines register by the laryngeal vibratory mechanisms. She identifies four physiologic registers designated as "laryngeal mechanisms": Mechanism 0, Mechanism 1, Mechanism 2, and Mechanism 3, (M0, M1, M2, and M3), which correspond to Vocal fry, Modal voice, Head voice/Falsetto, and Whistle. In singing, although this reality can be dealt with intellectually, we also are coping with resonance and kinesthetic sensations that muddy the water considerably for us. I propose to discuss registers from the point of view of my own pedagogy while recognizing that, as yet, there is no scientific consensus on the singing voice registers (Figure 5–2).

MALE VOICES

In men's voices I recognize four registers:

- Vocal fry
- Modal register
- Head register
- Falsetto

I recognize these as registers because singers need technical strategies to make transitions between them.

Vocal Fry (Male Voices)

The vocal folds are held in a way that provides a loose closure with air allowed to bubble through this loose glottis, with a resulting low-frequency popping sound. McKinney (1982) points out that fry can be used to obtain low pitches that would not be possible in modal register. He also states that the use of fry should not be carried up into the range of the modal register. Vocal fry is sometimes employed by the deep bass choral singers in the Russian repertoire, but personally I do not find it a very useful quality for solo singers in that it has such severe limitations of dynamics, range, and color.

Modal Register (Male Voices)

This is the normal register for speaking and for much of singing. The vocal folds vibrate along their entire length with medial compression created by activity in the vocalis and cricothyroid muscles. (Medial compression is within the depth of the folds and therefore is vertical.) The pitch range in this register will be in the region of:

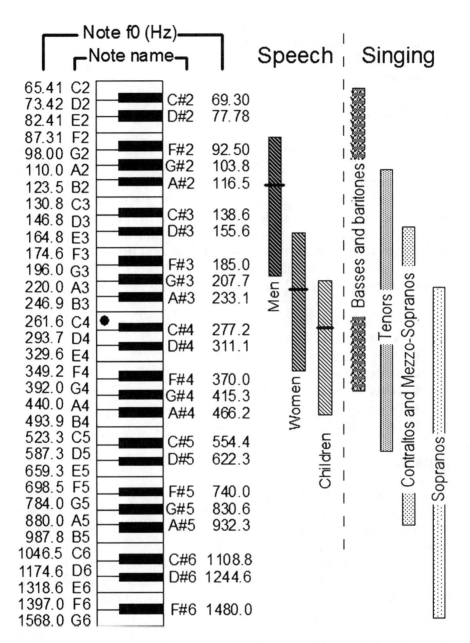

Figure 5–2. "Fundamental frequency values for notes of the musical scale extending two octaves either side of middle C (*marked with a black spot*). Approximate fundamental frequency ranges used in singing for sopranos, mezzo-sopranos/altos, tenors, and baritones/basses, and the speech of men, women, and children, are marked (Harris et al. 1998). Adapted from Howard (1998) by David Howard by permission of Whurr Publishers.

- Bass Eb2 to Bb3
- Bass baritone F2 to D4
- Baritone (heroic) A2 to Eb4

- Baritone (lyric) Bb2 to Eb4
- Tenor (heroic/spinto) Bb2 to E4
- Tenor lyric C3 to F4
- Tenor light C3 to F#4

Head Register

In head register, as the pitch rises, muscular changes are required in the larynx. Although the vibrating mass of the vocal folds becomes thinner with less vertical closure, the whole mass of the fold is still involved in the vibration cycle. At the upper end of this register, the cricothyroid and vocalis engagement is giving way to activity in the thryroarytenoid muscles. Usually, men are using Laryngeal Mechanism 1 with resonance adjustments that make this singing register different from modal register.

The range of pitches in this register (which will include some overlap into the modal register) are in the region of:

- Bass A3 to F#4
- Bass baritone C4 to G4
- Baritone (heroic) D4 to G4
- Baritone (lyric) D4 to Ab4
- Tenor (heroic/spinto) E4 to C5
- Tenor (lyric) E4 to D5
- Tenor (light) F4 to Eb5

Falsetto

This register is the highest in the male voice and sounds to the listener to have a female quality. In this register, only the vocal fold margins vibrate and the closed phase is either very short or nonexistent, that is, the vocal folds do not actually approximate.

The countertenor/falsettist voice is in common use in some musical cultures. This register is available in all male voices regardless of their fach, but needs to be dealt with for the purposes of gaining better understanding in two main categories:

- The choral type countertenor, mostly singing in sacred music
- The operatic falsettist

In both singing styles, I have trained singers to use full abdominal support. This allows the development of dynamic range and color and the voice has more carrying power and stamina. A recent preliminary study using "Voce Vista" suggests that the fully trained counter tenor voice uses Laryngeal Mechanism 2 but the closed quotient (CQ) as measured by electroglottography is very similar to a female singing in this register with a CQ of around 50%.

The usual pitching mechanism of the untrained, unsupported choral countertenor is via their ear (controlling pitch aurally). These singers often are excellent sight readers having evolved in the British-type choral tradition from childhood. This type of singing can be very limited if they wish to become soloists, and I have found it essential to help them build a full vocal technique.

There often is a large overlap between the registers of head and falsetto. When a falsettist has a fully developed vocal technique, choices of where and how the register is managed can be made for artistic and dramatic reasons rather than from vocal limitation. Other male voice types have the option of changing into falsetto register to sing high notes, but this should be used only for artistic purposes or at the behest of the composer. In singers (not falsettists) with a solid vocal technique, there will be little need to use this register at all in performance unless so dictated by the composer. Certainly, I would not encourage singers to change to falsetto in normal singing although this register may be useful in the studio as a tool for technical development.

Countertenors and falsettists often think that their modal/head registers are "no go" areas. However, once their vocal technique is adequately developed, especially abdominal support and breath flow, it is possible to negotiate the transition from head voice into falsetto and back again smoothly. It is easier for a falsettist with a tenor-type larynx to make this transition than it is for those who have a physiologically larger baritone and bass larynx.

Ranges for transition are in the region of:

Tenor-type falsettist:
- Head voice to C#4
- Falsetto from Ab3 upward

Baritone-type falsettist:
- Head voice to A3
- Falsetto from F3 upward

Larynx structure and flexibility will determine the upper range of the falsetto register.

FEMALE VOICE

In female voices I recognize five registers:

- Vocal fry
- Modal (chest)
- Middle register
- Head register
- Whistle register

Vocal Fry

In the female voice, this would rarely be used in classical singing. It may be called for in some contemporary compositions for effect. (It is almost inaudible without amplification.) The mechanism is the same as described for male voices.

Modal (Chest) Register

Modal register should be the main speaking voice quality. Sometimes females use a head voice register for speech and this often can generate vocal problems. In the singer, this constitutes a potential vocal misuse and should be corrected with speech therapy. In modal register, the vocal folds are short, vibrating with their full mass. On viewing with stroboscopy, the vocal folds appear thick and show a large amplitude mucosal wave. The thyroarytenoid and vocalis muscles are active and the cricothyroid is passive. This means that the visor of the larynx remains open. In this register, the need for abdominal support easily can be ignored or underestimated, although in some singers (especially extroverts), it is intuitively supported very well. I have found that, in singers whose speaking voices are disassociated (i.e., the Daddy's little girl type of phonation), support is rarely present. The need for some engagement of the muscles of the abdominal girdle is especially strong when easy access to, and transition from, this modal register is needed.

Ranges

- Contralto: (the "rare as hen's teeth" fach) D3 to E4
- Mezzo-soprano (dramatic) F3 to F4
- Mezzo-soprano (lyric/light) G3 to F4
- Soprano (dramatic/spinto) G3 to G4
- Soprano (lyric) Ab3 to F4
- Soprano (light/stratospheric) Bb3 to F4

Middle Register

Much of the female singer's time is spent in this range and the most crucial feature of its management is, in my experience, abdominal support. The vocal folds now are being controlled by the medial compression muscles (vocalis and cricothyroid) in conjunction with the anterior/posterior pull of the thyroarytenoids. As pitch rises within this register, the medial compression begins to give way to the anterior/posterior control of the thyroarytenoids via the gradual closing of the thyroid visor (see chapter 11). Henrich (2006) suggests that female singers very easily use Laryngeal Mechanism 2 with resonance enhancement to produce this middle register.

With strong abdominal support, it is possible to raise the pitch without closing the visor, but in doing so the transition into the next register will not be smooth or easy. The middle voice will have a thick and unwieldy sound, which can develop a wobble over time, as the vocal folds need too much breath pressure to operate efficiently.

Ranges

- Contralto Bb4 to D5
- Mezzo-soprano (dramatic) C4 to E5
- Mezzo-soprano (lyric/light) C4 to F5
- Soprano (dramatic/spinto) D4 to F5
- Soprano (lyric) D4 to F#5
- Soprano (light/stratospheric) Eb4 to Ab5

Transition from the middle into the head registers requires training and can be difficult for some singers but the benefits provided by the puffy cheeks exercise (see Exercise Section Appendix 1) can greatly assist this process.

Head Register

In head register, the medial compression muscles are no longer active and pitching is controlled by the thyroarytenoid muscles. This sounds similar to the falsetto register in the male voice but the vocal folds continue to meet, allowing the head register in females to have a full range of dynamics and color (Figure 5–3). Singers are now firmly in Laryngeal Mechanism 2.

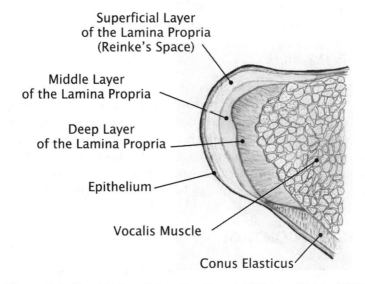

Figure 5–3. Vocal fold sagittal section. Copyright Richard Webber, 2005.

Ranges

- Contralto C5 to Bb5
- Mezzo-soprano (dramatic) D5 to C6
- Mezzo-soprano (lyric/light) Eb5 to C6
- Soprano (dramatic/spinto) Eb5 to C#6
- Soprano (lyric) E5 to Eb6
- Soprano (light/stratospheric) F#5 to E6

Whistle Register

McKinney (1982) indicated that this register was underresearched. This same comment can be made today. We do know that the larynx forms a small triangular opening between the arytenoid cartilages through which air is passed to form a simple sinusoidal wave. The vocal folds are thin and very tensed. This gives the high whistlelike sound, which can be made by most women and children. In the female singing voice, it is possible and advantageous to explore and develop this capability for most singers. Using a good supported airstream and a rolled "rr" scale, the upper whistle register can be easily connected to the top of the head voice and further practiced into normal singing. The use of additional 'twang' (aryepiglottic narrowing) in this register greatly assists the vocal efficiency, power, and transition from head voice into whistle register.

Ranges

- Contralto Bb5 upward
- Mezzo-soprano (dramatic) Bb5 upward
- Mezzo-soprano (lyric/light) B5 upward
- Soprano (dramatic/spinto) C6 upward
- Soprano (lyric) Db6 upward
- Soprano (light/stratospheric) Eb6 upward

Overlap in Registers

In each voice type, there are areas where there is a choice of which registration to use, often dictated by the shape of the phrase, whether the pitch within the musical phrase is rising or falling, the dramatic or vocal intensity of the music, and the general tessitura of the section being sung. This area may consist of a few semitones at the upper end of one register and the lower end of the next register, where a well-trained singer will have real choices available that can be made for artistic purposes.

LARYNGEAL CONTROL

In the past, singers and teachers often have been reluctant to address the larynx itself and to seek knowledge and understanding about its function. Since the invention and development of the fiberoptics industry in the 1980s, it has been possible to view the larynx and its functions from the inside. This has led to a great opening up of the knowledge base, not just for medicine and science, but with a huge potential for singers and teachers to become acquainted and comfortable with the larynx as a strong, discrete, and highly sophisticated machine.

This knowledge has allowed pedagogues to develop skills in both diagnosing and correcting vocal faults based on what they hear. They are able to listen to the machinery working in much the same way as a highly skilled motor mechanic can listen to an engine and know what is wrong with it and where to look for the problem. For these skills to develop, pedagogues have needed a clear system that allows them to codify and define voice quality in terms of laryngeal function. Experience in using this sort of listening and diagnosing of vocal faults when allied with physiologic and biomechanical knowledge can save much time and wasted effort for both the singer and the teacher.

The American researcher Jo Estill in her early studies with Ray Colton and others produced a system of voice figures whereby a person could practice various vocalizations and maneuvers and achieve predicted results. She called this system "Estill Voicecraft" and developed "figures" in the same way as ice skaters practice maneuvers on the ice until near perfection, then have them available for their artistic endeavors. Similarly, Estill argued that these figures could be practiced by voice users and then appropriately remembered in the muscles during artistic use of the instrument. In particular, this system was most valuable for learning about and teaching the different configurations of the larynx and the resonators. Estill was able to validate her research with acoustic measurements and simultaneous videostroboscopy, which showed the tiny movements of the different areas of the singing instrument from within the larynx itself.

The Estill model has been an invaluable teaching tool, but I recognized very early on in my association with Jo Estill and the system, that, in order to do the figures and use the system effectively, considerable demands were automatically being made on the breathing and support mechanism. The work I had previously done to understand abdominal support seemed even more valid when aligned with the discrete maneuvers of the Estill figures, which often called on primal sounds (e.g., sob, cry, etc.) as the vocal template. My own understanding of the physical and neural underpinning of these primal sounds reinforced my belief that the Estill Voicecraft model worked best when allied with my own breathing/support model.

During the last two decades, great strides have been made in the understanding of the extrinsic musculature of the vocal mechanism and how such things as posture and alignment can affect the way the larynx itself operates. This has meant that physiotherapists, osteopaths, and massage therapists now have a role in managing vocal tension and their skills can be called on to help singers.

Pioneers in the field of vocal manual therapy have been the Voice Clinic team at Queen Mary's Hospital, Sidcup (Harris et al., 1998) and in particular Jacob Lieberman, the osteopath attached to this clinic. Muscle tension dysphonia problems in singers are now part of the "vocal health agenda" and can be solved before the vocal folds themselves are compromised or damaged (see Harris et al., 1998).

THE POSITION OF THE LARYNX IN THE NECK

It is generally accepted by pedagogues that the ideal laryngeal setting for classical singing is a low one. This is because the richer harmonics that result from a longer vocal tract are expected in this genre. The means of attaining this low laryngeal setting is of paramount importance as we have true depressor muscles, and what has been identified as false depressors of the larynx available for this task. The false depressors normally are used in swallowing, eating, and other nonvocal tasks and can involve inappropriate tensions not conducive to good voicing. Of particular concern is the use of tongue root and jaw muscles. The only true depressors of the larynx are the sternothyroid, the sternohyoid, and omohyoid muscles. In singing, the most important of these is the sternothyroid (Figure 5–4).

This pair of strap muscles is particularly active in primal sounds and in some inhalations such as the "pre-yawn" (see Chapter 4).

In the training of singers, great care should be taken to avoid activation of the false depressors during both inhalation and in singing. Acti-

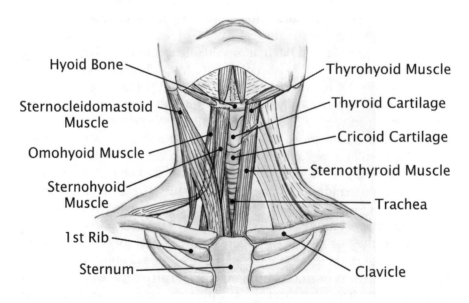

Figure 5–4. Strap muscles of the larynx. Copyright Richard Webber, 2005.

vation of the false depressors can provide a low-larynx position but there
are considerable negative effects:

- The resonating spaces above the larynx are distorted and, in particular, the laryngopharyngeal space is made smaller, creating a dark, woolly, and bottled sound.
- Increased muscular tension limits the ability of the thyroid cartilage to tilt, creating difficulties with upper registers.
- Register transitions are not smooth, due to increased muscular tension.
- The low position of the tongue base limits articulatory clarity (i.e., the vowels tend to sound homogeneous, and some consonants weak).
- The palate is pulled down by the activity of the palatoglossus muscle.
- Wobble can develop as the tongue root and jaw move in sympathy with the vibrato.
- Vibrato can become unstable in both pitch and speed because of the pressure from the muscle tension.
- Acoustic energy will be dampened affecting vocal carrying power.
- The singer's own pitch perception can be distorted resulting in "flattening" (which the singer cannot detect).
- Vocal stamina is compromised.

Sometimes singers cling to the sensation of singing with tongue
root constriction as it gives aural feedback via bone conduction, which
makes them feel that they are "making a really rich sound." This is
because the higher harmonics in the sound are being dampened, and
bone conduction is not as efficient as air conduction in the transfer of
sound. This can be a real "red herring," and they need to be convinced
of the danger and weaned away from the habit. Usually, the advantages,
such as increase in range and ease, begin to kick in quite quickly, which
helps them make the change intellectually and psychologically. I use the
analogy of a child's comfort blanket with the singer being cocooned in
his or her own sound world. Sometimes people who have the personality traits of "perfectionism and/or control freakery" find it extremely difficult to relinquish this perceived monitor of their sound. (See Exercises
in Appendix 1 for tips on how to eradicate this problem.)

The ability of a singer to operate the muscles that affect both the
vertical position of the larynx and the palate itself sometimes is restricted
by various sorts of tension in the extrinsic muscles of the larynx. In my
experience, reasons for this sort of "throat holding" can be many and varied, and include psychological "guarding," past trauma, poor posture,
past experience of poor teaching, especially breath locking, excessive
use of "straight" tone in early music styles, and vocal pressing. Once

these extrinsic muscles are in a state of rigidity, they must be dealt with as a priority, either before singing interventions are made, or in tandem with them. I have found that manual therapy techniques employed by voice-trained physiotherapists and osteopaths, who have had experience in dealing with the larynx, are the most potent and quick way of starting the changes, but equally important is the singer's awareness of the muscular holding and their agreement to make changes. Resistance is most evident in the successful "early music singer" who has probably already made a good living from this sort of singing, but who may be experiencing dysfunction at the level of the vocal folds. The term "muscle tension dysphonia" is a commonly used expression among the medical profession but usually relates to speech-based problems. I would like to propose that when related to the singing voice the term used becomes *muscle tension dysphonia in singers* (MTDS).

I have found that the safest and quickest way to help a student access an appropriate low-larynx position is to use a "pre-yawn" maneuver (see Exercise section in Appendix 1). Care must be taken that the tongue root does not get involved in this action. Phonation with the larynx in this position usually feels easy and, provided there is a good supported airflow and head/neck posture, the base of the throat will widen at the start of phonation. Singers report this "collar connection" as a feeling of complete freedom from throat tension. When this collar connection is active, the singer has limited kinesthetic awareness of it, and needs to see this inflation with a mirror, or feel it by placing a hand loosely at the base of the throat with the fingers spread like a necklace. When the collar connection is established, singers describe the feeling as akin to the stabilizers on an ocean liner.

As yet, the collar connection has not been researched, but I postulate that this interaction of muscle and breath constitutes the "open throat" or "gola aperta" of the Italian bel canto school of singing. Added to this can be the Estill "sob" or "suppressed laugh" figure (see Exercises in Appendix 1), which gives clean phonation within the larynx. My experience is that, once the collar connection is accessible, the need for tongue root and jaw tension to depress the larynx is minimized. In teaching, I sometimes speak of the "collar connection" as being the upper margin of the support mechanism, while recognizing that there are major phonation and resonance components within its use.

In scientific vocal studies, there is a general acceptance that, as pitch rises, there is a natural excursion of the larynx upward and forward in the neck. Although this excursion should not be consciously resisted, the goal of classical singing is to maintain a *relatively* low-larynx position. The addition of the collar connection appears to provide a relatively lower and more stable base for this excursion, which results in a more even vocal quality throughout the registers. Singers also report that high notes feel "lower" when the collar connection is activated. Research into this phenomenon is required.

Saul: A Case Study

Saul, a tenor, came for consultation having already spent his student years at music colleges and in a young artists' program by which time he was about 32 years old. He was very tall and built like a tank; although overweight, it was clear that his body type was "macro." His voice, however, was small and tight, unable to access his upper notes, and lacking stamina and ease of use. On examination, I discovered a total lack of any abdominal support, a forward slung jaw misalignment, and habitual pressed phonation. The work commenced based on the core components of my model, namely, breathing, support, primal sound, and postural alignment and showed that this voice was completely in the wrong fach. In fact, the voice matched the body type and was a true "heldentenor." The physical engagement of energy and muscular development required to support this voice took nearly 18 months to grow to a point where it could be used with unself-conscious reliance. Only then was it possible to address successfully the problems of the jaw setting and the lack of pharyngeal space.

Once this was sorted out, the true beauty of his instrument was obvious. The lower and middle registers sounded truly baritonal and this glorious sound progressed upward (as it should in the true "heldentenor" fach). Ventricular constriction was addressed by the use of collar connection and Estill "sob" maneuvers, and the deeper throat position for the larynx was accessed once the jaw had stopped jamming forward and down. This singer is a "gentle giant" and still has a problem or two related to being so constantly vocally "loud," and to the development and maintenance of the aerobic fitness required to maintain this sort of singing. He is so intensely musical and also such a "stage animal" that I am hopeful he will become fully committed to his talent. This type of voice requires a "Mack truck" engine that is not only strong but is finely tuned. I live in hope!

SINGERS AND THE SPEAKING VOICE

There is a wide variety in the way singers use their speaking voices. The style of their speaking voice will reflect their total personality construct, and not just their laryngeal physiology. There are many singers with enormous operatic voices who habitually use a gentle light phonation for speech, a voice that sounds quite unrelated to their singing voice. This is of no vocal consequence provided that the speaking voice they are using is not inefficient or vocally harmful.

When a student appears on the doorstep for a lesson, a great deal of information can be gained by the teacher about his or her vocal and psychological condition on that day. By being actively aware of the student's speaking voice and how it is being used, a teacher can receive valuable information about the student's health, mood, and general vocal state.

Some speaking voice behaviors can adversely affect the singing voice. It is important to remember that, even for professional singers, up to 85% of their vocalizations during a normal day are speaking rather than singing.

Examples of poor speaking voice behaviors and their causes include:

- Hard glottal attack
- Pressed phonation
- Resting tongue root constriction
- Habitual muscle tension in neck and shoulders
- Poor breath flow
- Insufficient hydration
- Vocal abuse (shouting, yelling, screeching, etc.)
- Excessive talking
- Habitual use of breathy voice
- Inappropriate speaking voice pitch
- Throaty voice production

In some girls/women, there is a tendency for their speaking voices to be produced with a glottal chink, giving them a breathy and "girlie" quality, which although acceptable in a social sense may carry the seeds of vocal inefficiency into the singing voice. Once good vocal habits are learned via singing, the speaking voice should modify and correct in tandem. If this does not occur, it is worthwhile to refer the singer to a voice clinic for a checkup and possible speech therapy.

In young male singers (particularly baritones), there can be a tendency to use an artificially dark and forceful speaking voice to create an impression of gravitas and authority, to mask personality traits, or to convince themselves that they are going to grow into a bass. This often carries over into the singing voice generally manifesting in tongue-root constriction problems. These young singers need to be encouraged to find their true vocal identity in both singing and speaking. Occasionally, it is necessary to refer them to a voice clinic for assessment and possible therapy.

PROFESSIONAL VOICE USERS WHO ALSO SING

Professional voice users, such as schoolteachers, lawyers, clergymen, and so forth who have singing as an important hobby may find difficulties combining their voice uses. Sometimes, their vocal technique is adequate for the type of singing they are doing; however, if their speaking voice is not efficient, this will often have a detrimental effect on their singing. Many of these amateur singers have never had singing lessons and can benefit greatly from seeing a good pedagogue. Unless these amateur singers have experienced vocal problems either in their speaking or singing voice, they may have only limited awareness of the dual demands on their voices. In many cases, it is the use of their speaking voice that needs attention. Sometimes the speaking voice improves as a result of regular singing lessons, but if these problems continue, they are best managed by a speech and language therapist with an interest in voice disorders or by a voice clinic.

Schoolteachers have particular difficulties because of the vocal demands of their profession and the lack of training and vocal awareness during the teacher training programs. Research currently is being done in this field but preliminary results suggest that most schoolteachers could benefit from vocal skills training. In the United Kingdom, the Voice Care Network offers specialist support in this field.

NATIONAL AND REGIONAL ACCENTS

Accents are predominantly influenced by tongue position in the mouth, which affects both vowel sounds and, to a lesser degree, consonants. Some accents have additional phonatory characteristics: for example, "twang" in Australian and southern accents in the United States, "creak" in the affected Oxbridge accent, constriction in the so-called Kensington accent, the "breathy-girlie" quality used by some nicely brought up South of England "gels," and the "pressed-creak" of the Glaswegian Scot.

Some of these vocal characteristics can be quite helpful to the singing voice. As an example, the antipodean "twang" can contain a very powerful resonance potential in some styles of music. Music theatre, rock, pop, and country use this twang almost in its pure state, whereas operatic singers benefit from its incorporation into the larger spaces of the singer's vocal setup when it becomes an integral component of "the singer's formant." Some accents, however, can interfere with singing phonation and need to be modified for professional use. Singers should not seek to lose their natural accent in their speaking voice but rather to modify any detrimental elements. In fact, I have found that the better they sing technically, the better their speaking voices sound without conscious effort. Only on rare occasions is it necessary to seek the help of the speech and language therapist for modification of their accent per se. As a general rule when singing in English, I would recommend a more standard pronunciation, also known as received pronunciation.

RELATION TO THE PEDAGOGICAL MODEL

Certainly people respond negatively to such things as hoarseness, huskiness, constriction, and breathiness, especially in the singing voice. Teachers often attempt to address phonation issues early because of the immediacy of the way phonation deficits present in the singer. However, phonation problems often are a symptom rather than a cause. In the long run, it usually is more efficient to ensure that the core components of the teaching model are developed to an adequate level before meddling with phonation. If phonation is addressed before the core components have been established, the new phonation pattern is unlikely to carry over and may never be produced correctly.

As an example, if a singer with pressed phonation corrects only the hypervalving of the larynx without dealing with the posture, underlying support, and breathing issues, he or she will produce either breathy phonation or healthy phonation that is fleeting rather than appropriate long-term change.

Similarly, a singer who presents with pressed phonation and a slow wobble (which usually is due to insufficient breath flow) will not be able to maintain changes to the laryngeal set without changing the underlying airflow issues that often are related to a locked abdominal wall.

> **Phonation is the first thing that the listener responds to unconsciously, and although it is vitally important in singing, it should not be the first thing that a teacher should try to change. Phonation issues in singing nearly always indicate a problem in breathing and support and/or postural alignment. Habitual use of the speaking voice also may be a significant contributing factor. In dealing with phonation issues, it is imperative that the teacher looks first to the rest of the singing system and makes appropriate corrections before tackling phonation itself.**

REFERENCES

Baken, R. J., in Sataloff, R. T. (1998). *Vocal health and pedagogy.* San Diego, CA: Singular.

Cooksey, J. M. (1992). *Working with the adolescent voice.* St. Louis, MO: Concordia.

Harris, T., Harris, S., Rubin, J. M., & Howard, D. M. (1998). *The voice clinic handbook.* London, UK: Whurr.

Henrich, N. (2006). Mirroring the voice from Garcia to the present day: Some insights into singing voice registers. *Logopedics Phoniatrics Vocology*, *31*, 3-14.

Hirano, M. (1981). *Clinical examination of voice*. Wien, Austria: Springer-Verlag.

McKinney, J. C. (1982). *The diagnosis and correction of vocal faults*. Nashville, TN: Broadman Press.

Sundberg, J. (1987). *The science of the singing voice*. Dekalb: Northern Illinois Press.

Thyme-Frøkjær, K., & Frøkjær-Jensen, B. (2001). *The accent method: A rational voice therapy in theory and practice*. Bicester, UK: Speechmark.

Titze, I. R. (1994). *Principles of voice production*. Inglewood Cliffs, NJ: Prentice-Hall.

Chapter 6

RESONANCE

Janice Chapman and Ron Morris

$\mathcal{M}$cKinney (1982, p. 125) states that, "resonation is the process by which the basic product of phonation is enhanced in timbre and/or intensity by the air filled cavities through which it passes." He goes on to say that in terms of a singer, the end result of resonance is to make a better sound. Bunch (2000, p. 37) says, "aesthetically the most important area of the voice is resonance. The quality of the human voice is unique with every individual and at the same time is the most difficult to study and quantify."

Resonance is an area of long-standing argument among pedagogues. Resonance, or sympathetic vibration, can be felt in the bones of the skull as well as in the chest wall and neck, but although these sensations are good monitors for the singer, they appear to have very little effect on the sound a listener hears. McKinney lists the following possible resonators for the voice:

- Chest
- Tracheal tree
- Larynx
- Pharynx
- Oral cavity
- Nasal cavity
- Sinuses

Resonating chambers have different characteristics and effects. These are due to the size, shape, type of opening, composition and thickness of the walls, surface, and combination (McKinney, 1982). Larger resonators respond most to low frequencies whereas the shape of the resonator determines which frequencies will be enhanced. When the walls of the resonating chamber are rigid or tense, damping is least; it will be very specific as to which frequency it will enhance, whereas resonating chamber walls that are soft and flexible tend to be associated with greater damping and are more universal in enhancement. Figure 6–1 shows a sagittal section of a head showing the vocal tract.

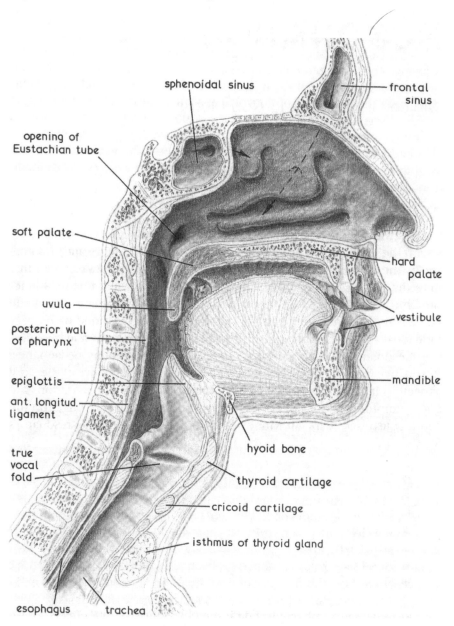

Figure 6–1. Sagittal view of head cavities. Reproduced with permission from *Dynamics of the Singing Voice* by M. Bunch (2000), Springer-Verlag.

THE CHEST

Although strong vibrations can be easily felt in the chest with the hand, especially for low notes, the chest is thought to have no significant effects on the resonance within the vocal system. McKinney (1982) and Bunch (2000) both point out that the chest has no direct connection to the outside air, is below the vocal folds, and is filled with soft tissue, all of which make it an inappropriate resonating chamber. It is possible that this "sensation trap" has pedagogical uses, however, in that it is only possible to experience chest vibration when the upper chest area is free of tension and the phonation style is modal and healthy.

THE TRACHEAL TREE

This refers to the trachea and the bronchial tubes, which lie below the larynx and run to the lungs. They are air-filled cavities with relatively hard walls and a tubular shape, which make them good possible resonators. Unfortunately, the tracheal tree has very limited ability to change shape or size so its ability to resonate will be restricted to approximately its own resonant frequency (McKinney, 1982). Van den Berg (1958) states that the resonant frequency of the tracheal tree is around Eb4 for both males and females, although this does vary somewhat with the size of the singer. It is interesting to note that this pitch (Eb4) is a registration pivot in many voices, sometimes the change from modal to middle register in women and modal to head in men. This is an area begging further research.

THE LARYNX

Although the larynx is where phonation occurs, it also is a chamber that can be adjusted in terms of size, shape, and opening. McKinney states that the larynx itself is the source of the so-called "singer's formant," which is in the region of 2500 to 3000 hertz. This allows a classically trained singer's voice to carry over a large orchestra. Jo Estill refers to "twang," a supercharged carrying power component, as being generated in the collar of the larynx or the aryepiglottic area. This is referred to in the Italian singing traditions as "squillo." Sundberg suggests that lowering of the larynx combined with changes in the area of the outlet of the larynx into the pharynx contribute to the singer's formant (see Sundberg, 1987). This seems to suggest that the higher frequency components of the singer's output are enhanced in the area just above the vocal folds (the epilarynx). At the present time, some of the medical/scientific terminology being used to describe this part of the vocal tract includes "the twanger," "the aryepiglottic sphincter," "the collar of the larynx," the "epilaryngeal tube," and "the epilarynx." There is another important contribution to resonance which occurs as a direct result of the Bernoulli effect at the level of the vocal folds themselves. This is the "closed quotient" (the amount of time the vocal folds are in the closed phase compared with the open phase of their vibratory cycle). During the open phase, acoustic energy is lost to the "chest" via the trachea where the bronchi damp the sound signal. Clearly, the speed at which the vocal folds snap shut is of great importance to resonance and it is interesting to note that the major factor contributing to this closing speed is subglottal air pressure (see Chapter 5 for explanation).

THE PHARYNX

McKinney (1982, p. 130) states that "by virtue of its position, size, and degree of adjustability the pharynx has to qualify as the most important resonator." The pharynx, due to its many muscular attachments can change:

- Its size in terms of both horizontal and vertical dimensions
- Its overall shape
- The tension of its walls
- The sizes/shapes of the openings to mouth, nose, and larynx (McKinney 1982).

The pharynx can be influenced greatly by postural alignment in that its resonating characteristics can be varied by adjustment to head and neck position. Lowering the larynx significantly increases pharyngeal length, which changes the resonance characteristics of the chamber. Because of the size of the pharynx, its variability, and the flexibility of its walls, it usually is responsible for the lower harmonics that create a warmer, richer sound. Thus, it is a crucial component when dealing with beauty of timbre.

The vocal tract constrictors involve the laryngeal and pharyngeal resonators, and are responsible for swallowing maneuvers. In general, these muscles need to be relaxed for classical singing (Figure 6–2); however, recent videostroboscopic recordings obtained using the puffy cheeks exercise suggests that as pitch rises the middle constrictor can become advantageously involved to adjust the length and width of the laryngopharynx.

The interaction of airflow and the resonating system cannot be ignored. Inadequate airflow will cause the pharyngeal space to reduce, which will affect beauty of tone. I (J.C.) teach that activating the torso/collar connection maintains the "open throat" position for singing as

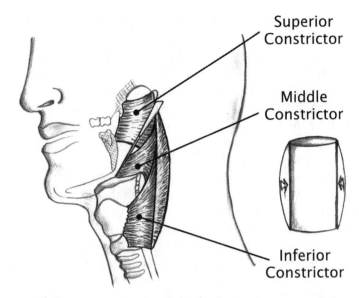

Figure 6–2. Sagittal view of the constrictors. Copyright Richard Webber, 2005.

described in various writings on the Italian bel canto tradition. Good airflow is an active component of the torso/collar connection (see Chapter 4).

THE ORAL CAVITY

The mouth is another important resonating chamber, as it is used to shape the vocal tone emanating from the pharynx into vowels and consonants. Because the pharynx and the oral cavity play an integrated role in both resonance and articulation, it is difficult to tease out their specific contributions. Each singer's personal physiology will have a bearing on resonance capacity, but in general we are of the opinion that resonance in the oral cavity should take a secondary role to the clear articulation of vowels and consonants. When a singer has good breath support, alignment, and a classical setting within the laryngopharynx, the tone produced will already be resonant and the front of the mouth will contribute only a small amount more to that existing resonance.

McKinney (1982) points out that the mouth is well-suited to the demands of resonance due to its location, size, and adjustability. My view is that, in classical voice production, the mouth cavity should be viewed primarily as a flexible articulator and not as a major source of resonance. Rather that there are "sweet spots" in the mouth cavity where resonance formants are tuned and which enhance both the clarity of the vowel and its resonance. This is achieved by experimenting with vocal tract shape and tongue position for each individual singer (see Dial-a-Vowel exercise in Appendix 1).

Wide frontal opening of the mouth often is taught by singing teachers in an effort to increase loudness. This can have an overall detrimental effect, in that the pharyngeal spaces can be compromised, which adversely affects vocal timbre. The jaw, of course, will need to open, but in a way that does not make the space in the pharynx smaller. This can be achieved by encouraging singers to drop the jaw back and down rather than jutting it forward and jamming it open. In the studio, we have used a variety of instructions the most effective of which is, "Close the back teeth, feel the position of the jaw internally and with the fingers externally, and then gently open the back teeth." This brings the jaw appropriately into position one (Figure 3–2), which is the best starting position for classical sound. Conversely, when a singer opens the jaw frontally, like a crocodile, the beauty of tone and vowel clarity may be sacrificed to vocal loudness (see Figure 3–2 in Chapter 3).

The tongue is the other major modifier of the oral cavity. It is a large muscular structure that is capable of almost infinite variability in shape, position, and tension. The vowel sounds are made predominantly by tongue action but the range of possibilities is large in terms of tongue position for any given vowel. In singing, the tongue position for vowels is a significant resonance issue. Choice of one tongue position over another should be made based on timbre, voice quality, and clarity.

The vowel quadrilateral, which is used as a map for spoken vowels, does not give singers a true picture of vowel articulation for classical singing. Although this diagram of different articulatory positions originally was based on what the French language teachers of the day (in the 1880s) thought were the positions of the tongue and was meant to be an aid to learning a foreign language, it has now acquired a different status. The modern use of the vowel quadrilateral is not based on anatomic but rather psychoacoustic considerations, and although these are useful for spoken vowel contrasts, they do need to be explored and extended for singing.

The classical demands of consistency of timbre across the vowel spectrum are best met when the tongue is in an Italian articulatory setting. This setting generally is higher in the mouth than for English. The part of the tongue that modifies each vowel change is not the same when the tongue is in this higher setting. Pedagogues who urge singers to make bright clear Italian vowels are correct in their demands but often try to create this brightness by the manipulation of facial muscles ("the smiling school of singing"). The facial muscles are not the best place to change vowel acoustics. Rather, they are better modified between the pharynx and mouth with the assistance of the tongue and palate (see Dial-a-Vowel exercise in Appendix 1).

The velum or soft palate acts to close off the nasal cavities from the mouth and pharynx. In speech articulation, its action is limited to opening and closing to produce nasal or oral sounds, but in classical singing, its function greatly influences resonance. A fully active velum will ensure a good closure of the nasopharyngeal port (doorway to the nose) and a good balance of high and low resonance. If the nasopharyngeal port is not properly closed, hypernasality can result. There is some question about whether the French nasal vowels should be sung with the nasopharyngeal port partially open. If it is possible that this can be achieved without a loss of pharyngeal space, it may well prove to be a viable and useful technical strategy. Studio experience leads us to believe (at this stage) that leaving the nasopharyngeal port partly open nearly always results in a lowered velum and loss of brightness in the singer's sound. Research is needed to show whether elite singers are indeed able to sing with a combination of high palate and open velar port.

The muscles that are active in elevating the soft palate are levator palatini and tensor palatini. Pedagogues often speak about sensations of a "dome" shape to the soft palate, which equates to full closure of the nasopharyngeal port with elevation of the velum. There is a strong interaction between the soft palate and the tongue. The palatoglossus muscle runs between the sides of the soft palate and the sides of the tongue and its action depends on one end being fixed. If the palate is high and arched, there is a tendency for the palatoglossus muscle to draw the sides of the tongue up and slightly back. Conversely, if the tongue root is depressed, the palatoglossus muscle will act to draw the soft palate down. As muscles can contract and relax but not expand, this makes it impossible to have a high-domed soft palate in combination with a depressed tongue root. Some teachers seek a high-domed palate in combination with a low tongue position for their students; however, if the low-tongue position involves tongue root compression, this will go against the natural order of muscular interaction. In some pedagogy books, you will see the tongue drawn with a broad central groove. This is a result of the sides of the tongue being pulled up by a tight palatoglossus muscle as the palate tries to lift against the downward movement of the tongue body. It is much easier to achieve a high-domed palate following the principles of natural muscular interaction if the tongue is in an elevated (i.e., Italianate) position (Figure 6–3).

In order for a singer to experience what a truly high-domed palate feels like and can achieve in terms of vocal quality, the puffy cheeks exercise can be used as a template (see Exercise section in Appendix 1, Semioccluded vocal tract exercises).

NASAL CAVITIES

The nose (the nasal passages and the nasal pharynx) can be switched on and off from the resonance system at will by the action of the velum. McKinney reminds us that only three English sounds require nasal

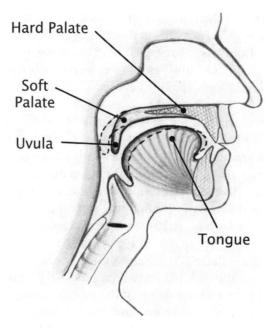

Figure 6–3. Sagittal view of the vocal tract showing palate and tongue. Copyright Richard Webber, 2005.

resonance (m, n, ng), and although some languages such as French and Portuguese have some nasalized vowel sounds, the use of the nasal cavities in classical singing should be very limited.

The nasal cavities, like the chest, are areas where singers perceive large amounts of vibratory feedback, but this is nothing more than a sensation monitoring system, not a resonating issue. In a now classic study, Wooldridge as reported in Vennard (1967) blocked singers' nasal passages with gauze and an expert panel was unable to tell the difference between blocked and unblocked singing. McKinney reminds us that these vibrations in the skull, nasal cavities, and on the hard and soft palates, are as a result of a well-produced and well-resonated voice, *not the cause of it*.

THE SINUSES

Similar to the chest and nasal cavities, the sinuses are sensation traps, not resonating chambers. Singers can use these sensations to monitor the quality of their singing but they must remember that these sensations are not the *cause* of their vocal quality.

There appear to be many options for the voice to resonate within the vocal tract, but in reality only the larynx, pharynx, and mouth are major contributors with the nasal cavities useful only for nasalized sounds. Bunch (2000) summarized this by stating "physically for optimum resonance, a singer will have maximum pharyngeal space, a lifted soft palate, a flexible ready tongue and a jaw that hangs nicely in place. These are the ingredients for a responsive mechanism of resonance" (p. 37), and it must be added, a good closed vocal-fold phase ratio.

Working with my pedagogical model, resonance is dependent on the core components being established, followed by corrections or development of skills in phonation and the speaking voice. Resonance, however, is constantly changing during these processes. For example, as the posture becomes better aligned, resonance is affected; as breathing and support are developed, resonance is affected; as phonation issues are sorted out, resonance is affected. And primal sound often can give the student and the teacher a glimpse of the potential timbre of the voice, unfettered by vocal inadequacies and problems. These flashes of the true sound of the student's voice are like a guiding beam for the teacher, even though the full development of the vocal technique that allows this holistic sound to be constantly present may take time to achieve.

The resonance of the human voice is miraculous. Babies' cries are designed to achieve responses from the parents, particularly the mother, and are part of our heritage as defined by Charles Darwin. The loudest and most emotionally imbued cries achieved the "survival of the fittest," bringing responses that resulted in feeding or nurture. The resonance present in the newborn child is in the 3000-hertz area, which corresponds to the most sensitive part of the human ear. A baby's cries are "primal sound" at its most potent as it is the only communication mode available to the newborn child, whose very survival depends on its ability to communicate its needs when it leaves the womb. Babies practice vocalizations in utero, and emerge from the womb with a highly effective vocal system ready for use.

In childhood we copy and imitate as our voices and our language skills develop. This sets up a vocal template that includes resonance as a major component. It is impossible to tease out the strands of resonance from articulation as both are interdependent.

THE SINGER'S FORMANT AND "TWANG"

Resonance is one of the most important parts of operatic singers' stock-in-trade because their voices must carry unamplified through a large orchestra, and fill a large auditorium. Not only do opera singers need big voices, they also need a vocal technique that will allow the text they are singing to be clearly audible. Research in the past four decades has been carried out on a phenomenon called "the singer's formant," which is a desirable alignment and use of the vocal resonating areas resulting in a "supercharger" effect, a bonus of resonance (which equates to loudness) over and above that which would be normally predicted for a given vowel (Figure 6–4). To read an explanation of the complex acoustics, see books such as *The Science of the Singing Voice* (Sundberg, 1987) or articles by Titze and Storey, (1997) and others.

Long before the singer's formant was understood from an acoustic point of view, opera singers in particular were using this vocal tract maneuver. (Yanagisawa, Estill, Kmucha, & Leder, 1989). There is a question about whether it is available to all singers or only to those with a particular type and shape of vocal tract, but I believe that any singer can learn to use it. In my studio, I teach it as a component, when everything else is perceived to be in place. In some singers, it is present already as a result of their vocal physiology and perhaps linguistic accent. For example, Australians and Americans have easy access to nasal and oral twang. Estill pioneered the understanding and specific use of this component (twang) in her valuable work in the 1980s where she identified "twang" as the (desirable) laryngeal constriction that creates the bright harmonics known also as "ring" in the voice. When this "twang" is actively present, it can be combined with a low larynx and wide pharynx to create the acoustic environment where the 3rd, 4th, and 5th formants cluster together and gain their "singer's formant" bonus of the extra 6 dB (Titze & Storey, 1997).

To teach this, I work first on the epilarynx constrictor using a witch's cackle, a peacock call, or the sound of a cockatoo, in the singer's

Figure 6–4. *"Who needs a microphone"?* Copyright Simon Pearsall, 2005.

upper range. In male voices, it is sometimes easier to attain this twang by using a quacking sound like a duck call. To make sure that oral twang rather than nasal twang is produced, simply squeeze the nostrils. To ensure that the student's tongue root is not engaging, I encourage them to make this sound with the tongue fully extended, then to gradually allow the tongue to regain its normal position for the vowel. Once this phonation trick is in the muscle memory, it is easy to return to normal classical voice production, adding the low-larynx position and the wide expanded pharynx (using torso/collar connection) to achieve an end product, a rich operatic quality containing the singer's formant. This can be checked using available computer technology with the aid of a suitable software package such as VoceVista, but once this sort of sound is available to a singer, they have no trouble recognizing and reproducing it at will. It is important to note that, although this sound requires considerably less effort at the level of the larynx, it is dependent on supported airflow and postural alignment for its attainment. It is important to remind singers that the action of the twang mechanism is within the larynx itself just above the vocal folds and does not involve facial grimacing.

Research from an Australian study in 2004 (Barnes et al., 2004) suggests that the perceptually "best" operatic voices appear on laryngoscopy to show the epilarynx collar almost fully covering the view of the vocal folds as normally seen. This anterior/posterior constriction is part of the desirable "purse string" type constriction which constitutes the "twang" component. With this type of viewing of the vocal machinery now possible, the diagnosis of what opera singers (and others) actually do to create their healthy and efficient voicing must be re-evaluated, as this type of (desirable) constriction maneuver may be misinterpreted as vocal abuse to speech therapists or physicians when in fact it is healthy, efficient, and necessary for the task.

The presence of "squillo" or "twang" in the operatic voice is crucial for vocal efficiency and longevity. Sometimes singers and teachers misunderstand this desirable constriction at the level of the aryepiglottic sphincter and mistakenly employ the constrictors of the throat instead. This produces a "neck-tie" tenor sound and should be avoided (Figure 6–5).

Figure 6–5. *"Is my collar too tight"?* Copyright Simon Pearsall, 2005.

REGISTRATION

I suggest that the reader first refer to Chapter 5 on Phonation and the Speaking Voice for the function and technical backup to registers. However, because registration has important resonance issues, they are addressed in this chapter.

For most but not all vocal tasks in classical style singing, it is desirable to disguise register transitions. Most operatic composers, especially those who really loved the voices for whom they were writing, composed their characters' music using vocal registration as another artistic/dramatic tool at their disposal (e.g., Fiordiligi's dramatic drops into the modal/chest voice in "Come Scoglio," Verdi's use of falsetto for Falstaff, and Puccini's Gianni Schicchi). A clever singing actor who also has control of his or her registers can make great dramatic effect without hurting the voice at all. I have observed that this sort of high drama can be very exciting for the audience in perhaps the same way as the trapeze artist makes leaps. It is worth pointing out that the safety net required under these feats is the basic abdominal support, especially the sides and back of the waistband, which remain stable regardless of pitch, volume, or color.

DISGUISING REGISTER TRANSITIONS

I have found that the disguise of register transitions is dependent on a number of factors:

1. Excellent abdominal support with good airflow, (allowing the fine discrete maneuvers within the larynx to take place free of unnecessary tension)
2. Ability to trust that the sound the singer is hearing internally is not what the listener perceives
3. Voluntary control of the larynx/pharynx (Estill figures are helpful here)
4. Good postural alignment (the head and neck in particular)

My priorities when dealing with register transitions are to:

- Maintain vocal quality
- Maintain clarity of text
- Maintain vibrato rate and pulse

Maintenance of the vocal quality must be across both the pitches and vowels. There should not be a perceptual change in timbre from one register to the other in the ears of the listener. The singer, who hears his or her own voice mainly through bone conduction, is likely to hear a distortion in timbre at register changes. The inexperienced singer may try to match his or her own perception of quality in this region and in doing so compromise the voice production. Resonance matching in the upper passagio is described in the exercise section in Appendix 1.

Register transitions nearly always are an area of suspicion and doubt for students, but this anxiety is alleviated once the work has been done. The rolled "rr" scale is one of the most valuable tools in the singing teacher's armory, as it encourages the gradual appropriate engagement and disengagement of the cricothyroid and thyroarytenoid systems, without the singer needing to monitor everything consciously. Another set of exercises involves vowel modification, and this too is described in the exercises section in Appendix 1.

RELATION TO THE PEDAGOGICAL MODEL ("THE ZONE")

Once the resonance issues are dealt with in the pedagogical model, the singer will experience an ease of singing that can equate to "finding the zone" for athletes, in terms of their sound palette. Important corrections still may need to be made in the area of articulation, which can prevent this holistic experience from happening, but once most of the technical components are in place, these excursions into the "zone" happen more and more often and remain for increasingly longer periods.

To put it simply, when the singer has correctly balanced his or her sound, other things become easy too. For example, once the tongue and jaw are no longer trying to "hold or manage the sound," they are free to make the text in a simple speechlike manner. The tongue's liberation from a "sound-controlling" role is an enormous breakthrough for many students. For the singer experiencing this for the first time in the studio, it can feel ridiculously easy. They may express themselves with such words as, "This can't be right, it's too natural." At this point in time, I would replay the lesson tape for them immediately, while their sensations of ease and lack of effort are still familiar. Common feedback at moments like these includes, "This sort of singing feels like nothing at all in the throat, lots of buzz in the head, and much more activity in the abdominal muscles."

Maria: A Case Study

Maria is a light soprano and sings professionally in a radio chorus, coping with a constant diet of sightreading and rapid learning of highly complex music. She was in her early 30s when she approached me for assistance. She had been experiencing vocal symptoms of fatigue, hoarseness, throat pain, and loss of range. Otolaryngologic assessment had shown that her vocal folds were healthy and functional but that there was supraglottic constriction and evidence of muscle tension dysphonia. During her consultation, I noted that her support and breathing were clavicular, and her tongue root constantly engaged in a rocklike setting during classical singing. Her tone was small and dull and her vowels were undifferentiated. Although she was able to sing quite good high coloratura, her middle register was dysfunctional and breathy and her voice tired very quickly. In classical mode, she, was loath to use her natural chest register.

She mentioned that she also sang folk and country songs, and when I asked her to demonstrate this style of singing she showed no tongue root constriction, had clear bright vowels, and easy phonation. This style of singing was a useful phonatory tool toward changing her classical sound but did not engage the necessary mechanisms to support the breath for classical voicing.

We began by using the pedagogical model in order, that is, starting with the core components. This led to immediate improvement in phonation but resonance remained clouded and dull.

Because this singer was singing professionally every day, I felt that we needed to address the tongue root problems early on. Once her awareness had been raised, she was able to monitor her tongue root manually during rehearsals. As the tongue root gradually released, a whole new voice emerged. Her primal sound and her new way of supporting her breath gave her the template from which to work and the resonance adjusted radically over the next 6 months. The voice grew in size, the resonance was full and bright, the vowels became clearly differentiated, and her facility for high coloratura was even greater. Her middle and chest registers were fully usable and she suffered no further symptoms of vocal fatigue.

Resonance is the sexy end of the vocal product, and in recent years, science has been caught up in the study of the "singer's formant." The discovery and acceptance of this phenomenon has progressed to the point where mathematical equations have been developed to describe it accurately. What has not been appreciated is that the ability of a singer to produce the "singer's formant" is dependent on a whole complex set of physical and vocal components being fully developed and synchronized. Making a sound rich in "twang" (like a demented peacock) demands a set of physical engagements within the torso. If you only make this one brief sound, you will not have time to notice what the torso has to do to produce it, but if you are on an operatic stage and producing sustained "opera quality" (rich in twang) for two hours, then your body must be a very highly developed athletic machine. This is the "squillo" sought by the Italian school of bel canto that ensures that the singer is audible over the orchestra without damage to the voice. The fact that the training of singers in this vocal school took seven years of supervised rigorous vocal exercises meant that not only the larynx but also the body would have been vocally athletic. The singer's aural expectation would also have been trained to accept these seemingly distorted perceptions of what is a correctly produced and resonated sound.

> **In my pedagogical model, issues of resonance are addressed directly once the core components are adequately achieved and developed to a sufficient standard. There are methods of teaching singing that focus on resonance very early in the process, in the hope that support, breathing, posture, and phonation will fall into place once resonance is achieved. This is a very poor approach as it is impossible to determine the true primal sound of the voice when resonance has been "fiddled with" cosmetically to the exclusion of all the other building blocks of a vocal technique. The "cart is before the horse" and improvements are not sustainable when other aspects of the singer's technique remain uncorrected.**

REFERENCES

Barnes, J., Davis, P., Oates, J., & Chapman, J. (2004). The relationship between professional operatic soprano voice and high range spectral energy. *Journal of the Acoustical Society of America, 116,* 530–538.

Bunch, M. (2000). *A handbook of the singing voice.* London, UK. Author.

McKinney, C. (1982). *The diagnosis and correction of vocal faults.* Nashville, TN: Broadman Press.

Sundberg, J. (1987). *The science of the singing voice.* Dekalb: Northern Illinois University Press.

Titze, I., & Storey, B. (1997). Acoustic interactions of the voice source with the lower vocal tract. *Journal of the Acoustical Society of America, 101,* 2234–2243.

Van den Berg, J. (1958, May) On the myloelastic-aerodynamic theory of voice production. *NATS Bulletin, 14,* 6.

Vennard, W. (1967). *Singing the mechanism and the technique.* New York, NY: Carl Fischer.

Yanagisawa, E., Estill, J., Kmucha, S., & Leder, S. (1989). The contribution of aryepiglottic constriction to "ringing" voice quality—a videolaryngoscopic study with acoustic analysis. *Journal of Voice, 3,* 342–350.

Chapter 7

ARTICULATION

Ron Morris and Janice Chapman

$\mathcal{T}$he articulatory system and its uses form one of the core components of the speech and language therapist's (SLT) work. SLTs aim to change unusual or atypical articulation so that it fits what is considered to be normal for the society in which the person lives or functions. Primarily, SLTs are interested in making articulation intelligible so that the person can be easily understood by those around him. In performing this vital task, SLTs also become keepers of a formidable store of knowledge about the articulatory system, the sounds that comprise it, how those sounds are made, and how sounds can be changed. This knowledge can be used by the singing teacher and the singer to improve not only the sound of the text, but also overall vocal quality. An intimate knowledge of the articulatory system also allows the SLT to view articulation in terms of its efficiency not just in the end result of correct or incorrect sound production.

ARTICULATORY SYSTEM WITHIN THE VOCAL TRACT

The articulatory system has always been regarded by singing pedagogues as important but it is usually seen as the last place to change resonance or the place where the beautifully produced vocal tone is shaped into vowels and consonants. In fact, we now know (particularly through work with the deaf, for example, Daniel Ling, 2002) that the articulatory system can have a direct impact on the voice and vocal quality. The articulatory system certainly does change resonance and is, of course, responsible for articulating vowels and consonants but:

- Deviations in articulatory postures can influence vocal tone.
- Inefficient use of the speech physiology can affect voice quality and vocal tone.
- The articulatory system can act as a monitor to what is occurring at the level of the larynx and even below at the level of the breath support system.

Bearing these points in mind, it is obvious that the articulatory system should receive much more attention from singers and singing teachers than it currently does.

COMPONENTS OF THE ARTICULATORY SYSTEM

Textbooks on the anatomy, physiology, and function of the articulatory system abound so only a brief overview of the system is provided here. Major components are listed below (Figure 7–1):

Vocal Folds →	Determine whether sounds will be voiced or unvoiced
Velum →	Determines whether sounds will be nasal or nonnasal (these can either be vowels or consonants)
Tongue →	Major determiner of vowel shape and is the principal organ of articulation for most consonants
Teeth/Alveolus →	Point of articulation for a number of consonant sounds especially the most common English consonants /t/ and /s/
Jaw →	Provides opening for vowel sounds and affects oral resonance but its main function is for eating not for speech. This could be one reason why it can be so recalcitrant in singing.
Lips →	Rounding or spreading of vowels and the articulation of some consonants. Can also elongate and modify the vocal tract.

The structure, function and actions of the vocal folds are dealt with elsewhere in this book but a brief overview of the other articulatory structures is necessary.

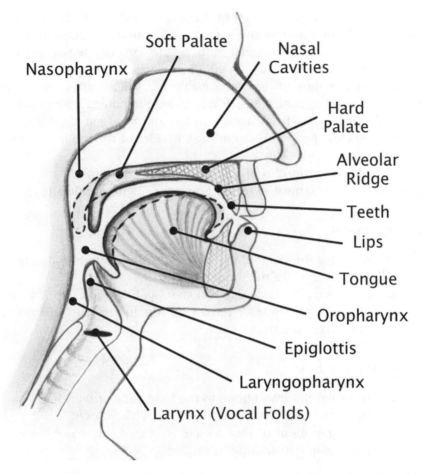

Figure 7–1. Side-on view of the articulation system. Dotted lines show the velum raised and the tongue root released slightly forward. Copyright Richard Webber, 2005.

TONGUE

The tongue is a purely muscular organ containing no bone or cartilage so it is capable of vast variation in terms of shape, position, and function. The tongue also is very strong with at least 1 kg of pressure exerted on the alveolar ridge during each swallow. This strength cannot be underestimated when it comes to misuse of the tongue and the mayhem such misuse causes to the development of a balanced vocal tract.

The tongue generally is seen as being composed of two sets of muscles:

- Intrinsic → completely within the tongue
- Extrinsic → run to the tongue from elsewhere in the head and neck.

The intrinsic muscles form part of the tongue body and often are intermingled with the fibers of the genioglossus muscle, which forms most of the tongue's bulk. The intrinsic muscles are named based on the direction of the muscle fibers as: longitudinal, vertical, and transverse. The intrinsic tongue muscles are responsible for tongue shape within the mouth and assist in tongue tip elevation, tongue curling, and bunching. Their function varies from person to person with genetic differences that inhibit some people from curling the sides of the tongue up into a tube or rolling an /r/ easily.

The extrinsic muscles of the tongue run from outside the tongue and attach to it. The most significant ones for singers are detailed below.

Genioglossus

- Runs from the point of the jaw to the tongue body and indeed it forms the bulk of the tongue body.
- Actions vary depending on which set of fibers is active. For example, it can protrude or retract the tongue tip and depress the body of the tongue.

Hyoglossus

- Runs from the hyoid bone to the base/back of the tongue.
- Main action is to draw the tongue back and down.
- Overengagement of this muscle is one of the major causes of tongue root constriction in singing.

Styloglossus

- Runs from the styloid process on the skull to the sides of the tongue.
- Major action is to lift the sides of the tongue up and back.

Palatoglossus

- Runs from the velum to the back and sides of the tongue.
- Action varies dependent on which end of the muscle is the most stable: can either raise the back and sides of the tongue or pull the velum down (Figure 7–2).

Vocal Effects of Tongue Movement or Use

The tongue can have a direct effect on the position of the hyoid bone and hence the larynx. In particular, the tongue can act as a false depressor of the larynx causing the hyoid bone and the tongue root to be pressed down on top of the larynx. This tends to give a dark woolly

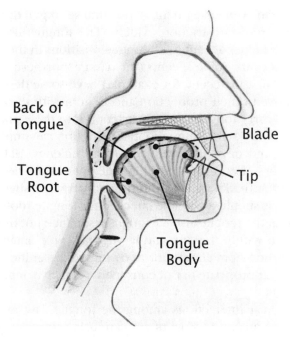

Figure 7–2. View of the tongue with the various subsections labeled. Copyright Richard Webber, 2005.

sound that is not flexible as laryngeal efficiency and resonance are hampered. This dark, bottled sound is often heard in the speech of the deaf where the deaf person attempts to increase kinesthetic feedback by pulling the tongue back into a retracted position. Singers also can be guilty of this fault, often in an attempt to "lower the larynx" to acquire an operatic sound. This fault usually is reinforced by the changes that occur in the singer's aural perception of his or her own voice with a tongue depressed sound being "warm and full" to their ear (but dark, woolly, bottled, or muffled to the listeners). This fault can be easily tested:

- Say an /i/ sound, place the thumb under the base of the tongue, feel how little downward pressure there is.
- Continue to say /i/ but gradually pull the tongue back and downward; notice how much additional feedback you have, not only under the tongue with your thumb but also within your mouth. Note how the sound changes.
- Repeat the experiment but this time sing the /i/.
- Try with other vowels. Some low central vowels such as /a/ often demonstrate the effect even more significantly.

Once a habit of tongue retraction or tongue root constriction develops, it can take many weeks or even months to "undo" this fault. In some people, tongue root constriction crosses from their singing into their speaking and can even develop into a postural setting of the tongue with resting tongue root constriction evident. The tongue also is the main organ that determines accent, with tongue positions in the mouth different for many accents. Some accents (the darker "northern" accent or the throaty South African accent, for example) have some degree of tongue retraction native to their production and singers with these accents are more likely to carry tongue root constriction into their singing.

Tongue retraction or tongue root constriction can impinge on vocal fold vibration and most importantly vocal efficiency. Habitual tongue root constrictors often report vocal fatigue, loss or restriction of range, and loss of pitch flexibility (coloratura) and certainly singers reporting these symptoms should always be checked for tongue root constriction.

Position of the tongue also can affect resonance not only within the mouth but also within the oro- and laryngopharynx. Small adjustments of tongue position (a millimeter or two) can have significant resonance effects and the appropriate use of consonants can give immediate access to this resetting.

The muscular interactions among the tongue, jaw, and palate also can affect voice quality. In singers who are using these structures inefficiently or incorrectly an interdependence rather than an independence can develop. These are singers for whom the tongue, jaw, and palate function as a unit rather than as separate entities so that changes in one structure automatically dictate changes in another. For example, as the tongue moves downward to articulate an /a/ vowel, the jaw and palate automatically also descend, which can greatly affect voice quality and resonance (Figure 7–3).

JAW

The jaw (anatomically known as the mandible) has its major function in chewing and mastication and only a very secondary role in articulation. Actually, it is possible to speak quite clearly without moving the jaw at all! The jaw is served by very powerful muscles to aid in mastication but, like the tongue, their strength can have marked negative effects on singing.

Temporalis

- Runs from the horn of the mandible to the temporal bone.
- Acts to close and retract the jaw.

Masseter

- Runs from the cheek bone (zygomatic arch) to the jaw.
- Acts to close the jaw and clench the teeth.

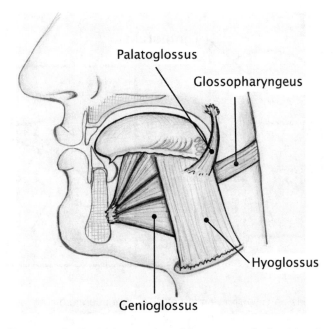

Figure 7–3. Extrinsic muscles of the tongue. A view showing the most important extrinsic tongue muscles for singers. Note the close relationships among the tongue, velum, jaw, hyoid bone, and pharynx, which can have a direct impact on the larynx. Copyright Richard Webber, 2005.

Medial Pterygoid

■ Runs from the back of the upper jaw (maxilla) to the base of the mandible.

■ Acts to close and slightly back the jaw.

Lateral Pterygoid

■ Runs from the back of the upper jaw to the horn of the mandible.

■ Acts to protrude the jaw and assist in forced opening of the jaw (Figure 7-4).

Vocal Effects of Jaw Movement or Use

The jaw is discussed in terms of having two opening positions. In position one, the jaw falls because of the effects of gravity and hangs loosely, in essence opening slightly backward and down. Very little if any muscular activity is needed to achieve this position. Further opening reaches position two where the jaw, on maximal opening, has also moved forward.

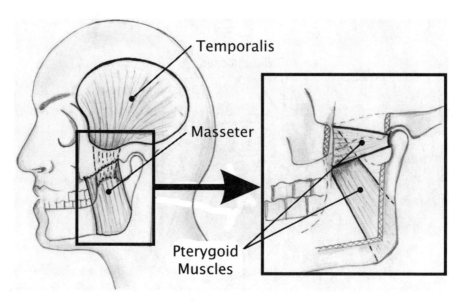

Figure 7–4. Side-on view showing the muscles that operate on the jaw. All but one of the pterygoid muscles act to close the jaw. Copyright Richard Webber, 2005.

This second position usually is not conducive to good singing because of the increased tension that can be felt around the whole oral capsule. This large crocodile opening of the jaw creates a sensation of "space" certainly but this extra room is in the front of the oral cavity, not at the back of the mouth in the oro- and laryngopharynx where it is needed. Increased tension in the floor of the mouth can be felt easily in position two, which is absent in position one. Once again, this can be readily demonstrated:

- Locate the temporomandibular joint (jaw joint) just in front of the ears. Place fingertips on this joint.
- Slowly open the jaw noting how the joint seems to pivot but does not move forward.
- Continue to open the jaw noting how the movement changes from one of pivoting only to one that involves both pivoting and sliding forward.
- Maximal opening corresponds to jaw position two.
- Gradually close the jaw again and try to identify the point where the pivot only mechanism is operating. This is position one.
- Place a thumb under the floor of the mouth, jaw closed, and monitor the tension.
- Open the jaw to position one and notice how there is very little, if any difference, in the activity of the floor of the mouth.
- Open the jaw to position two and feel how much additional tension there is in the floor of the mouth. This situation becomes

more detrimental to singing if the tongue root is also engaged (see Figure 3-2 in Chapter 3).

Occasionally, the jaw opening appears to be appropriate but the large muscles that surround the jaw can become involved in setting the oral capsule, which encourages tension to refer into other oral and pharyngeal muscles affecting vocal efficiency and tone. The pterygoid muscles in particular can act to protrude the jaw which has a direct impact on vocal efficiency.

There are a small number of singers, however, whose vocal function can be efficient with the jaw in position two. This appears to be an anatomical difference because with the jaw in a fully open position their oral capsule is not affected by additional muscular tension. In these few cases, it is best not to try to correct this posture.

In general, the jaw has little role to play in articulation but, for people who demonstrate tongue root constriction or who have interdependence of the jaw and tongue, the jaw can be seen to compensate for some tongue movements, particularly elevation of the tongue for tongue-tip alveolar sounds. This often gives the text a "chewed" quality as the jaw movement usually is not quick enough to make the consonants cleanly. The jaw can also become involved in the articulation of some palatal sounds such as /ʃ, tʃ, ʒ, and dʒ/ by swinging forward to assist their articulation, especially when the blade of the tongue rather than the tip is used to make these sounds. These compensations are not efficient and thus can affect vocal quality.

VELUM

The velum (soft palate) is used to close off the nasal passages for speech, swallowing, and other pneumatic activities such as blowing and sucking. The velum has no bone or cartilage being constructed only of muscle and mucous membrane, which makes the organ flexible and mobile. The velum is under voluntary control but there appears to be only limited kinesthetic awareness of its position.

Levator Veli Palatini

- Paired muscles that run from the skull base to help form the body of the velum.
- Act to raise the velum and close the nasal port.

Tensor Palatini

- Runs along the sides of the levators across the velum body.
- Tenses the soft palate and acts to open the eustachian tubes.

Palatopharyngeus

■ Runs from the palate to the lateral pharyngeal walls.
■ Acts to elevate the pharynx and reduce oropharyngeal space.

Palatoglossus

■ Runs from the velum to the back and sides of the tongue.
■ Action varies dependent on which end of the muscle is the most stable: can either raise the back and sides of the tongue or pull the velum down.

Vocal Effects of the Velum (Soft Palate) Movement or Use

The velum is concerned primarily with the control of the oral/nasal contrast. The palate affects resonance greatly, not only in adjusting nasal resonance but also in modifying or adjusting pharyngeal resonance. Once the velum is closed, the palatopharyngeus muscle is able to adjust or modify the pharynx depth and to some extent the shape. The velum, through the palatoglossus muscle, also can affect tongue position. This muscle's action is dependent on one of the structures being fixed. If the tongue root is constricted with the tongue body pulled back and down the palatoglossus muscle will also tend to draw the palate down. This will add to the dark, woolly, bottled sound of tongue-root constriction by changing the oral and oropharyngeal resonances. Similarly, a high arched velum will encourage the body of the tongue to lift, which usually will produce the better balanced oral and oropharyngeal resonance that is required for classical singing. Interaction between the tongue and the velum have very significant effects on the singing voice.

The palatoglossus muscle, because of its clear attachment to two mobile structures, allows us to see the interaction of one articulatory structure with another easily. This interaction or combination of actions is not unique and occurs throughout the entire articulatory system. This also helps explain why adjustments of a millimeter or two can create significant and obvious differences in vocal tone or quality.

LIPS AND MUSCLES OF FACIAL EXPRESSION

The muscles of the face (including the lips) attach into the skin, which leads to the infinite variety of facial expressions that we can create. Humans have more muscles of facial expression than any other animal, which give us access to this infinite variety of expressions. Facial expressions appear to be only on the surface as we can produce most expressions at will, but the connection to the emotional system means that links to other muscles or systems also occur.

Obicularis Oris

- Surrounds the mouth.
- Acts to close the mouth and protrude the lips.

Levator Labii Superioris

- Runs from the top lip up into the face.
- Acts to raise the top lip.

Depressor Labii

- Runs from the corners of the mouth down and outward.
- Acts to depress the corners of the mouth.

Levator Labii Alaequae Nasi

- Runs from the top lip up into the nostrils.
- Acts to scrunch up the top lip.

The actions of the facial muscles often subtly change the activity or function of other deeper muscles that can affect the voice. This appears to be due to direct interaction, emotional connection, or realignment of the muscular environment. This can be demonstrated by attempting the following actions and feeling what happens to other parts of the articulatory system:

- Tucking the lower lip under the top teeth resets the jaw position, acts to reduce pterygoid activity, and thus encourages release of pharyngeal constriction.
  - Try this maneuver with the jaw in position one and feel how easy it is. Now open the jaw to position two and try the maneuver. It is more difficult and the immediate reaction is to close the jaw toward position one.
- Lip protrusion often encourages activation of the genioglossus which helps pull the tongue forward.
  - With the tongue tip resting on the bottom teeth, protrude the lips; notice how the tongue tip moves forward (unless it is prevented from doing so). Repeat this maneuver with the tongue tip purposely held retracted and notice how much additional tension is felt in the lips.

SPEECH SOUNDS

The structures of the articulatory system have two main functions, swallowing (deglutition) and speech. This duality of purpose (as in the larynx) can lead to interference, mostly where the swallowing reflexes are wrongly recruited for a vocal/speech task. Good understanding of the way in which speech sounds are made can assist the singing teacher or singer in identifying this interference.

Speech sounds are divided into vowels and consonants. Two separate systems, neither of which is perfect, are used to classify them. However, these systems give a practical way of classifying speech sounds that can assist the singer and teacher.

Vowels are classified in terms of tongue height, tongue placement in the mouth, and lip rounding, while consonants are described in terms of manner of articulation, place of articulation, and voicing.

Historically, vowels often have been expressed on a quadrilateral shape that shows tongue height and place. This was once thought to be useful for teaching purposes but, because it does not exactly correlate to actual tongue movements, especially in singing, we prefer not to use it. In classical singing, the gold standard has always been the bel canto tradition, which is based on the Italian language. We now know that every language has its own articulatory setting (especially for the tongue) so the ideal for classical singing should be to acquire an Italianate position for the tongue. Studies have shown that the Italian language uses a higher back of tongue resting position. The articulation of the vowels then occurs from this higher resting position, which facilitates the speed and flexibility of the organ itself. Sung Italian vowels therefore, will not match the vowel quadrilateral exactly.

The vowel sounds are the most variable because the tongue does not touch a particular point in the mouth as it would to articulate a consonant sound. Instead there are target zones in the mouth that also interact with pharyngeal spaces to create the necessary resonances that are required for each vowel. Accents are mostly determined by subtle changes in tongue position on vowels.

The production of clear vowel sounds is based much more strongly on tongue position than on lip rounding. All five cardinal Italian vowels can be made with neutral lip rounding (although /u/ is particularly tricky). Overuse of the lips as a compensation for indistinct vowels is common, and although this gives an impression of the vowel, particularly in isolation or in a single word, in connected speech or in singing the definition of the vowel can be easily lost.

Since the 1980s, phoneticians have looked at vowel sounds in different ways and the work carried out in order to make synthesized speech easier to understand suggests that vowels have a target shape not only in the mouth but also farther down in the vocal tract. Wood (1979) suggests that tongue height is used to differentiate between vowels that have similar "points of constriction" in the vocal tract. Wood believes in four points of constriction:

- Palatal
  - Vowels /ɪ,i,ɛ,e/
- Velar
  - Vowels /u,ʊ/
- Upper Pharyngeal (uvula)
  - Vowels /o,ɔ/
- Lower Pharyngeal (pharyngeal)
  - Vowels /a,æ,ʌ/

These were based on x-ray studies and he feels that lower vocal tract target shapes are vital to vowel production. When applied to the singing voice, this knowledge is extremely powerful. When the vowels are sung with the tongue in an Italianate setting, as in the "Dial-a-vowel" exercise, (see Appendix 1), these lower vocal tract target shapes are obvious as laryngeal height and therefore pharyngeal space can be felt to change for each vowel.

Consonants are classified based on manner of articulation, place of articulation, and whether the sound is voiced or unvoiced. In English, the following categories are used:

- Manner
  - Stop (air is trapped and then released as an explosion)
  - Fricative/affricate (air is forced through a narrow gap)
  - Liquid (continuous airflow, usually voiced around an articulatory position)
  - Nasal (sound is allowed into the nasal cavities)
  - Semivowel (vowel-like in formation)
- Place
  - Lips (labial)
  - Teeth (dental)
  - Alveolar ridge (ridge just behind the top teeth)
  - Palatal (hard palate)
  - Velar (velum or soft palate)
  - Glottis (level of the vocal folds)
- Voicing
  - On/off

See Table 7–1.

Differences especially in the position of the tongue can occur in both vowels and consonants depending on the phonological environment (the sounds that are around them). This phenomenon known as

Table 7–1. Table of consonants showing English consonants (in International Phonetic Alphabet form), detailed by manner, place, and voicing. Manner of articulation is noted along the horizontal axis of the table; place of articulation is noted along the vertical axis. Voiced consonants are in **bold**.

Place	Stop	Fricative/Affricate	Liquid	Nasal	Semivowel
Labial	p/**b**			**m**	**w**
Interdental		/θ/**ð** (voiceless/ voiced th)			
Labiodental		f/**v**			
Alveolar	t/**d**	s/**z**	**l**	**n**	
Palatal		ʃ/**ʒ** (Sh in wa<u>sh</u>, s in mea<u>s</u>ure— fricatives) tʃ/**dʒ** (ch in <u>ch</u>urch, j as in <u>j</u>ug— affricates)	**r**		**j** (y as in <u>y</u>ou)
Velar	k/**g**			**ŋ** (ng in ring)	
Glottal	ʔ (Glottal stop buʔer)	h			

coarticulation or allophonic variation can be exploited by the singing teacher to obtain changes in the sound produced vocally. For example, the consonant /k/ is produced in a more forward position in the mouth in the syllable /ki/ than in the syllable /kɔ/. Similarly, the /a/ vowel is produced with the back of the tongue higher in the mouth in the syllable /ka/ than in the syllable /ta/.

So, with this knowledge, /a/ vowels that are too dark can be adjusted with /k/ syllables until the correct kinesthetic awareness and sound is obtained. Once the correct sound is settled, then other consonants can be used to ensure that the correct sound is truly stable. In the same way, consonants that are being produced too far back in the mouth (as can happen when tongue-root constriction is present) can be realigned by using other vowels or consonants to place them better. A /k/ that is too dark or guttural can be adjusted by using a /ki/ syllable or by alternating /ta-ka/ syllables to bring the consonant /k/ more forward in the mouth.

Knowledge of consonant and vowel production, especially placement of the tongue within the mouth, can be used as a shortcut to correct vocal faults or to rapidly improve vocal tone. Once the correct kinesthetic sensations have been experienced and practiced, the singer should have a template of articulatory postures to work from.

COMMON FAULTS WITH ARTICULATOR USAGE

Many faults can exist, dependent on the singer's anatomy, speech sound system, or habit and each singer must be looked at individually. Observation of the articulators in speech, at rest, in oromotor function, and, finally, in singing is required. Many articulatory faults in singers are subtle and the speech sounds they produce usually are acoustically correct (at least to a less trained ear) but have inefficiencies in the use of the articulators, which can have an impact on vocal quality and tone. These articulatory inefficiencies should be addressed and corrected wherever possible either by the singing teacher alone or in combination with the speech therapist.

Singers who have frank errors of articulation such as lisps, defective /r/ sounds, or /f/ for /θ/ are relatively rare but certainly every effort should be made to bring these singers to speech therapy to have these errors corrected. Such defects often are seen by the speech therapist as a minor articulation deficit that does not affect intelligibility but these errors can cause great difficulties for the singer.

Singing teachers often feel underconfident when diagnosing or working with subtle inefficiencies of articulation but they are excellent observers, have well developed ears, and are alert to subtle changes in vocal production which help them perform this task well.

DIAGNOSIS IN SPEECH

During conversation with the singer, or in simple speech tasks such as saying the days of the week and months of the year, the following signs of articulatory inefficiency should be looked for:

- Excursion of the jaw.
  - How wide is the jaw opening on vowels and consonants?
    - This should identify clenched or held jaws, asymmetric jaw opening, or overopened "jammed" jaws.
  - Is there excessive jaw movement on the articulation of lingual (tongue articulated) sounds?
    - This should identify jaws and tongues that are inappropriately working as a unit.

- Postural deviations of the jaw and neck.
  - Are the head and neck in alignment with the rest of the torso?
    - This should identify jaw jutters and people whose jaw opening distorts their head and neck alignment.
- Unusual tongue/jaw position on the articulation of speech sounds.
  - Does the jaw move forward on the articulation of the palatal fricatives or affricates?
  - Does the jaw move forward or back to assist in the articulation of other consonant sounds (especially /s, z, θ, ð, k, or g/)?
    - This should help to identify tongue blade users that need a jaw compensation to ensure that the speech sounds are acoustically acceptable.
- Consonants that are acoustically acceptable but look different.
  - Are there any speech sounds that look awkward, uncomfortable, or unusual?
    - /l/ and /r/ sounds that are produced with excessive lip activity but sound correct may suggest some tongue tip weakness or incoordination.
- Muffled or slurred consonants.
  - Does the articulation sound clear and crisp?
    - Imprecise consonants or a generalized lack of clarity is usually associated with tongue control or strength issues.
- Neutralized vowels.
  - Are the vowels and diphthongs produced precisely and clearly?
    - Deficits in vowel precision are often associated with tongue retraction and may show as problems with diphthongs in the presence of good monopthong vowels.
- Frank speech sound errors (lisps, weak /r/, /f/, for /θ/)
  - Even if these are regional accents, singers should be able to articulate all the consonant sounds clearly. Some of these minor deficits may be residual from a more significant speech disorder as a child, which could indicate some basic problems with articulator control.

DIAGNOSIS AT REST

Observation and palpation can both be used to identify inefficiencies of the articulators at rest.

- Size and shape of the visible articulatory structures.
  - How large are the lips or jaw?
    - This can identify large or cumbersome jaws or lips that may cause additional muscular tensions or activities while singing.

- Can any obvious defect be observed?
  - Singers who have had surgery to the face or jaw may have some reduction in the range or strength of movement in some of the articulators.
- Postural deviations of the jaw/neck (including clenching of the jaw).
  - Is postural alignment adequate?
    - This identifies jaws that are jutting forward and distorting the head and neck alignment.
- Open mouth behavior.
  - Does the singer have difficulties breathing through the nose?
    - This could be due to enlarged adenoids or tonsils or other medical problems such as rhinitis or allergy. Alternatively, it may be a habit, left over from previous problems with nasal breathing.
  - Is the singer able to close the mouth?
    - Problems maintaining mouth closure could be due to neuro-muscular conditions but more likely they are due to habit or physical difficulties caused by a severe open bite where the singer is unable to close the lips over the teeth.
- Tongue thrust swallow
  - Does the tongue protrude forward, pressing on the teeth or between the lips when swallowing?
    - This usually is associated with dental problems such as overbites and, in most cases, is combined with tongue-tip weakness.

DIAGNOSIS IN OROMOTOR FUNCTION

The structure and function of the articulators can be checked using some simple oromotor movements. Practice, by giving these tasks to a number of people, will help the teacher identify what is within the realm of normal functioning as there is some variation within the normal population.

- Check range and strength of movement of the articulators.
  - Do the lips move freely and flexibly? Are the pout and the smile equal on both sides?
    - Lip protrusion and retraction, ability to maintain a seal, and flexibility should be noted.
  - Does the tongue move freely and flexibly? Does the tip lift? Can the person lick his top lip? Does the tongue look particularly large within the mouth? These points should be noted:
    - Tongue excursion, especially tip elevation both inside and outside of the mouth.

- ◦ Ability to articulate a /k or g/ and /t or d/ sound with the jaw opened to two fingers width.
  - ◦ Ability to make rapid tongue tip taps (/t,t,t,t,t/).
- Does the jaw open as expected into two positions? Does the jaw click or swing to one side on opening? The following points should be noted:
  - ◦ Jaw opening, especially the movement forward on forced opening of the jaw.
  - ◦ Jaw flexibility with movement from side to side.

DIAGNOSIS IN SINGING

Careful observation of the articulators during the singing of songs and exercises is required. Often, a view from the side of the singer, rather than from the front makes it easier to see deviations of jaw, head, and neck positioning. Confirmation of what is being heard or seen can be made with gentle palpation.

- ■ Patterns of sound.
  - Are there patterns of sound? For example, all the /a/ vowels have tongue root but the /i/ vowels do not.
    - ◦ Sound patterns such as the one involving the /a/ vowel can indicate tongue-root constriction. Singers with a degree of tongue tie or tongue-tip weakness may show changes in vocal quality when faced with text that has a plethora of tongue-tip sounds.
  - Is there jaw jamming or incorrect positioning of the jaw, especially on /tʃ, ʃ, dʒ, and ʒ/?
    - ◦ This suggests the possibility of a tongue blade user. The jaw has to move forward to allow correct sounding articulation of these sounds if the blade rather than the tip of the tongue is used.
  - Are there postural deviations relating to the in-breath or certain consonant sounds?
    - ◦ Singers with articulation problems such as a lateral lisp may show unusual jaw movement when articulating /s/, which can affect the vocal tone. Similarly, singers with weak /r/ sounds may show overinvolvement of the lips. Distortions of posture during inhalation can come from collapsing of the upper body, thrusting of the head forward, or from jaw tension.
  - Are there muffled vowel sounds or imprecise consonants?
    - ◦ Lingual consonants that are poor in the presence of good labial ones may suggest some problems with tongue movement or control. Vowel sounds that are muffled could be due to clenched jaws or imprecise tongue positions.

The articulatory system is complex as its components have many interactions that can affect not only articulation but also resonance and vocal tone and quality. The possibilities for faults, misuses, and deficits are almost boundless but most singers have somewhat predictable difficulties that are summarized below.

The most common faults with articulator use/function are:

- Tongue-root tension
- Jaw tension
- Tongue-jaw-larynx functioning as a unit
- Tongue blade articulation/Tongue-tip weakness or imprecision
- Inability to roll /r/
- Tongue tie

TONGUE-ROOT TENSION

This basically occurs through a desire for increased kinesthetic feedback when speaking or singing. Deaf children are known to use a retracted tongue position to compensate for not being able to hear clearly. Tongue retraction improves kinesthetic awareness of the tongue's position during articulation. This can be easily felt by saying the days of the week with the tongue purposely retracted in the mouth. Over time, this tongue retraction becomes habitual and marked tongue-root tension is developed.

Singers use tongue retraction and tongue-root tension to increase auditory feedback. Tongue-root tension gives the singer a more pleasurable auditory experience of his or her own singing. Many singers also use the tongue root as a false depressor of the larynx when attempting to sing with the lowered larynx position that is desirable in classical singing. This false depression of the larynx also occurs when a singer is trying to sing in a lower "fach" than is natural for his or her vocal apparatus. Once again, this use of the tongue root can develop into a strong habitual pattern.

Tongue-root tension also occurs when there is inadequate breath support for the singing voice. To sing classically or, more specifically, operatically the voice (including the larynx, the resonating system, and the articulators) must receive active muscular support. If this support is not provided correctly by the large muscles of the torso, the muscles of the articulators especially the tongue root and jaw will take over this function. The voice simply has to be supported from somewhere.

Articulatory signs of tongue-root tension include:

- Distorted or homogenized vowel articulation. This is particularly evident in the central vowels. Listeners have difficulty in discriminating /a/ from /o/. In less severe cases or in singers who are well-advanced in their training, it may be difficult for them to clearly define open and closed Italian /o/.

- Tongue-tip consonants may sound weak or imprecise.
- Velar consonants also may be backed so that articulation sounds swallowed.

There are many exercises to release tongue-root tension in singing such as *lizard tongue* (where the tongue is thrust out of the mouth while vocalizing). These types of exercises are effective but can be supplemented (or in some cases replaced) with articulatory options.
Articulatory options include:

- Use of "th" (/θ or ð/) to pull whole tongue body forward.
  - Vocal exercises or songs can be "sung" through on /ð/ to help release the tongue-root tension. This can be followed by /ð/ plus the singer's best vowel, /ð/ plus the vowels from the exercise or song, and finally with the correct text. One hopes the singer will experience enough of the "free" sound to match the kinesthetic sensations of the "free" sound with the text. Recording this type of session also adds to the re-education of the singer's aural perception of his or her own sound.
  - For example, using the first line of "Caro Mio Ben" by Giordani.
    - The melody is sung through using /ð/.
    - This is repeated using /ði/ for each syllable
    - Repeated again using /ð/ plus the correct vowel, that is: /ða, ðou, ðiou, ðɛ/ and so forth.
    - Finally sung again with the correct text.
- Use of /k, g, or ŋ/ to raise the back of the tongue. This can be used in a similar way to the /ð/ by following the steps exactly with /ŋ/. With /k/ or /g/ commence at the point where the consonant is used followed by the singer's best vowel.
- Use higher tongue position vowels /i, ɛ, æ, or u/. The use of these vowels will tend to raise the whole tongue body but, in more severe cases of tongue-root tension, these vowels alone may not be enough to make the corrections. Use of consonants described above with these higher vowels may be necessary.

It is important to watch the position of the jaw and the amount of tension in the oral capsule while using articulatory exercises for tongue root, as inappropriate tension can reduce their efficacy.

Some singers have such a strong tongue-root tension habit that its engagement is visible or palpable on inhalation or even at rest. If this is the case, releasing the tongue-root tension during vocalization usually will be successful but may not carry over into repertoire tasks. Singers with resting tongue-root tension find it difficult to change their habit and replace it with a new muscle memory. It can take up to 6 weeks to bring about this change.

The exercises listed below will help the singer break old habits and experience appropriate kinesthetic sensations of normal tongue root use:

■ Accent Method breathing (see Chapter 4) using /θ and ð/ with the tongue fully protruded. The fricatives in isolation first, followed by syllable babble with these fricatives. Initially higher tongue position vowels should be used in this babble.

■ Tongue base stretches with jaw two fingers wide and a forceful /k/ held for 3 to 5 seconds.

■ Tongue tip curled under its own body (inside the mouth) and a /θ/ held for 3 to 5 seconds.

■ Tongue click with jaw two fingers open (hold for 3 seconds then click).

These exercises should be done three times each two or three times each day for up to 6 weeks.

Recalcitrant tongue-root users also may need deep tissue massage and manual therapy to assist the release of these tensions. There is a group of singers for whom their tongue root-tension may have a psychogenic cause, and if this is suspected (e.g., after 6 weeks of tongue root exercises they continue to revert), they should be referred for appropriate counseling or psychotherapy.

JAW TENSION

Jaw tension often occurs through an erroneous concept that a bigger mouth opening is better for singing. Many singers believe that opening the mouth will improve resonance and provide "space." In reality, most people have two position jaws. In the first position, the jaw opens almost solely under the influence of gravity and opens slightly downward and backward. There is little or no muscular tension in the temporomandibular joint (TMJ) or floor of mouth. In the second position, pterygoid muscles operate to assist protrusion of the jaw, which can distort the oral and pharyngeal spaces. Tension can be felt at the TMJ and in the floor of the mouth. Wide opening of the jaw can even pull the larynx up, which often is compensated for with tongue-root tension to reset the larynx. When the jaw is widely open (position 2) and the tongue root is inappropriately engaged, the palatoglossus muscle will activate to drag the palate down to create a dull and muffled sound.

Jaw tension can present as:

■ Consonant sounds that are imprecise or sound chewed.
■ Vibrato that can be detected in the floor of the mouth.
■ Jaw appears to be involved in the pitching mechanism.

- Overopening and jamming the jaw open, particularly through the upper passaggio.

If the jaw is being used excessively or with too wide an opening, it is often advantageous to have the singer use the jaw less. Exercises to moderate jaw opening or movement include:

- Singing with a finger or a pencil held between the teeth.
  - This prevents the jaw from moving and helps remove it from the sound production. It is important to monitor the forward position of the jaw during this exercise as some singers will close the jaw appropriately but then push it forward.
- Singing with a finger pushing the jaw back and down.
  - This encourages the jaw to open only to position one. If the opening is wider than position one, the pressure of the finger should prevent the jaw jamming open and forward.
- Singing with the thumbnail just behind the top teeth with the knuckle pressing the point of the jaw back and down.
  - This position encourages opening to position one only, as the knuckle can help prevent the jaw from moving beyond this position.
- Jaw waggling and lateral movement.
  - A combination of up and down and gentle side-to-side motion can ensure that the temporomandibular joint is not set and tight. This movement also helps loosen the floor of the mouth.
- Monitoring pterygoid bulge on jaw opening to define the extent of excursion.
  - It is possible to feel the difference between position one and position two with the fingers on the temporomandibular joint and this can be used as additional feedback to identify the extent of jaw opening.

The jaw has only a minor part to play in correct articulation so articulatory options are somewhat limited. Articulatory options include:

- Use of /j/ ("y" as in yes) sound with high tongue position vowels.
  - This encourages minimal but essential jaw opening and can be used with any type of vocal exercise or repertoire practice.
- Use of /j/ with open or central vowels to define the upper limit of jaw excursion.
  - This slightly greater opening also can help with loosening tight jaws.
- Use of contrasting syllables such as /laja/or /taja/ so that the jaw remains relaxed and the tongue functions correctly.

- The amount of jaw movement on these contrasting syllables should be very small if at all. The tongue should be able to work independently of the jaw to make the articulatory changes.

Once again, it is important to monitor the position of the jaw during these exercises. Jaw jutting or tension in the floor of the mouth should be monitored and avoided, otherwise the benefits of these exercises can be lost.

TONGUE/JAW/LARYNX FUNCTIONING AS A UNIT

Due to muscular connections through the hyoid bone, it is possible for these three structures to work together as a unit instead of maintaining their separate functions as articulators or as a phonator. This undifferentiated functioning usually is a sign that there is marked tongue-root and jaw tension, which have an impact on the hyoid bone and thus on the larynx. The lack of independence of these structures is very inefficient from both an articulatory and phonatory point of view. This inappropriate interdependence often occurs because of lack of abdominal support for breath flow, as structures such as the tongue root and jaw assume responsibility for supporting the voice. Tongue/jaw/larynx interdependence presents as a severe case of tongue-root or jaw tension but usually with some additional features such as:

- Tongue and jaw choreographing pitch changes.
  - Changes of pitch can be seen to be occurring on the jaw or can be felt at the tongue base. Usually, it is easier to see this phenomenon when wider pitch intervals are required. Singing octave exercises or triads often highlights these deficits, which may be masked in scalar passages.
- Jaw articulates a number of tongue-tip sounds with some consonant imprecision.
  - Excessive jaw movement is seen on the articulation of tongue-tip sounds. This can be seen more easily when open vowels are used. The text in repertoire often is muffled or has a chewed quality caused by the overactivity of the jaw in articulation.
- Vibrato is seen in the floor of the mouth.
  - The sympathetic and healthy oscillation of the supralaryngeal structures (vibrato) is transferred by tight muscular activity and connection from the pharynx to the tongue base and jaw. These structures can be seen to vibrate at the same frequency as the heard vibrato. This vibrato can be of any speed and may not be unpleasant or intolerable although it is often unstable or wide.

Improving the state of affairs in the singer where the tongue/jaw/larynx is functioning as a unit requires the getting of a "divorce," especially between the tongue and the jaw. Work to regain the freedom of these structures also will serve to release the larynx from its bondage so that all three structures can resume their proper functions. This can take some time to become the new habit pattern (typically measured in months rather than weeks), but immediate improvement in the sound should be noted. It is common for the freedom obtained in exercises to begin to be evident in the singing of repertoire after a few weeks, once old muscle patterns have had time to melt away.

Exercises to develop independence of these articulators include:

- Jaw exercises with the tongue in various positions (especially protruded).
  - This encourages the jaw opening and positioning to be independent of the tongue. At least three tongue positions should be used: backed with the sides of the tongue touching the upper molars, neutral with the tongue tip resting on the lower front incisors, and protruded with the tongue thrust out of the mouth.
- Tongue root exercises (as described above).
- Tongue exercises with the jaw at two fingers opening.
  - This encourages the tongue to move alone and ensures that the tongue tip is stretching to make articulatory postures. Five exercises all done with the jaw at two fingers opening are useful.
    - Tongue protruded to its fullest extent then retracted.
    - Tongue protruded to its fullest extent then the tip is elevated and relaxed.
    - Tongue tip is alternated between the gum ridge behind the top and bottom teeth (this exercise can be gradually increased in speed as long as accuracy of position is not sacrificed).
    - Tongue tip is used to lick the lips in a circular motion, first in one direction then in the other.
    - Tongue tip is run along the top then the bottom teeth, first in one direction then the other.

These exercises should be done six times each two or three times a day. Additional articulatory exercises include:

- Tongue tip sounds babbled with jaw held immobile at various openings (/t, d, l, n, s, and z/) using low central vowels.
  - This encourages tongue tip independence of the jaw. Commence with the jaw essentially loosely closed then gradually increase the opening of the jaw over a couple of weeks until the exercise can be done with the jaw in a two-finger position.

■ Tongue tip and back babble with jaw position held constant (/t-k, k-t, k-l, l-k, d-g, g-d/).
   • This exercise should follow a similar course to the previous one.
■ Sing phrases with a combination of tongue tip and tongue back consonants with whichever vowel sounds best.
   • Monitor the position of the jaw during this exercise. The jaw should not open beyond position one and should not be involved in the articulation of the consonant or vowel sounds.
■ Articulatory exercises for tongue-root tension also are appropriate

TONGUE BLADE USERS

There is a group of speakers in the normal population who use the blade (middle of the tongue) to articulate some of the tongue tip sounds. Consequently, there is a group of singers who also do so. Speech sounds absolutely normal and indeed, in a nonsinger, this type of articulation is of no importance. Unfortunately, tongue blade articulation leads to inefficiencies in articulator use that also can affect vocal tone and quality in singers. Generally, students/singers who are tongue blade users are good aural musicians as their ears have driven adjustments in tongue and jaw position so that these phonemes sound correct. The articulation of the palatal fricatives and affricates (/tʃ, ʃ, dʒ, and ʒ/) are of most concern as the jaw usually becomes involved to make these consonants sound acceptable. It is a worthwhile experiment to try to make at least /ʃ/ in this way. Anchor the tongue tip behind the bottom teeth and now try to produce a /ʃ/. The sound has reduced frication and usually does not sound sharp. Notice how the sound becomes acceptable if the jaw is protruded forward. Tongue blade users often have this jaw compensation (which is quite slight) active during all their speech and, therefore, singing attempts. Over time in singing, this jaw setting becomes a habit and can greatly affect vocal tone causing a "white tone" on certain vowels (especially /a/).

Identification of tongue blade users requires a combination of both ear and eye. Slight lack of sharpness sometimes can be detected in the production of some of the fricatives and atypical jaw movement can be seen during speech or singing.

Look for:

■ "Lazy" articulators—something is not quite right with the articulation but you can't put your finger on it.
   • The teacher may have concerns about the articulation during singing but not during speech. Consonant sounds appear weak or imprecise but only with some vowels or in only some environments.

■ Articulation deteriorates at speed.
  • More problems are noted when rapid articulation is required as the tongue blade/jaw team are usually slower and more cumbersome than the tongue tip alone. Passages of rapid recitative or wordy coloratura often highlight problems.
■ "Darker" sound especially in the /s and z/ phonemes.
  • This often is more obvious in singing than in speech and may be more noticeable when back vowels such as /a, o, or u/ are used.
■ Jaw compensations for /ʃ, tʃ, ʒ, and dʒ/.
  • These usually are more obvious in singing than in speech.
■ Tendency for the tongue and jaw to work as a unit, especially on the articulation of the tongue tip sounds.

Exercises to encourage tongue tip function form the basis of modifying the articulation of the tongue blade user. Most tongue blade users find the concept of using the tongue tip to articulate very foreign, and it may not be possible to change all their sounds to this new setting. /s and z/ usually prove the most difficult to change but the jaw compensation for these sounds is much less than for /ʃ, tʃ, ʒ, and dʒ/, which should always be tackled first. Developing increased awareness and strength of the tongue tip makes the chances of successful adjustment of the articulation better. Exercises without singing would include the following tongue tip exercises:

■ Protrude the tongue to its fullest extent and then raise the tip. Do not allow the jaw or lower lip to help.
■ Lift the tongue tip to the alveolar ridge then open the jaw to its fullest extent maintaining contact of the tongue tip on the alveolus.
■ With the jaw open to position two, deliberately curl the tongue tip up and down always touching behind the teeth, never on them. Gradually build up speed.
■ Move the tongue back from an extended /θ/ position with the tip running back along the roof of the mouth through /s/ to a /ʃ/.
■ Articulate tongue tip sounds from a two-finger jaw aiming for precise tongue tip movement.
  • /t, d, n, l/ are the most appropriate sounds to use as /s and ʃ/ are difficult to articulate clearly with the two-finger jaw opening.
  • Babbling tongue tip and tongue back sounds with a two-finger jaw opening. Low vowels usually provide the best environment to encourage tongue tip activity.
  • Articulation of /ʃ, tʃ, ʒ, and dʒ/ with the correct jaw and tongue position.
    ○ Articulatory positioning techniques usually are required with instructions as follows: Lift the tongue tip up and place it on the alveolar ridge then make an /s/-like sound. Draw the tip back (usually only a millimeter or two) and the sound will

become more /ʃ/ like. To this sound add lip rounding and gently close the teeth, making sure that the jaw does not move forward (close the teeth at the back rather than the front of the mouth). This should provide a correct /ʃ/ sound. This should be practiced until the singer can produce the sound without preliminary adjustment. The other palatal fricatives can be acquired from the /ʃ/.

- ○ In cases where these sounds are quite recalcitrant, referral to the speech and language therapist may be needed.

Changes to articulation can take as long as 3 months to achieve. Ideally, tongue blade users would become tongue tip users in all speech and singing attempts, as this would stop their old habit from re-establishing itself. Some singers are able to separate their singing from their speech, however, so that the old habit continues in speech but is eradicated in singing. These singers need constant monitoring to ensure that the old habit does not re-emerge in singing.

Once some preliminary work has been done with the tongue tip or in singers who are kinesthetically aware, singing with some articulatory adjustments should lead to rapid, if not immediate, changes to their vocal tone.

Articulatory options could include:

- ■ Singing with /ð/ to disengage the middle of the tongue.
  - • Tongue protrusion can free the middle as well as the root of the tongue. /ð/ plus vowels can give a good awareness of a freer tone which can then be matched with the text.
- ■ Singing with /ʒ/ while monitoring the jaw position so that the tongue tip has to elevate appropriately.
  - • If correct jaw/tongue position for this fricative can be achieved, it can be used to retrain the singer's kinesthetic awareness and to help him or her identify the correct freer sound.
  - • Exercises or repertoire can be sung with /ʒ/ alone or /ʒ/ plus a vowel to access the improved vocal tone.
- ■ Singing with voiced fricative babble to maintain tongue tip activity.
  - • This should be done on the student's best vowel initially and then expanded to include all the vowels.
- ■ Use of /tʃ and dʒ/ with correct jaw posture to develop new kinesthetic awareness.
  - • If these affricate sounds are produced correctly, the combination of the stop and fricative appears to have some ability to promote an open throat (these sounds are used to assist patients who have had a laryngectomy to open their throat to achieve esophageal speech).
- ■ Exercises for jaw and tongue-root tension also may be useful if these faults are associated with the tongue blade use.

INABILITY TO ROLL /r/

The ability to roll an /r/ sound (produce a voiced tongue tip trill) appears to be genetically driven. A small number of people appear to have a lack of movement or some reduction in the flexibility in the intrinsic muscles of the tongue. Even so, every singer can be taught to roll an /r/ well enough for the purposes of articulation in Italian, if not for the extended rolled /r/ needed in some vocal exercises. The inability to roll an /r/ usually is due to stiffness or weakness in the tongue tip so it is valuable to commence with tongue tip exercises as described above to promote strength and flexibility. Once again, it may take 3 to 6 months of work to achieve an acceptable rolled /r/ and students should be encouraged to keep practicing for at least this length of time. When tongue tip flexibility is improved, the tasks listed below can assist the development of the rolled /r/:

- Commence with lots of tiny tongue tip /t/, breathy and aspirated.
- Leading into a loose tongue flip with lots of air.
- When the vibration is continuous, voice can be added.
- This may take a number of months to settle and voice should not be added too soon.
  - It also is useful to use a word such as "parto'" as the articulatory setting for the "t" will encourage correct tip activity for the rolled /r/.

The development of a rolled /r/ for a singer who initially appears unable to produce one may take many months and daily practice for success to be achieved. Careful attention to the tongue tip exercises and the position of the jaw will smooth the way for a rolled /r/ to develop. The student can use a lip trill instead of the rolled /r/ in singing exercises and, once the tongue tip is released, it may be possible to do both the lip and tongue trill together as an intermediate step for achieving the rolled /r/ alone.

TONGUE TIE

Tongue tie (where the lingual frenulum, the band of tissue underneath the tongue, is too short) is quite rare. Prior to the 1960s, many children were submitted to "tongue tie" release surgery to improve their speech, usually with very little to no effect. There are many degrees of tongue tie not all of which will interfere with articulation or singing. Some children are so adept at compensating for their tongue tie that it is quite common for children who cannot protrude their tongue past their teeth to have completely normal speech. Just as with the tongue blade user, if speech sounds normal and the person is not a singer, tongue ties, even quite severe ones, are really of no importance. For the singer, the presence of even a moderate tongue tie can lead to jaw compensations, tongue-root constriction, or articulatory adjustments that would be counterproductive to good singing.

If a person can protrude the tongue tip to the top lip without obvious tension, he or she does not have a significant tie (from the speech and language therapy point of view). They may benefit from tongue tip exercises to strengthen and improve the function of the tongue tip and they may require articulatory adjustments to achieve the best singing but surgery usually is not required. Surgery for these cases should only be considered if the tongue tie (despite the best effort to improve tongue function and articulation) is hampering the singing voice.

When surgical intervention is required, tongue tip exercises should always be given as simple snipping alone will release the frenulum but usually will not change the function of the tongue. The tongue musculature will have a memory and a habit of movement based on its former motility restrictions that can only be changed by active intervention with stretching and exercise. A selection of the tongue exercises provided above with an emphasis on those for the use of the tongue tip will be required.

PEDAGOGICAL IMPLICATIONS

In my teaching model (J.C.), the articulation satellite is placed on a par with the phonation and resonance satellites; however, I normally refrain from working on articulation until phonation and resonance management have been reasonably well established. It is clear from the discussion above that the articulators themselves can greatly influence these other components. My experience in the studio is that, once the core components are established, it is possible and valuable to make adjustments to the other satellite components as and when necessary. For example, the exercises described for releasing jaw and tongue-root tension will affect articulation just as attaining a good clean phonation setup will allow the articulators to function with precision and ease (a "chicken and egg" situation).

SOME PEDAGOGIC TIPS

When singing Italian recitative, never use the jaw as a declamatory tool. In young singers, it often happens on the strong beat of the bar and this habit needs to be corrected early on. The articulators should retain their linguistic setting and flexibility at all times.

When singing in Italian, if the text is not clear, check that the pressure of sound at the level of the larynx is balanced, that is, there may be too much pressure on the vocal folds caused by the singer trying to be as loud as possible. The amount of voice that allows one to sing perfectly intelligible Italian also can be a clear indicator of the voice being well balanced.

Singing in Nasalizing Languages (French and Portuguese)

Dealing with the demands of singing in a "low palatal" language like French, for example, can be very undermining of a singer's confidence. The teacher's repeated exhortations to maintain the elevation of the soft palate in spite of the nasalization of many of the vowels can sound like constant nagging, but I have found that, once the core components of the teaching model are in place, it is relatively easy for singers to educate their vocal tract to behave properly. There needs to be a shift in awareness and one of the shortcuts I have made in this respect is to suggest that singers imagine that they are singing in Italian with the tongue and palate while pronouncing the French simultaneously as accurately as possible at the front of the mouth.

What this aims to do is to have the singer set up the vocal tract in the optimal singing position with the high domed palate and high tongue back. The addition of nasalization to the vowel is then a very fine, small adjustment of the velar port. If the velum descends for the nasalization, as it would in the spoken language, there is a danger that the larynx will rise and the tongue root compensate by pressing downward in an effort by the singer to maintain the "deep-throat" sensation.

One of the best ways to encourage the palate to remain high is to use the "puffy cheeks" exercise to set up the vocal tract correctly then add a "just a soupçon" of nasality as required.

The "Smiling" School of Singing

There is a fundamental belief that raising the cheeks will produce a high palate. This is the "smiling school of singing" to which I do not subscribe. Initially, there can be benefit for a student to experience a general lifting that includes the facial muscles, but this practice ultimately has the opposite effect to that desired. Employing the muscles of the mouth can cause the palate to drop rather than rise. It also has the effect of shortening the vocal tract and making the tone harsher. The elongated "duck bill" sort of mouth position will produce a different tonal quality and is more effective in the maintenance of the high-palate position. The Italian vowels demand a high palate and tongue for their production, not an artificially produced "smile." The muscles of the mouth and lips are employed in the pronunciation of the text and in my teaching are not considered to contribute to voice production.

For students who have a habit of excessive use of facial muscles, I use the "puffy cheeks" exercise to set up the vocal tract correctly and to minimize facial muscle tension.

SUPPORTING THE CONSONANTS

Singers often have problems with consonants. There can be many reasons for this, but the most important one, I believe, is a lack of support under the airstream.

For singers with "mushy" consonants, I use Jo Still's consonant exercise, but with the addition of a strongly supported torso. This exercise involves leaving out all the vowels and going from consonant to consonant while also vocalizing. It is difficult to do this unless the body is well engaged, and should be used only for a few phrases at a time to upgrade the oral muscularity of the articulators. Once the student gains awareness of this level of muscular precision, it is a pleasure (and relief) for them to reinsert the vowels. My only caution with this exercise is that it **must** have good support from the abdominal muscles. When a consonant is supported, the following vowel will also be "on the body." Many singers and singing teachers view consonants as their enemies; however, given our understanding of the anatomy and physiology of articulation, synchronized with good abdominal support, it is obvious that they also can be the singer's friend.

Tongue Twister Exercises

To assist singers in developing muscular flexibility and precision in the tongue, I use a set of tongue twisters (see Appendix 1). These exercises also help to bring about independence of tongue and jaw. They also require a good supported airstream.

Violetta: A Case Study

Violetta is a highly gifted instrumental musician and singer who came for lessons having completed postgraduate courses at a major conservatory. She had fallen in love with singing, and even though her own opinion of her voice was that it was perhaps not a top quality instrument, she was keen to make the very best use of it and hoped to make a good career as a professional singer.

She had inadequate breathing, no support, and limited technique but with her talent and hard work, she was very soon singing to a high standard. However, there remained an area at the top of the range that gave her trouble and did not always contain the matching timbre of the lower part of the voice. In lessons, this problem was improving but did not carry over well from lesson to lesson. She complained that this ease of voice production did not always hold during performances.

My own awareness of the articulatory mechanism was limited at the time, and when Ron Morris sat in on a lesson with Violetta, he was able to diagnose that she had a forward slung jaw and in her normal everyday speech was a tongue blade user. He was able to give this singer appropriate exercises to remediate the problem, which has resulted in her vocal inefficiency at the top being quickly and permanently resolved. The main reason that these articulatory adjustments worked so quickly and efficiently was that everything else was in place and this became not just the icing on the cake, but the cherry on the icing on the cake.

This case study highlights the value of the multidisciplinary team work, which is transforming the singing teacher's ability to learn more and function better. It also is an indicator for speech and language therapists who are interested in the singing voice that much can be gained on both sides from sitting in with vocal pedagogues. Singing teachers and speech and language therapists have complementary bodies of knowledge, some of which are shared. There are areas that are more highly developed in each group and there needs to be a free interchange of information between the disciplines.

This is particularly highlighted in relation to the articulatory mechanism.

Singing pedagogues have always considered the articulatory system to be important but usually have considered it only in terms of clear text. Through multidisciplinary interaction, we now know that the articulators can impinge directly on vocal function and tonal quality. Singing teachers need to view the articulatory system with new eyes and become educated to its interactions with the whole vocal mechanism.

REFERENCES

Ling, D. (2002). *Speech and the hearing-impaired child: Theory and practice* (2nd ed.). Washington, DC: Alexander Graham Bell Association for the Deaf.

Wood, S. (1979). A radiographic analysis of constriction locations for vowels. *Journal of Phonetics*, 7, 25–43.

Chapter 8

ARTISTRY AND PERFORMANCE

"If I screw up one more high C, I'll do it for real!" Copyright Simon Pearsall 2005

Vocal technique underpins artistry in a way that is both complex and simple. By starting at the beginning with "primal sound" and its emotional and physical manifestations, it is possible to build a vocal technique that can withstand all pressures put upon it and yet still maintain the "singing from the heart" potency desired by all artists and audiences alike.

Performances can take place at any time in a singer's development. Indeed, it is vital that a singer has the experience of performing regularly at a suitable level throughout his or her training. This constantly reinforces the singer's pleasure in musical communication and should be encouraged by teachers even though the singer may not be fully in control of his or her instrument. It is essential to explain to singers that, when they sing in public, they should not be thinking about vocal technique but enjoying the communication, and yet this is not the reality. When a student is grappling with technical changes, I have found it realistic to suggest to them that they have 90% of their mental focus on the performance and 10% overseeing their technical performance. Singers who have "perfectionist" traits find this very difficult, wanting to reverse the percentages.

Working with my teaching model, during a singer's development we need to step away from the technical issues at regular intervals and test the performing and artistry component. This is essential for the confidence and emotional courage of the student no matter at what level they are working. A regular revisiting of their inner artist can be both reassuring and frustrating in that they become aware of how much they have achieved and how far they still need to go. But usually these experiences are positive ones.

Beryl: A Case Study

Beryl, a singer who had already achieved fame at a national level on the strength of an immense performing talent but very faulty technique, had sung the role of Constanze 4 years earlier and been severely technically challenged and frightened by the experience. After about 2 years' tuition in my studio, she was again offered the role and reluctantly brought the arias to her lesson. After a "sing-through" of "Marten alle Arten" she burst into tears. My response was along the lines of, "That was really good, so why are you crying?" "Because it was so damn easy," she wailed. Although her technique was still evolving and her confidence still shaky, she had developed far enough for the whole experience of singing this difficult aria to move from negative to positive.

In the studio, I work with singers at differing levels of development, and with various abilities for taking on information. Although the student's pathway is individually tailored, there are some recognizable principles that apply to all of them.

1. During the early phase of working where the core components of the model are paramount, we are working technically for most of each lesson but always allowing time for the singing of one or two simple pieces of music with the student concentrating mostly on technical changes.
2. As the singer develops technical confidence, it is important to suggest singing both their exercises and their songs "with emotion."
3. Attaining a "zone" state of synchronization allows the singer to concentrate on musicality, text, and emotion with only a small part of awareness given over to technical monitoring.

When all the other components of the model are fully synchronized, the singers arrive at the performance and artistry component and can virtually "forget all about technique." This desired state, after all, is the reason for studying to be a singer in the first place. To be true to the composer is paramount and the technically confident singer has the ability to communicate the composer's intentions to the audience on all levels (musical, mental, emotional, spiritual, artistic).

The development of artistry seems to follow an interesting timetable in singers. There often is a relatively slow development of the main components of the teaching model, but once these are in place, artistry seems to flourish very quickly in those with talent. Once the technical building blocks are in place and functioning on "automatic pilot," the imagination seems to forge a direct channel to the voice (without left brain/will power/analytic type interference). This equates to "the zone" experienced by athletes.

MUSICIANSHIP

Today, singers also must be musicians. No matter how stunning and special their vocal instrument may be, it is not enough to be just a "voice on legs." As a young singer, I was amazed to find that some of my colleagues in the opera company for whom I worked could hardly read music and had to be spoon-fed their repertoire by the music staff. But it was clear that these also were the rare voices, the Verdi/Wagner type instruments, for which special rules seemed applicable. These singers had to work really hard and often it was in their interests vocally as their vocal muscles learned how to sing the music rather than just their brain. However, now it is no longer tolerated for a singer to be musically illiterate or even semiliterate. In my studio, I insist on music being studied to a high standard before it is presented to me to work on. Only occasionally do we "read through" repertoire in a singing lesson. I do believe that musicianship can and should be taught—it is a set of skills available to all.

TALENT FOR THE SINGING

There is another area of a singer's talent that is harder to teach (perhaps impossible) and that is a "feel for the instrument." When a singer opens up to sing, at whatever level of technical achievement he or she has, it is possible for some ears to recognize that indefinable "something," which equates to this "feel for the instrument." How can it be quantified? Indeed, should we even try? When I hear this raw talent (for that is what it really is), I always make a point of acknowledging it to the singer, for often they do not know consciously that they are possessed of it and by it. The possibility that a young singer will become arrogant if presented with an evaluation of his or her talent is a reasonable risk. However, this knowledge carries with it a huge burden of responsibility to develop and use this talent and it is of great importance that the entire package is aired at an appropriate time in a singer's journey, that is, an acknowledgment that the talent exists, and discussion about the responsibility for carrying that talent around.

Part of the student's responsibility of preparing to be an artist is to listen to all sorts of music, vocal and nonvocal. They need to attend performances and listen to recordings of lots of different music and different styles of singing. They also need to immerse themselves in their own potential field of activity. It is particularly important for students to listen to the vocal music of different countries as sung by native singers for the sake of style and language. At tertiary level, it is very helpful for students to make a record of the performances they have attended and to make critical comments for their own education. Discussion with their vocal teacher and coaches also can aid their ability to develop discrimination.

PERFORMANCE AND ARTISTRY: PEDAGOGICAL IMPLICATIONS

Some students seem to have all the pieces of the jigsaw ready and need only a push in the right direction to be able to experience "holistic" performing. Some of the strategies I use to help them make this last leap are described below.

SINGING ENERGY

Singing energy is not the same as the energy contained in the music, that is, the singing of "droopy" music often undermines the vocalization in the inexperienced or developing singer. The idea that the energy required to "play the instrument" is different from that of the expression of the music is not often discussed.

The instrumental equivalent would be for a string player to play an instrument without using the appropriate tension in the fingers or bowing arm because the music was soft and sad. The energy to play the vocal instrument must transcend the music itself. Young singers tend to sing soft and sad without any support. The emotional energy produced by anger is a good stimulus for singing energy to be experienced. I sometimes ask students to sing their scales in a state of synthesized anger. This quickly produces a very positive result from which they can get an awareness of what vocal energy should be like and then extrapolate to their vocal tasks. For example, a page of Handelian runs and divisions sung first "as though in a state of anger" can help in building awareness of the sort of energy the voice demands to execute this sort of vocal writing with zest and flourish.

TIPS ON SOFT SINGING

Young singers often feel nervous about the demands of singing softly. I have found that, once a singer's support is active (i.e., the "engine room" is up and running), and their voice is well-schooled in focusing the tone, soft singing is easier to manage. Less pressure and less resistance are the key. In the low and middle voice, a very forward and high focus point is useful imagery, and if this focus is maintained, the air pressure and support will probably be maintained automatically. When singing softly above the passaggio, it is helpful for singers to first sing loudly to locate the area where they experience the focus of each note, then place the soft version of that pitch and vowel similarly.

However, some problems do occur and teachers should watch out for them. If the pitching becomes suspect (i.e., dips below the note), the culprit probably is the airflow. Students need to be reminded that singing softly still requires that the air be "feeding" the voice at all times. If the air is insufficient, the tongue root and jaw probably will become tense and the palate sometimes falls as a result. This too results in pitch "flattening."

Another important issue around "soft singing" is the size of the vowels. If the vowels become mean and restricted, the pitching and tonal quality automatically will be affected. I have found it to be quite important to correct students on the question of the vowels at regular intervals (I am guilty of nagging them). The Italian vowels are a great guide here, high tongue, high palate, and gently lowered larynx (as occurs naturally in a "pre-yawn" inspiration). I have found that a very focused /u/ vowel is excellent for practicing soft singing especially into the upper passaggio and top of the vocal range.

A quick and easy way to achieve the necessary pharyngeal configuration for soft singing is to use the "puffy cheeks" exercise to balance the airflow and resistance. First, sing the melody with puffy cheeks only, at the desired dynamic, then add some text while maintaining the puffy cheeks to allow the tongue and oral cavity to practice. It is then simple to merely open the mouth a little farther to achieve the end product. This should result in appropriately balanced soft singing with generous Italianate vowel sounds; however, this technique is effective only if core components of the model, particularly alignment, breathing, and support, are adequately developed.

SINGING RECITATIVE

This can be a minefield for young singers whose support is not established. I feel that recitative requires the same support from the torso as singing the aria itself. However, especially in *recitativo secco*, the absence of sustained accompaniment can have the effect of subtly divorcing the singer from the body. Conductors, coaches, and directors are always asking for clear diction in recitative but rarely have any concept of the acoustic and technical underlay to this problem. Unsupported consonants do not have much acoustic energy and urging a singer to do ever more in the way of spitting out the consonants without dealing with the underlying air compression factor only makes the problems worse. Maintaining the same sort of abdominal support in recitative as that required in arias ensures that it will be easy for the singer to make the text clear.

When singing an aria, the musical phrase drives the singer's breath and support, but in recitative, it is the text and more importantly the meaning of the words that have to take over this function. I use a technique in teaching the singing of recitatives which includes:

- Speaking the text on full support.
- Vocalizing the tune of the recitative on full support using only vowels and maintaining a legato line.
- Singing the recitative at full voice (text and melody together).
- Singing the text in a lighter recitative style but still with full support. The use of the jaw should be minimized while the activity of the tongue and lips is upgraded. This ensures that consonant sounds are clear and well articulated without affecting vocal stability.

The gaps between the notes still have air compression under them, which has the effect of binding together the whole thought rather than individual words or even syllables. This creates the impression of lightness.

Regarding the energy levels at the vocal folds, never try to make the sound bigger at the level of the folds. Rather, increase the abdominal support and the resonance spaces while keeping the small vocal fold signal constant (like in the rolled rr). This prevents the development of stressed and pressed phonation and wobble.

WHAT DOES THE COMPOSER WANT?

How far should the singer go in interpretation of the music? As far as they are technically able. I have found that very musical singers who for various reasons have not been "connected up" to their support have great problems when dealing with "being musical" while singing. Sometimes, their musicality (if aligned with emotion) can act as a stimulus for the body to become engaged under the singing, but quite often it can be a minefield. Many composers state very clearly on their scores what they want the performers to do to express their music. Strict adherence to the score often gives very clear clues for the interpretation of the underlying messages the composer wishes to impart. I worked with Benjamin Britten on a number of his operas during my singing career, and this maxim certainly applied to the interpretation of his music. There are many, many writings dealing with interpretation to help in the preparation of performances and I do not think it serves any purpose for me to add my two cents here. This is not the purpose of this book.

VOCAL COACHING

Once a singer is able to access the performance and artistry part of the model, vocal coaching can be extremely valuable and is a vital part of his or her evolution as an artist. Indeed, I use the analogy of my own work being like that of a car mechanic, getting the machinery up and running to an optimal level. Then it can be the responsibility of the vocal coaches to help the singer "drive the vehicle around the race track" with increasing finesse. My experience has been that there are particular coaches whose way of working is easily compatible with my teaching model. Singers at a professional level usually are very smart at locating the "right" person to coach their repertoire but still come regularly for technical checkups. Vocal coaching is not a substitute for teaching singing.

DEALING WITH CONDUCTORS, VOCAL COACHES, AND REPETITEURS

Simon: A Case Study

Many years ago, I was working with a young artist, Simon, who was employed on an Apprentice Scheme in a major opera house. He was in his mid-20s and a very good artist at the start of his apprenticeship program. During his second season, he was cast in a major role and rehearsed for the customary 4 to 6 weeks. I was aware that he seemed to be less and less confident as the rehearsal period progressed, and encouraged him as much as possible. I normally would try very hard to be present at the general rehearsal under these circumstances, in order to assess and feed back to him anything he might want to deal with before the opening performance (here, I would be very careful to give him only specific notes about things he was ready and able to deal with at that moment in time). Unfortunately, I was unable to go on one occasion. Next morning he rang me and said, "You know Janice, after the rehearsal, 14 different people gave me notes and none of them told me anything good."

It seemed that because he was young and "the new boy on the block" everyone in the Opera Company thought he was "fair game," even stage management and wigs and costumes people felt it was okay to make comments, possibly even valid ones. And as for the music staff, without any overall supervision from the Head of Music, or the Music Director, they all "had a go." Many of the comments were directly in opposition to one to another, for example, one coach said, "in this part of the duet, you are singing too loudly," whereas another said, "in this part of the duet you couldn't be heard and need to sing louder." He was so undermined by the whole experience he could not say, "Get lost!" to any of them.

Young singers have almost no political clout within these Apprentice/Young Artist schemes and, in their first couple of years in the profession, are exceedingly vulnerable to the overcriticism problems that arise (with the best intentions, I hasten to add) from eager young coaches and repetiteurs who "only want to help." It is possible that some repetiteurs and coaches are endeavoring to raise their own importance within the companies, but most only want to feel that they are truly earning their pay (a laudable ambition). But the overall impact on the singer needs to be filtered through a very wise senior member of staff who knows the singer well and has his or her welfare at heart. After all, the investment in these programs is considerable and everyone within the company wants the artists to succeed.

"COSMETIC TINKERING"

I believe that the "craft" underlying the "art" often is ignored in the vocal studio. Singing teachers sometimes do not recognize the fact that the voice is a musical instrument that needs to obey natural laws and undergo continuous incremental training if it is to function at optimum level. This leads to a sort of "wing and a prayer" style of teaching. Corrections to repertoire at a cosmetic level sometimes engender better singing at that moment in time, but often do not carry over beyond that moment. Teachers sometimes blame their students for being stupid or lazy when in fact this sort of cosmetic tinkering by a teacher is, in itself, the cause of many problems. Cosmetic tinkering alone will not build a vocal technique.

A model of how I perceive the holistic process from technique to performance is shown in Figure 8–1.

This model may appear simplistic. However, the strange thing is that once the singer is "connected up" and his or her training achieves synchronicity, singing does indeed feel simple. There often is a direct route from the imagination to the voice without the need for self-conscious management. Getting singers to trust this process though can be a problem and here it is useful to have them record their lessons so that they can judge for themselves. As an example, if you suggest a singer sing a particular phrase with "great sadness," the color of the sound he or she is making will change without the singer thinking of a technical way of changing the vocal color. In my opinion, this is the way it should be.

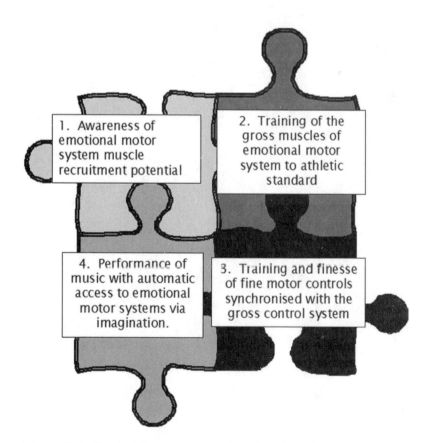

1. Awareness of emotional motor system muscle recruitment potential

2. Training of the gross muscles of emotional motor system to athletic standard

4. Performance of music with automatic access to emotional motor systems via imagination.

3. Training and finesse of fine motor controls synchronised with the gross control system

Figure 8–1. The holistic process from technique to performance.

In the human brain, performance and artistry belong in the talent/personality/intuition/imagination/communication realm. Sometimes, teachers state that these are not skills but talents and cannot be taught. I agree up to a point with this view; however (and it is a big however), on many occasions, my experience has been that singers who are locked up by technical problems are unable to access and show if this talent is present. It has been a great joy to me to "connect up" an apparently stilted and seemingly unmusical student and find a hidden treasure of talent for the expression of vocal music lurking beneath the surface and desperate to be liberated. Time, patience, and skill are required by teachers but I have found it immensely worthwhile giving singers the benefit of the doubt for as long as possible in the belief that they will find their "holistic singer" within.

Chapter 9

THE TEACHING AND LEARNING PARTNERSHIP PART 1.

The Singer's Journey: A Case Study of Eleven Singers Associated with the Studio

Marilyn McCarthy

> *The youth desired to sing to the Immortals. It is a law with us that no one shall sing a song who cannot be the hero of his tale, who cannot live the song he sings, for what right hath he else to devise great things and to take holy deeds into his mouth.*
>
> N`Óirin Ni Riain
> *And Deep Things Are Song* in Armstrong and Pearson (2000)

> *We shall not cease from exploration and the end of all our exploring will be to arrive where we started and know the place for the first time.*
>
> T. S. Eliot
> *Little Giddings* Complete Poems and Plays

This chapter presents a case study that explores the meaning some singers attribute to their art and craft. The singer's journey is described and examined for themes that illuminate the inner world of the singer.

Interviews were conducted with eleven singers, four of whom were also singer/teachers associated with this method. The findings are presented as stages of a journey that appears to be cyclical and without end and are offered as a case study.[1] The core assumption exercised here is that, in order to deepen understanding of the process involved in teaching and learning singing, it is important to appreciate the different meaning each student attributes to singing in the wider context of his or her life.

INTRODUCTION

The students in this case study are adults who are emerging as, or already making their way as, professional singers. Of these, five were women and six men. Their ages ranged from 22 to 50, with all except two over 30. They have traveled the singer's path with some acclaim, travailed rough terrain, stumbled often, and arrived at a place in themselves where being a singer has become a primary identity in the world. They are attracted to the studio having heard stories which bring hope that they can develop further and strengthen their resources for the road ahead. They come with many gifts, a passion to sing, and a willingness to risk themselves as learners on a journey. Along with their talent, they bring rich life experience and high aspirations.

What is the passion that attracts people to sing? They give a multitude of reasons—for love, fame, fun, as a career option, to heal, because singing is what they do best, or sometimes to express their soul. At their core, they sense that the voice connects a singer's inner experience of self with the external world, be it with events, friends, family, community, audience, in a theatre, or on the world stage. Some, like the singers in this study, are attracted to the path of the professional singer. One thing is clear: voice is central to their identity and sense of belonging. It can give expression to the fullness of their being, which tends to be lost in the course of daily living, and has the potential to bring them into relationship with themselves, their community, and the world around them.

Common themes emerged from the diverse stories that the singers in this study described. They tell of awakening to the beauty of singing, setting out with a sense of vocation, following their vision to cross thresholds of intense loss and great challenge, moments of turning that change their direction, and achievements that sustain and remind them of their purpose.

The journey is different for each singer, never orderly nor linear. Instead, the stages are visited and revisited in cycles. Like Parsifal, or Tamino from *The Magic Flute*, the singers conceive of themselves as ordinary human beings living in the mundane world, who sometimes are swept up in the archetypal dimensions of theatre, performance, and soul. In committing to the singer's path, they dare to test their limits.

Although they may be perceived as heroic by audiences, the singers are only too aware of their humanity on a journey without end.

There are many different paths for people who love to sing. Although the themes that unfold in this journey pertain to the singers and singer/teachers in the study, some elements may be recognized by those who travel on a different path. It is hoped that these stories will provide another perspective from which teachers can consider their own work with students. Seven stages can be discerned.[2]

THE SINGER'S JOURNEY—7 STAGES

1. ONCE UPON A TIME . . .

. . . a child was born into a family where there was music. The child felt happy. The people sang stories, hummed, clapped, danced, drummed their joy, and wailed their sadness.

For most of the participants in this study, singing is an integral part of childhood—in the family, at school, and in the wider culture. Asked when they first knew they wanted to be singers one said, *You don't decide. It was always in me.*[3] Another: *"It was sewn into the fabric of life."* Imagine another who as a child sang, *"to the streets, pegging out the washing, on the toilet. Everywhere! They couldn't stop me."* Yet another whose parents were involved in the music industry looked puzzled and said, *"My voice and singing are part of me. Without my voice I wouldn't exist. That's how I give expression to my emotions . . . it makes me alive."* Music and singing are as much part of their sense of self as breath. As children, they love to sing and know they are loved when they sing. They are connected into the wider community and feel a strong sense of belonging through their music.

2. AWAKENING—HEARING THE CALL

The path to becoming a singer often begins with an awakening, a numinous experience that remains forever engraved in their psyche. In formative years, they hear music that touches them to the core. In hindsight, it is described as, *"like falling in love, a feeling of wholeness."* At the time of this awakening, their experience is of something, *"so beautiful that I cried"* and sensed as a connection with the soul. Sometimes a relative or mentor introduces them to this experience. One woman, who as a child was surrounded by traditional Irish music, was taken by her aunt to her first singing lesson at age 10. She was skeptical but, *"The minute the teacher played (Panis Angelicus and Ave Maria), and I sang, I went into a trance. I cried all the way home because I couldn't believe the beauty of the sounds."* She thought that she might be able to do this.

Sometimes it happens while listening to another singer. One young man felt freedom and happiness while singing on the streets of European cities. Then he was introduced to a record of Fritz Wunderlich by a mentor-friend. He said, *"I listened . . . and fell in love with the sound. I'd never heard anything like that before,"* and quietly added, *"I thought I might be able to do that too."* Another experienced an epiphany when singing the solos of an oratorio with a choir. *"I sang one note, and I knew. At that moment all things made sense."* These awakenings mark the beginning of a conscious relationship with the Inner Singer, the sense of self or soul.

As they grow, it is typical for young singers to develop gracefully and naturally, relying on intuition and gathering experience. They are supported by their community. There is usually little awareness of the journey ahead or the craft required to sustain a career. For some, opportunities to study, perform, or even record may come their way without effort. The young person reaches toward his or her joy, believing that *"love and talent would be enough."*

3. SETTING OUT—THE DOOR TO SELF-KNOWLEDGE

The path leads to separation. Like Dick Whittington accompanied by Puss in Boots, young singers often leave home with great hopes to study in a foreign environment, which they hope will be welcoming. They may be severed from family, friends, and community with only their vision, talent, and willful courage to survive in an often unfriendly, political, and competitive world.

Several talked about the excitement and shock of their experience in academies and colleges where they relished the range of opportunity and exposure to new people and experiences. And here, for perhaps the first time, they may feel the chill of being ignored, the stress of meeting performance standards in tight time frames, and the humiliation of being compared with others and criticized clumsily and publicly. Here, there can be loneliness and friends who also are competitors. The Inner Singer may begin to fade.

All but one experienced a relationship with a teacher that unhinged their ability to trust themselves and tested their sense of vocation. *"I had a feeling of not moving on at all. I was frustrated and couldn't work it out. The pressure made it worse. I put myself under it."* Another who had lost trust in herself was confounded by her teacher. *"She said I had a great talent and she accused me of being lazy. I was frantic but no one could tell me how to get there."* In a similar situation, another young woman tried to learn by herself, sitting nose to television watching divas sing, trying to *"get it."* But, *"I just knew there was something wrong. No one could help me and I was abusing myself. I was put down by teachers and lost a lot of self-belief."* Yet another was told by her singing teacher that she *"couldn't sing"* and so she severed herself from failure immersed herself in mastering the violin, studying under the tutelage of a strict teacher. Years later, she was able to recognize that this training had helped her develop musicianship, but deadened her spirit.

During this stage, fear can creep in, a stealthy enemy, crippling, freezing the spirit, killing love and dulling the Inner Singer. In a sort of desperation, they may drive themselves by calling on the Inner Critic, with thoughts such as: *"You'll never be good enough; you're a fraud; you don't work hard enough to deserve success; everything you've worked for will come to nothing."*

On this crisis stage on the journey, one man reflected, *"The measure of a singer is how to survive (the journey) without becoming emotionally dead."* The journey has just begun.

4. LOST TO SELF AND VOICE

Here is an existential turning point. Doubting the memory of their beloved Inner Singer, many fear that they are in life or death struggles. They enter a wilderness period, which may last weeks or many years, and which many come to revisit as an old friend. In this period, unresolved trauma or personal woundings may surface; some women lose their way, experiencing a conflict of roles when they become mothers; relationships may need to be sorted out. One man whose life and identity as a singer was in tumult recognized that he was so close and yet so far. Frustrated that he could not yet find the small key that would open the doorway, he eventually realized that he had to sort our some draining life issues to clear the way for new opportunities. In this phase, things do not always make sense. The technique they strive for may not be the magic bullet they had hoped. *"I was singing good roles, but by the time I was in my 30s my career had dried up."* Or another who flourished as a protégé, *"gave up at age 22, gutted out, lost. I had no sense of self-esteem or trust in myself. No ownership of my voice. My Muse died. I had dead eyes and the voice was dysfunctional."*

This experience of facing a death of self is common for singers and with it comes either intense and restless longing, or a slow, gray suspension of feeling. A young woman who could not find a teacher to help her with technical problems says, *"I thought I might as well hang myself."*

5. REMEMBERING AND TRUSTING THE SELF

The return home is triggered differently for each person. Often, when all seems lost, the shock and recognition of their plight sometimes triggers the very thing that turns it all around—they let go and listen to their own voice again. One said, *"I learned to listen to myself. I didn't realize how much feedback I was giving myself."* The young woman who had pursued her violin career was unexpectedly reminded of the Inner Singer by colleagues. One heard her singing after practicing and said, *"You should be a singer."* This reconnected her with her dream and her voice. *"I knew what I wanted from my voice, but realized I didn't really know how to sing."* The problem was clear and a solution could be found.

Remembering and trusting often requires that the singer confront fear and confusion, stand strong in the self, and demonstrate an ability to protect the Inner Singer. In order to claim the right to share the joy of singing, fear needs to be faced and dealt with. *"I faced my fears and wrote about them, then allowed myself to be emotionally connected on stage, in the moment. It's not an optional extra, but a key element to sing well."*

Claiming the connection with the Inner Singer is associated with two main things. First, learning to recognize and listen to their inner voice, which guides them toward mastery of their own destiny. Some singers reported needing to say no to situations or to offers that others deemed highly desirable. Others had to learn to value their own judgment. One who had stayed too long in a stagnant relationship said, *"When I finally listened to myself and left my teacher, I realized I could trust my intuition and value myself."*

Second, the singer needs support from the environment, mostly in the form of a teacher or mentor. Recognizing that, over time, there had been a number of teachers who were right for different stages of development, one woman said, *"When you find the right one, a teacher can literally save your life."* Connecting with the right teacher at the right time can bring breakthrough. *"I always thought that singing was so much harder than it really is. I was getting exhausted and (she) showed me how to support properly."* Part of the renewal depends on timing, and helping singers reconnect with their soul. A man said, *"I needed to reconnect with the part of me that loves singing and she's helping me do that."* After being lost in the wilderness, another man described his first consultation with such a teacher. *"She cried, and I cried. It was cathartic. I discovered something that had died. It's coming back to life."* In this situation, there is healing and reunion with parts of the self that have been shamed and exiled. There is self-respect and self-love. *"I am forming a new relationship with the singer in me. Now I'm more willing to nurture and to be there for the long haul."*

Because the voice so intimately reflects the development and integration of the whole person—body, mind, soul—the mastery of vocal technique for the singer is often central to empowerment. It can be a foundation for new life and voice. Musicality, voice and technique are indistinguishable. One man who searched long and hard for the beauty in his voice hung on with determination, eventually finding the "right teacher at the right time." *"He built a technique again and turned me around."* Then, with new trust and confidence they can say, *"My sense of competence and control is growing . . . I am learning to trust myself and my technique."*

One singer described the *"gradual, cumulative synthesis of mastering small things that I once found difficult"* as the key to remember the Inner Singer. They experience relief that at last they have the freedom to sing, to be as big as they *"really are."* Another said, *"I can express a fuller range of feeling, and be the things that one cannot be in "real life."*

At this point, the quest may be perceived to extend beyond mastery of the craft and art of singing to include mastery of the self.

6. ACCEPTING AND RENEWING

At this stage, singers claim themselves, their voice and their right to sing. It is experienced as acceptance and partnership with the Inner Singer. At a concert that marked a turning point in her career, a woman said, *"I knew that I couldn't be more than I am. I had the resources that I had, and I gave myself up to that fact. This surrender meant I could allow freedom of the sound and allow the warmth without over-reaching myself. I'm learning to trust my own artistic judgment as much as other people's."* A man who has learned from experience says, *"I am very discerning about who I trust these days . . . they need to be on the same team."*

With self-reliance, and a technique that supports artistry, there is a new freedom. Held within the structured "container" of the stage or performance, they feel confident to express the fullness of themselves. *"Singing allows me to feel and express a fuller range of emotions. On stage, I am more than who I am in "real life."* Another puts it differently, *"I am liberated to be all that I am—nothing more."* A turning point of acceptance and renewal came when one man was involved in a situation where the culture and connections supported intimacy and trust. *"I learned to BE, to do nothing . . . on stage. That has stayed with me throughout. It freed me to BE ME!"*

Feel the joy at this moment, the sense of ownership now that the Inner Singer is again part of the constellation. There is a commitment and willingness to risk the whole self to express the beauty of the music. One says, *"There's all this amazing music out there and I want to get into it."* For another, *"My entire life goes into singing. When I sing a role, it is the depth of my personality that comes out."* The goals are clear. *"My voice has been my salvation. My love of singing saved me. My task now is to bring the authentic artist more into my life, to express the amazing and intense things I feel, on a day-to-day basis."*

7. BEGINNING AGAIN . . . AND AGAIN. . .

"An Inner Singer is for life, not just for Christmas." Every day, singers commit to live out the dimensions of their lives—the ordinary, messy and human, and the luminous. It's for life, *"like being married and committing to a long-term relationship."* Another says, *"I have learned to relinquish the need for instant gratification to take the long journey."*

Other dimensions of life are involved in maintaining this relationship and finding the right balance is not always easy. Relationships change, agents promise, birthdays pass, houses are bought and sold. For some, this aspect of their lives claims much attention. *"It's sort of like being a martial artist, in a state of readiness and balance for performance, and having to pace myself between times."* Relationships ground them, *" . . . of course there are the profound and lasting ones, like spouses, children, soul mates and, if you are very lucky, a proper singing teacher."*

As singers enter more fully into the profession, they are tested to maintain their commitment to themselves, their talent, and career. The stressors and demands are many. One said, *"I can drop into it (despair) in the middle of rehearsals. I felt lonely and exhausted, as if I had reached some sort of plateau."* When asked what helped him through this slump he said with a grin, *"Oh, earning money is a great spur. But mostly, I am refreshed by the joy of performance."*

Some singers articulate an evolving "spirituality" of work—a wider perspective within which to make meaning of their lives and careers; a respect for the voice as "teacher." This gives them a place of retreat to gain a sense of the greater story unfolding within their lives. One man conceptualizes this as a life path. *"It's not a single point, but a Holy Grail, stretching out in front of you forever. But there are many cycles and small points along the way."* A young woman understands her vocation. *"I know why I'm here. It's because I've been given a great voice. I know I'm good, but I don't' treat my voice as if it were mine. It's not me that's amazing but this voice. I must respect and take care of it. Every day I feel lucky and cherish the opportunities."*

DISCUSSION

These singers either are already successful professional singers/teachers, or are on the verge. Their journey may be familiar to us, as we sense the singer, doctor, artist, therapist, or financial wizard within each of us. Once awakened to their passion, they begin a journey of adventure and misadventure where they must underscore each moment of triumph and celebration with courage, self-care, and resilience forged from experience.[4]

What is this "Inner Singer"? What is the soul that they speak of? In an age of science, it may sound fanciful to use such words, but the singers in this study seemed grateful for the chance to use metaphor and poetry, as well as fact to describe their experience. One described the Inner Singer as, *"Love that breathes life and inspiration into technique. It's not just a passion. If I couldn't sing I'd have to dance."* Another described it as, *"the beauty that I long to express."* Words like *spirituality* and *"something bigger than me"* indicate that the singers can access enhanced states of consciousness as they master their craft.

DIFFERENT PATHS

Although each story is different, the singers in this study recognize the themes that arise and welcome news that they are not alone. Each takes their own path in their own time. For instance, one man who was involved in music from childhood, awakened to the Inner Singer at 25 years old. For another, after an initial awakening, the Inner Singer lay dormant for many years, only to be breathed back to life again during a consultation when he was 50.

One woman did not experience the hunger to be a singer. As a child, she sang because people loved to listen. She is exceptional in many ways, displaying prodigious talent in science, on-stage, but especially as a singer. Just as in childhood, singing is easy for her. Audiences are moved by her voice. Her career unfolds almost without effort. In fact, she realizes that without really choosing, she has flowed along with the opportunities to study and sing as they presented themselves. She feels at home on stage but in ordinary life she finds more difficulty. She feels ambivalent, wondering whether she deserves this gift. She says, *"I didn't see the singer in me, nor did I ever look for it . . . until others saw it. Now I am chasing that bit."*

THE PATH

The voice connects singers with themselves, others, and events in the external world. The voyage of learning and discovery leads them through experience toward mastery, from Apprentice to Master Craftsman.[5]

From	**Toward**
Dependence on others	Self-reliance
Emotional fragility	Emotional awareness and resilience
Singing to be loved	Singing to express love
Untutored and instinctive	Educated and knowledgeable
External locus of control	Internal locus of control
Hidden potential	Fullness of expression

From	Toward
Unconscious instinctive	Conscious awareness
Giving others control	Taking responsibility for voice
Indiscriminate trust in instinct and intuition	Discrimination and trust in instinct and intuition

What sustains them? Naturally success and achievement fuel the journey, but there are many other preconditions including a sense of vocation; the confidence that comes with a *"solid technique and getting a grip on the emotional resources"*; and positive expectations and attitudes such as hope and love. Relationships are one key to being grounded in the self. One singer responded to the notion of "unlikely helpers"— those whose paths cross theirs briefly. *"The amazing ones stick out like a sore thumb when you meet them—almost always through intense and transient relationships."*

THE GAP BETWEEN WORLDS

Some singers feel they bridge at least two worlds, spanning the gap between performance and "real life." Others see their art and performance not as separate, but as an expression of who they are, *"a living explosion that cannot even be contained on the stage but gets out into the auditorium."* Imagine the joy when, in performance, they can give expression to a wide range of "selves" that they perceive do not easily fit in social settings. The stage or performance provides a space within which they extend their usual boundaries to include the archetypal energies of gods, heroines, evil seducers, faerie queens, prophets, saviors, and tragic lovers. Here they are stripped of the artifice and interference attached to daily life, free, congruent, whole, and powerful. In the service of their art, they can let go the small self to engage with the great story.[6] For them, stage is a refuge from the prison of ordinary life. The singer who left science behind says, *"I don't know how, but I seem to be able to leave my shit behind when I step onto the stage. I rely on being able to do that."*

ON LOSS AND GRIEF

"I quit college, got pissed as a fart and told my teacher who I loved that I would never sing again. All she could do was let me go."

Accompanying this journey like a constant shadow is the experience of loss and the grief that goes with it. Endings and beginnings, change and growth—grief is their constant companion. In claiming your own voice and life, there is fulfillment and also separation. On opening night, there is the inevitability of drawing the final curtain. Eventually, the luster in the voice of youth fades.[7] Grief that is sealed inside, unexamined and unresolved, can become locked into the body and reflected in the voice. Loss is encoded each stride forward, but when singers engage with archetypal roles, their capacity for grief, as well as joy and other emotions, is amplified.

As singers become more successful, relationships are inevitably put under pressure. One man who has grown in stature and confidence, describes how in the dedication to his art, some destructive relationships have been left behind. *"I can survive without certain relationships but I cannot survive without my voice . . . and there are few people who can understand this. It hurts, but it's necessary. I've learned to cultivate relationships with people who are at least facing in the same direction as me."* Another says that the excitement of travel and career *"takes a big toll on relationships. For myself, a supportive relationship is essential for sustaining success and happiness in life and career."* Either way, choices for the future are accompanied by their attending consequences.

Individuals approach grief differently, and make their own meaning of loss. For example, when early success withered, *"I thought then, that I'd never sing again, that I'd died."* When a family member was killed in an accident, *"I got really depressed. He knew me better than anyone else. He was a great support."* Or in closing a successful show, *"I really loved that experience. We all clicked and encouraged one another. When it finished, I just walked away because I thought I couldn't afford to hurt when I was preparing for the next one."*

When artists commit fully to life and voice, grief and loss are etched into the deal. Those who can learn to live with the flow of sun and shadow claim the right to the wealth of their experience from which art is made. They learn to live with grief as the appropriate and natural response to loss. In doing so, they are able to face the challenges on the journey, with or without their teachers, and remain in touch with their emotional breadth and depth. Certain emotional strengths stand out as enabling and supportive for singers: hope and optimism, faith and trust, courage, willingness to risk, self-appreciation, ebullience, calm focus, compassion, fierce determination, respect, beauty, passion, presence, and love.[8] The prize is self-control.

THE SINGER AS MARTIAL ARTIST

When a voice sings with truth it resonates distinctively in the being of both the singer and the listener. It has less to do with technique than with a direct and vital expression of the soul/psyche through sound, with or without words. In that moment, the singer and listener are united in a nondual state and the usual sense of everyday separateness dissolves. (Knottenbelt, 1998, p. 30)

There is a parallel to be drawn between singers and martial artists. Both require that the individual attains mastery of the physical, mental, emotional, and spiritual dimensions and to demonstrate this through a form of artistry. The journey to mastery involves learning to live with paradox,[9] developing, holding, harmonizing, focusing, and integrating different ways of being.[10] In Western cultures, these often are presented as contrary, but over time, as they master themselves and their craft, singers learn to value and integrate dual states:

- The ordinary "real world" and also the archetypal world of performance and stage
- External objectivity and internal subjectivity
- Being open to learning and being focused and self-directed
- Being spontaneous and also outcome-oriented
- Being permeable and resilient
- Being powerful, controlling, and in charge, and also being vulnerable, letting go
- Being practical, grounded and in the body, and also being in touch with the soulful, beautiful, artistic, and visionary
- Valuing individuality and also valuing self as part of the whole.

INTEGRATION

There is a tendency in Western cultures to perceive these states as opposing and yet each is valuable to the singer. Therefore, the challenge is to develop a third position which is able to be inclusive of these polarities. Reanney (1994, p. 137) suggests that bringing conscious awareness to the process of unifying opposites leads to "knowing," the deep-felt knowing that arises from the connectedness between all the parts. In his view, it is conscious awareness with love that integrates and binds that which is fragmented. He emphasizes that *"consciousness is an act of union . . . the act of union is an act of love."* For participants in the study, the unifying force is the relationship with the Inner Singer.

Thus, it should not be surprising that singers talk of love when it is such a powerful force for healing and integrating their science, art, and practice. Qualities such as love and courageous intelligence, respect, and dedication are required to learn the art of the martial artist—to find the balance in opposing states and use them at will. In exploring, integrating, and transcending these differing states something new is made possible. The end state is not an end point. For the singers, it is sensed as a homecoming, a return to the Inner Singer, or the self which is always there though often forgotten. Through the course of our lives, we make this return journey again and again.

TOWARD TEACHING

By now, whether you identify as teacher or singer, you may feel daunted by the immensity and seeming complexity of the task, which involves not only the whole person—mind, body, feeling, and soul—in singing, but also involves the elusive notion of love. Most singers know when they are fragmented and "out of tune." They also have glimpses or even extended periods when love infuses their work, when they are attuned and in "flow," their whole self participating in making glorious music. At those times, they say it feels simple. *"My voice works when I work."*

The implications of adopting a holistic approach are explored in Chapter 10.

> **The studies show that, at least for this cohort, singing is more than a talent to be developed or a career option. Voice connects them to the sense of self or soul, which is their primary source of expression in the world. The path of the singer is marked by recognizable phases and can be experienced as a "life and death" journey. The search for mastery of the art and craft of singing is not only a search for identity; it is the search for wholeness. Learning to appreciate and work with the Inner Singer is a task for both teacher and singer.**

REFERENCES

Armstrong, F., & Pearson, J. (Eds.). (2000). *Well-tuned women. Growing strong through voicework.* London, UK. The Women's Press.

Knottenbelt, H. (1998). *On the wings of voice. A role theory perspective on improvised singing and voice work.* Melbourne, Australia: ANZPA.

Reanney, D. (1994). *Music of the mind.* Melbourne, Australia: Hill of Content Publishing.

BIBLIOGRAPHY

Campbell, J. (1972). *Myths to live by.* New York, NY: Bantam Books.

Campbell, J., & Moyers, B (Flowers, B. S., Ed.). (1988). *The power of myth.* New York, NY: Doubleday.

Houston, J. (1987). *In search of the beloved—Journeys in mythology and sacred psychology.* Los Angeles, CA: Jeremy P. Tarcher.

Mindell, A. (1992). *Leader as martial artist.* Portland, OR: Lao Tse Press.

Mindell, A. (1995). *Sitting in the fire.* Portland, OR: Lao Tse Press.

Seligman, M. E. P. (2002). *Authentic happiness.* Sydney, Australia: Random House

Sheehy, G. (1976). *Passages. Predictable crisis of adult life.* New York, NY: Bantam Books.

Yalom, I. D. (2001). *The gift of therapy.* London, UK: Judy Piatkus.

NOTES

1. The data for this study were gathered during a visit to London in February 2005, and followed up with E-mail exchange. It was initially intended as background material to a similar study conducted in 2001 with 12 singers and singer/teachers to identify the capabilities which "make the difference" for successful singers and teachers (see Appendix 2). The description of capabilities represents a valid tool for teachers and singers, but like the tip of an iceberg, reflects surface behaviors that are sourced in the rich inner life of singers. As the journey stories unfolded, it became apparent that they allowed glimpses of the depths and it was decided to write them up separately. An iterative action-research approach was used, using open-ended questions in exploratory one-to-one interviews. The exploration began with the question, "When did you first know you wanted to be a singer?" Typical questions followed. Where did the journey begin? What challenged you on the way? What supported and sustained you? What conditions, qualities, and abilities promoted your learning in the teaching and learning partnership? The data were clarified and enriched through follow-up E-mail exchanges. Drafts of the core material developed for Parts I and II were provided for comment by participants and changes were incorporated into the body of the work. My own experience as consultant, counselor, and singer was valuable in enabling the singers to explore issues of identity and ultimate concern to them. As a second layer of analysis, the stories were sifted for capabilities which were embedded into their structure. These were matched and merged with findings of the study conducted in 2001.

2. Initially, I chose the mythologic framework of the heroine's adventure (Campbell, 1972; Campbell & Moyers, 1988) in which to describe the themes embedded in the stories because it mirrors and encapsulates the ordinary and extraordinary qualities that singers embody on the path. This emphasized the feats and agonies of the hero, but although it rang true for some, the singers were in accord when I de-emphasized this aspect. It felt more congruent to focus more on them as human beings aiming to express great things. Feedback from the participants validated this choice. "*I read the first part with tears in my eyes—it's powerful stuff and nothing short of a validation for (my) compulsion to follow 'the road less travelled.'*" Jung's concepts of *individualism*—the natural drive toward development and integration of the self, encompassing transcendental and spiritual areas of meaning, also are germane and referenced in the text. But most psychological models of human development such as those articulated by Erikson (1950, 1964, 1968) or Sheehy (1976) seemed too "small" to contain the largesse in the stories.

3. In using the stories and quoting participants, I have been mindful of their confidentiality. Thus, rich detail that could identify or compromise their future has been omitted.

4. Singing may not have the same meaning for all those who approach the voice. Some people hope for fame or fortune. Others may yearn to be heard, to improve themselves, or to have some fun. It is worth pondering how many young singers who also feel called to the path of the Inner Singer might have been discouraged or lost on the way. We hope that this story can enliven and encourage them to consider and reframe the meaning of singing in their lives.

5. In providing comments on drafts, many of the singers appreciated the clarity that this table offered. However, it needs to be emphasized that the reality of achieving all these states is, as one puts it, *"as likely as 10 atoms colliding at exactly the same time in the same space."*

6. *By Great Story, I mean story that enables us to see patterns of connections, as well as symbols and metaphors to help us contain and understand our existence* (Houston, 1987, p. 92).

7. See Yalom, I. D. (2001). *The gift of therapy*. London, UK: Judy Piatkus, Chapters 41–44. At 71 years, Yalom writes concisely and simply about his approach to existential psychotherapy. This book contains pithy reflections, many of which are relevant to the teaching and learning relationship.

8. Martin Seligman (2002) provides useful frameworks and tools for the development and integration of positive emotions. His work extends beyond problem-based psychology to positive psychology—understanding the place, developing and utilizing the strengths of positive emotions.

9. See p. 137, Reanney, D. (1994). *Music of the mind: An adventure into consciousness*. Melbourne, Australia: Hill of Content Publishing Co.

10. See Mindell, A. (1992). *The leader as martial artist*. Portland, OR: Lao Tse Press, and Mindell, A. (1995). *Sitting in the fire*. Portland, OR: Lao Tse Press.

Chapter 10

THE TEACHING AND LEARNING PARTNERSHIP PART 2.

The H-Factor: Working Holistically Within the Teaching and Learning Partnership

Marilyn McCarthy

"I have learned that exercises aren't enough.
Souls need to sing beautiful songs."

(Singer/teacher)

The opera performer is instrument and instrumentalist in one.
Their inner dialogue and outward physicality interact
as they create the moment of performance.
They are the art that is heard and seen.

(Hulcup, 2004, p. 15)

This chapter explores the implications for teachers of working holistically within the teaching and learning partnership. The focus is on four elements that contribute to creating and sustaining a vibrant learning environment. Quintessential issues that lie at the heart of a holistic approach have been identified and discussed. They are drawn from themes emerging within the study and sessions with singers and singer/

teachers who were observed in the studio. In addition, five conversations were conducted with Janice Chapman to explore and illuminate the issues and implications for teachers.[1] We drew on our experience and knowledge from the fields of education, human relations, and human development to formulate a grounded theory (Glaser & Strauss, 1967).

Although the underlying principles may be relevant for singers at other stages of development, they should be applied and adapted to each situation.

INTRODUCTION

Adult singers bring many gifts to the learning process. They come with their genetic potential as well as their hard won knowledge, skills, and attitudes gleaned from formal education and informal life experience. The singers and singer/teachers in the study have already been tested and honed and are committed to a path of singing and/or teaching. When singers commit to learning, they offer themselves with the expectation that the teacher will enter into a relationship with them to develop and unfold their potential. They carry dreams and hopes, which may be rooted deep within. Some dreams will be disclosed—about repairing or strengthening vocal technique, or performing with presence—and other dreams may remain as secrets to be revealed only when the teacher has earned their trust and the right to share in them. Therefore, what happens between the singer and the teacher is of great consequence.

Teachers adopting a holistic approach not only bring specialist information and expertise to the relationship, but also importantly, take responsibility for facilitating another's change and growth—mind, body, and soul. Thus, the journey taken by singer and teacher together can be as tender and tough as a marriage, for the voice is not an object, but the singer's connection between his or her inner experience and outer world. Much of what happens on this quest for mastery of the voice can be surprising to both singer and teacher.

What distinguishes a holistic approach from other methods for teaching singers? The following model outlines the elements that support a holistic approach in teaching and learning. In each of the four components of the model, we have selected ideas, tools, or practices that "make the difference"[2] (Figure 10–1).

1. H-LEARNING—FACILITATE AND MANAGE THE ART AND SCIENCE OF LEARNING AND CHANGE[3]

Whether in life or in the studio, learning essentially is about the whole person changing and developing behavior. Our knowledge, feelings, and skills are intricately involved in learning. For singers and others in the

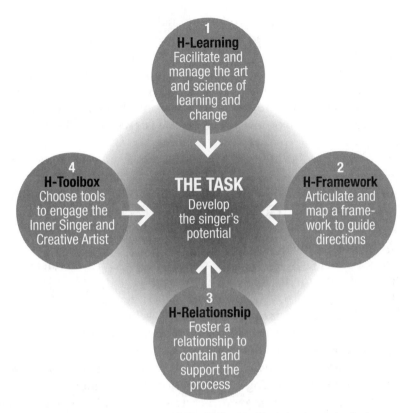

Figure 10–1. Four components of the H-Factor Model, elements that support a holistic approach in teaching and learning.

creative and performing arts, learning also involves high levels of experimentation and risk-taking with new and unknown techniques and ideas. Consequently, understanding the nature of multiple intelligences could assist teachers to stay connected to the singer in the process of learning. This section focuses on:

- Multiple intelligences and the singer
- The power of emotional intelligence to shape performance
- Pacing the singer.

MULTIPLE INTELLIGENCES AND THE SINGER

> *The human brain-mind-body system is capable of multiple ways of knowing. "Knowing" is deepened and amplified when there is an integration of our ways of knowing.* (Atkin, 1997, p. 25)

The human brain houses a variety of intelligences that are centered in different memory sites. In all human activity, these intelligences combine like parts of an orchestra to produce thought or action including voice. The greater the quantity and quality of these interconnected and interacting intelligences, the greater the quality of the result. The purpose in writing these few paragraphs is to raise your interest enough to investigate further. Only the tip of an iceberg is explored in this chapter and you are encouraged to investigate beyond this reading. For example, a useful book by Norman Doige (2007) is *The Brain That Changes Itself*.

According to Gardner (1983), we all have at least seven intelligences that are not fixed at birth but can each be developed.[4] Most people are strong in just a few of these intelligences, moderate in others, and borderline in the rest. The aim for learners is to exploit strengths and work on weaknesses enough to produce the best all round, or multi-intelligent performance possible.

Singers, especially opera singers, call on all seven intelligences at some time in performing their art. For example:

- *Logical/Mathematical Intelligence* is used to read music. It involves abstract reasoning for sequences and patterns and is, therefore, of central importance to the singer.
- *Visual/Spatial Intelligence* is used by the creative artist to image the scenery or setting of a song; or move confidently in relation to a stage setting. Singers who are strong in this intelligence will form vivid mental pictures and are likely to have a good sense of balance, harmony and design in their work.
- *Musical/Rhythmic Intelligence* is one source of musicality and is used to appreciate the structure and rhythm of music and sound. People with this intelligence have a "good ear," and may be pitch-perfect.
- *Body/Kinesthetic Intelligence* is used for expressive/creative and controlled/balanced movement. Singers strong in this intelligence will sense and learn through doing, feeling, and moving their body as instrument.
- *Interpersonal Intelligence* enables singers to establish rapport quickly and build relationships with people. Singers with this intelligence work well with others, are sensitive to dynamics in relationships, body language, and to differing cultural values.
- *Intrapersonal Intelligence* is grounded in self-awareness. It enables singers to know themselves, their strengths, and weaknesses; maintain confidence under pressure; read the emotions of others, and control their own emotions.
- *Verbal/Linguistic Intelligence* is used to remember words, phrases, and accents, and to interpret the text. Singers with verbal/linguistic intelligence are sensitive to the emotional content in language and enjoy reading and discussion.[5]

What are the implications for the teacher-learner partnership? From a multi-intelligence perspective, the purpose of teaching is to offer a variety of quality experiences that engage and connect as many intelligences as possible. This may involve using a full complement of sensory experience, including intuition, movement, and imagination, to awaken, develop, and utilize a student's potential. To teach a skill is to create a new memory pattern by involving and connecting different intelligences, connecting that memory to other skills, and grounding it in a context such as a particular scene, audience, or event.[6] Hulcup (2004, p. 11) encourages teachers to connect skills with context in their work, understanding that a skill acquired in a lesson may not necessarily translate to the stage or concert hall because other intelligences are also involved in a different context.

> If skills are taught and practiced in discrete modules, they conflict by competing for the singer's attention in the moment of performance, and no matter how much work the performer has invested, an uneven and ultimately unsatisfying performance results for the audience and artist alike. (Hulcup, 2004, p. 11)

Observing Janice Chapman conducting a session with a singer, I was struck by the range of approaches she used to achieve this. It seemed she opened as many doors and senses to learning as she could find.

In one single adjustment to vocal technique, the singer was invited to explore, extend, deepen, trust, and connect their learning through:

- Experiencing the physicality involved in singing by identifying and sensing musculature and posture and through touching, moving, and gesturing.
- Raising their awareness of the inner and outer senses:

    Hearing: *How does that sound on the inside? When you listen to the tape it will be different. You'll hear—*

    Touching: *I'm just going to put my hands here to help you remember where to support. What does that feel like to you?*

    Seeing: *When you make that sound it is like (draws image in the air with hands). What do you notice?*

- Understanding the rationale for change by using a model to demonstrate and provide factual and visual information about the vocal tract.
- Grounding the learning by imagining and role-playing in different settings: *When you practice, listen to the tape again.* Or, *Here is the audition panel—(sets out objects on the floor). Now, enter the room and stand before them. Notice how shallow your breathing is right now.*

- Breaking an old habit by counting backward silently while singing a song, a technique which appears to distract the left brain (Dennison & Dennison, 1989, p. 4), or supporting a vocal adjustment by changing the habitual gesture that accompanied the old way.
- Imagining and dreaming into the future.

THE POWER OF EMOTIONAL INTELLIGENCE TO SHAPE PERFORMANCE

JC: *A young woman in her early 20s came to the studio. She had great potential. She was intelligent, sensitive, with a fine voice and musicality that came with her ancestry. For a long time she avoided singing the songs her famous forebear wrote. Eventually she faced them in a lesson. A few bars in, she broke down and sobbed for a long time.*

What unlocked this sobbing for the young woman was singing a song that connected her to culture and family. We cannot know the meaning for her but we wonder how much unconscious effort went into protecting herself from being 'sprung' in public. We could guess that until she could face and claim her right she might be limited in what she could sing.

According to Seligman (2002. p. 31), "All emotions have a feeling component, a sensory component, a thinking component, and an action component." Although these components can be described, they cannot be separated from one another for they are interdependent. Goleman (1995, p. 6), says emotions are impulses to move and to act. This is illuminated further by Williams, Teasdale, Segal, and Cabat-Zinn (2007, p. 17) who define four interdependent dimensions—"feelings, thoughts, body sensations, and behaviors through which we respond to the events of life." The point is that singing is not possible without emotion and this requires that singers refine and forge emotions into a force to energize and enliven the work. Emotion conveys fire, power, and color in singing and having access and control of their emotional resources is critical for singers.[7]

Remaining open and responsive, rather than reactive to feeling, is likely to enhance performance. Yet this openness is often experienced as counterintuitive. As we have seen, strong negative feelings that are unknown or threatening can intrude into consciousness and may threaten to overwhelm a singer's ability to perform the task at hand. When fear or anger is aroused, flight or fight responses are triggered and battle stations readied to eradicate the intruder. Many singers have experienced the distress of freezing into a mechanical drone before an audience, or the dread that darkens the heart, mind, and voice. Energy and focus become fragmented in the fight, and the performance suffers along with the singer and the self-confidence.

In contrast, positive emotion buoys people and promotes confident creativity and risk-taking, generosity, an open and undefended attitude, quick thinking, flow, and success. Positive emotions act as buffers for stress and provide support in difficult times. The "good news" for the melancholy, is that positive emotions can be learned. For example, positive emotions like gratitude or forgiveness can change negative states such as cynicism or bitterness.[8] When teachers are aware, open, and confident in themselves, they may be able, not only to assist singers to tap and develop the resources of emotional intelligence, but also to transform and manage unhelpful emotional states. This requires that teachers are aware, and emotionally confident in themselves. Each will have limitations and it is critical to know these. Then they may either elicit support for clients or refer. It also may be helpful for teachers to be part of a multidisciplinary team.

Also see "The H-Toolbox: Metaskills—the transformative power of love, hope, and other qualities" later in this chapter.

PACING THE SINGER

Helping singers connect parts of the brain, and harness emotional intelligence requires teachers to have patience, knowledge, and skill. Among these are the abilities to determine readiness for learning and to pace singers. Pacing means staying in step with them, following their process, and also knowing when the time has come to teach, challenge, and stretch them.

Have we not all procrastinated while we gather the psychological or physical strength to take the next step? During times of transition and change, it is normal for people to move back and forth between their fear of the unknown and their desire to embrace the future, stepping from one side to the other as they gather perspective, resources, skills, and confidence to move on.

JC: *It takes patience to watch us people mark time before taking a big stride forward. The concepts and ideas that are used to teach singing are planted like seeds that grow. The timing matters and pushing singers too early only meets with resistance.*

Tending the psyche is part of a holistic approach. When to teach skills? When to wait or listen deeply? When to delve, facilitate, or challenge? Sensing when and how to shift roles from Knowledgeable Teacher to Creative Midwife to Mentor Companion is crucial. A singer who was grieving the suicide of a friend and experiencing tumultuous times in his private life described himself as, *"singing through a golf ball lodged in my throat."* At the beginning of his lesson, he blurted out all that was happening, in front of another singer who was acting as audience for the session. He wrote: *"Janice asked the other singer (audience) to leave and braced herself for the deluge. But a couple of exercises in she intuited that despite my recent personal crisis I was okay and then she asked the audience to come back in. We worked on the voice in a normal professional way. It was "ordinary." When I got home, I listened to the tape and I have never sounded better."* At this moment in his career, it was important for this singer to learn how to trust himself to sing, even when beset by sadness and chaos.

2. THE H-FRAMEWORK—ARTICULATE AND MAP A FRAMEWORK TO GUIDE DIRECTIONS

Frameworks are maps that provide directions for travelers. There are two parts to this section.

- Defining a holistic approach.
- A role framework to guide singers and teachers in developing capacity.

DEFINING A HOLISTIC APPROACH

What does it mean for a teacher when a singer writes,

S: *"I am my voice. My voice is me. Deep down, I always wanted to be a singer. I love the stage and on that stage I can take journeys with different aspects of my personality. When I'm singing well, the feeling is most rewarding. I have to be ready to be My True Self and show it to everyone."*

JC: *If I think about it too hard I could be overwhelmed because I need to feel equal to the task. I'm not a priest or a therapist. My work is to help singers connect to possibilities, to their sound, talent, body, weaknesses and strengths, and particularly to the Inner Singer. I work incrementally, in small manageable chunks, one piece at a time. But somehow, at the back of my brain there's an awareness of many things. What technical thing is blocking access to the Inner Singer? What's emerging? What will free, empower, or enable? I have these sorts of questions always hovering in my mind.*

Unlike other musicians such as a cellist, pianist, or even conductor, the singer and the instrument are inseparable. The instrument cannot be stowed at the end of a performance like a cello. Hulcup (2004, p. 30) says,

> It is vitally important to recognize that mind, body and emotion function as one during singing itself and when learning to sing. The ability of each element to function fully is interdependent on the strength of the other two.

If a voice were a bicycle, it could be dismantled, worn parts replaced, and put back together. But a voice is the intentional result of a living system, a human being in action—body, mind, emotions, and soul. The parts are not easily separated, yet teachers do work with "parts," bringing them to the foreground at the right moment, taking care to integrate them back into the whole.

JC: *You have to work with what's in front of you. Readiness and timing are critical to the task. When singers are strong they come with a shopping list, and I know that I can only provide answers for things singers are ready to deal with. One young extremely talented singer was not strong. She was so terrified that she almost ran out of her first lessons. I knew if I made too many technical adjustments quickly, she'd be unable to cope. It took 2 years to patiently build trust, in small increments. I knew what was possible in the long term, but worked with what she could deal with in the moment.*

It takes courage and awareness for teachers to work this way—being present to the particular issue at hand, and also to the well-being of the whole person. Over time, teachers can develop double awareness of the "big picture" as a background, and the specific element that is being addressed in the here-and-now, and with confidence learn to respond creatively and effectively to a singer's needs.

JC: *I watch and wait for unexpected moments of revelation. Just a few bars might reveal something.*

Figure 10–2 maps a way of conceiving this double awareness in the role relationship between teacher and singer.

The teacher is oriented like the martial artist, holding a soft focus on potential, history, and future aspirations, but remaining alive to the moment, ready to draw on his or her own resources or call forth those of the singer into the learning process. Working holistically is made more difficult because of the need to span the physical and nonphysical

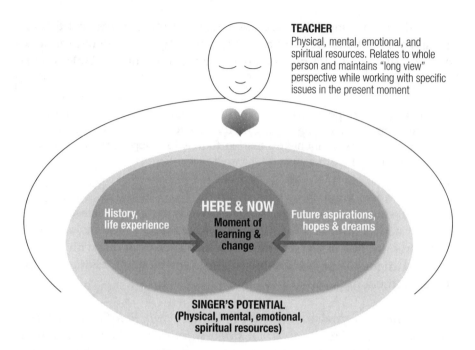

TEACHER
Physical, mental, emotional, and spiritual resources. Relates to whole person and maintains "long view" perspective while working with specific issues in the present moment

History, life experience

HERE & NOW
Moment of learning & change

Future aspirations, hopes & dreams

SINGER'S POTENTIAL
(Physical, mental, emotional, spiritual resources)

Figure 10–2. Teacher role: holding double awareness in the here and now.

dimensions of singing, which are at the heart of a holistic approach, as well as the science and art of singing.

JC: *As I work in this way, I hold a broad awareness of the sensing kind, and also draw on models and skills which I have developed over many years. Most important is that I continue to develop and articulate a framework to guide my practice. It needs to make sense to me, as well as to the singers and my peers in the field. So the principles underlying my approach must be rigorous enough to withstand critical appraisal in a scientific environment, and also be useful in teaching and in reflecting the experience of singers. Perhaps the most critical thing here is to create a framework and an environment in which all these perspectives can meet.*

A ROLE FRAMEWORK TO GUIDE SINGERS AND TEACHERS IN DEVELOPING CAPACITY

Several steps were taken to develop a framework that could begin to map milestones on the singer's journey. The first resulted in two dictionaries of capabilities, one for teachers and another for singers (see Appendix 2). These dictionaries are behavioral descriptions of abilities that "make the difference" to the development and success of a singer and a teacher. [9] However, in meeting the study participants' Inner Singers, we realized that a behavioral model was only a part of making sense of the singer's inner world or describing the elements of a holistic approach. We needed an approach that included behaviors and also reflected both the psychodynamics of the singer and the relationship with the teacher.

Using data from the case study, we found it useful to tease out the key functions and roles of the singer and the teacher. We employed the concept of role from Psychodrama[10] to develop a framework. Roles are described in terms of the *values/thinking, feeling/emotion, and action* components a person demonstrates within a given context and for this reason enable a richer description of singer and teacher abilities as they interact with each other and the changing environment.

We found that singers need to function with high levels of awareness and skill in eight main role areas[11]: Some of these will be well developed in singers, and others will be underdeveloped, needing the coaching and support of a teacher, mentor, or friend.

The roles of the audience have been introduced into the system as context, for there is always an audience present for the singer, whether it be it a teacher, a crowd, or the singer's inner listener (Figure 10-3).

- **Inner Singer**—is the core identity, or soul of the singer. It is also the organizing principle for the whole system. This aspect of a person enlivens and inspires; it is experienced both within the singer, and also as a Gestalt, a wholeness which includes and holds all the parts. The Inner Singer is characterized by awareness, a state of open knowing, or sense of self. The audience may know it as "presence" and feel inspired by the Inner Singer. It is accessed through insight and intuition.
- **Creative Artist**—an aspect of the creative genius[12] within each person; the Creative Artist may lie dormant unless it is cultivated. It may be cowed by bullying or discounting from significant others, or be robbed of confidence and courage. The Creative Artist responds to "messages" from the Inner Singer, other roles, and the events in the external environment. It works spontaneously, in the moment[13] ; to assess, interpret, invent, and formulate new or appropriate ways of being in the world. Its source is imagination and inspiration.
- **Martial Artist**—is mindful, balanced, and centered in the core self; disciplined and courageous in mastering and harmonizing the energies of mind, emotion, and body and focusing them toward the art; is present to the moment, balanced and poised in readiness; responds rather than reacts; moves with the flow of

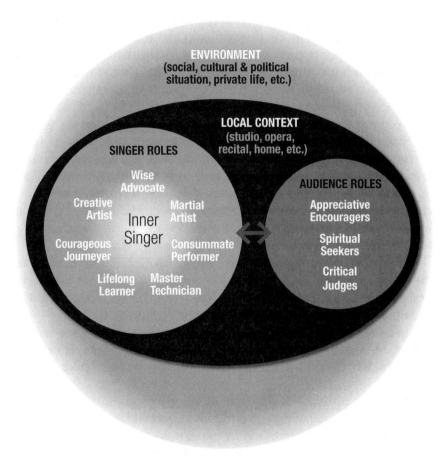

Figure 10–3. The eight main roles of the singer: the Inner Singer, Martial Artist, Creative Artist, Master Technician, Consummate Performer, Courageous Journeyer, Wise Advocate, and Lifelong Learner.

energies in self and environment toward destination; sees through, and challenges the Critical Judge. The Martial Artist is accessed through mindful movement.

■ **Master Technician**—is the instrument, the instrument maker, and carer. The Master Technician understands the living interplay between the physical body, the Inner Singer, and the Creative Artist. The Master Technician tunes the instrument and seeks those with arcane knowledge as well as scientific expertise to extend expression and bring forth its true nature and potential. The Master Technician also cares for the instrument, listening and interpreting the language of body/mind—instinct, movement, sensation, and feeling—to bring forth its beauty. The Master Technician monitors stress on the instrument and ensures that it is strong, flexible, and permeable enough to allow the give and take involved in living and singing.

- **Consummate Performer**—expresses in action; crafts the performance with presence, artistry, voice, movement, and emotional power to engage and change people in an audience. The Consummate Performer is aware of self, senses and responds to the audience attention and mood, and communicates in such a way that their mindsets and feelings are altered. Consummate Performer is present to self and audience, masters fear, listens to Creative Artist, and works with spontaneity in the moment.

- **Courageous Journeyer**—takes the journey; chooses and maps the goal and the destination by consulting the Inner Singer and all the other players. Courageous Journeyer is flexible and determined, changing direction to take advantage of the prevailing winds, knowing when to rest and when to move on. Courageous Journeyer gleans knowledge and life skills along the way, fostering resilience, psychological and emotional hardiness, and compassion for the self; over time, discovers that the "destination" is a new beginning, celebrating milestones on the way. As the load becomes too heavy, Courageous Journeyer throws unwanted baggage overboard and seeks companionship and help from fellow travelers and those who have gone before.

- **Wise Advocate**—the Wise Advocate interfaces with the world, keeping vigil, advising, communicating and advocating, containing and protecting the integrity and interests of the singer. It is the personal face of the singer. The Wise Advocate is astute in discriminating, clear in advocating, skilful in engaging, interacting, and negotiating in situations. The Wise Advocate is also strategic, seeking opportunities, monitoring directions, and managing a wide range of personal and professional issues that affect the singer. To be effective, the Wise Advocate needs the life skills gathered by the Courageous Journeyer, the support of a strong and resilient ego, psychological and emotional hardiness and maturity, and wisdom of the compassionate carer. The Wise Advocate works with the Martial Artist to deal with criticism. Most importantly, the Wise Advocate acts to balance the private and the professional, advising the singer how to maintain a life beyond that of the singer-performer.[14]

- **Lifelong Learner**—seeks to learn from life as well as from others with relevant expertise; is courageous in taking risks to learn about self. A Lifelong Learner is open to learning from many situations that at first may not seem relevant; is curious about discovering and applying new approaches; continually reviews practice for improvement.

These roles—soulfulness of the Inner Singer, creativity of the Artist, finesse and control of the Martial Artist, vigor and fitness of the Instrument, mastery of the Technician, craftsmanship and capacity of the Consummate Performer to galvanize, persistence of the Courageous Journeyer, containment of the Wise Advocate; and voracious appetite of the Lifelong Learner—populate the psyche and ideally interact like a well-oiled team to produce voice and performance. This is a living organism of exquisite complexity, each element consciously attuned and ready to contribute to the task. An absence, weakness, or conflict within the roles distracts focus and robs energy. For instance, if the Master Technician is lacking knowledge, or the body-instrument itself is physically hampered, it cannot express what is inside the person. Alternatively, if the Inner Singer is dispirited, the music probably will be lifeless. If fear rules the Consummate Performer, the body and voice will constrict.

Whose responsibility is it to develop these roles? First, it is the singer as the journeyer on the path. Although young singers often need encouragement to develop a sense of ownership and direction, experienced singers learn to champion their own cause, sometimes even with their teachers. Ownership and responsibility for learning belong with the experienced singer and teachers ideally are their wise servants. They may bring specific knowledge and expertise to the Master Technician, Consummate Performer, or other roles, and also need to recognize that one role cannot be developed in isolation from the others. Thus, in working with a singer, the Master Technician may be in the foreground while other roles remain in soft focus in the background, ready to contribute to the learning.

THE AUDIENCE AS CONTEXT

Singing does not take place within a vacuum and Figure 10-4 attempts to illustrate the singer's relationship with audience as integral to the act of singing. The audience is always present for the singer, whether imagined or real.

JC: *The audience adds the fourth dimension to the singer, music, and text. Sometimes I encourage singers to imagine an audience or I invite other students into a session. The audience focuses the concentration and energy for a singer. When singers engage and connect with the audience as well as the music, they can create something that transcends the ordinary.*

Three audience role clusters have been identified to provide examples of how the dynamics with the audience influence singing. Most of

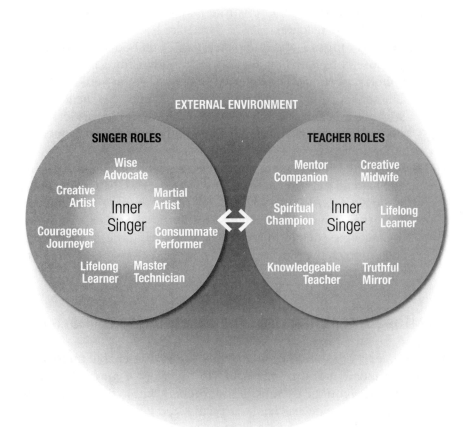

Figure 10–4. Core roles of the teacher in relation to the singer.

us recognize these roles in ourselves; they are present in each audience and individually in each person, including the singer and the teacher. Warming an audience up to the Spiritual Seeker or Appreciative Encourager, rather than the Critical Judge is part of the Consummate Performer's craft:

- **Appreciative Encouragers**—attend with an expectation of pleasure in the performance; they are open to the experience and hopeful they will undergo a change of heart or mind; they participate in the performance, even if it is in allowing themselves to be captured by a moment, and they rejoice when a singer helps them transform in some way. Appreciative Encouragers have a "glass half-full" approach, looking for opportunities to add more, rather than criticizing what is missing. It is not always easy for singers to be Appreciative Encouragers of their own performances and this role may need coaching and developing by the teacher.

- **Critical Judges**—audition panels usually embody this role. Their purpose is to discriminate and make judgment. Critical Judges uphold institutional or external standards. As an audience, they aim to improve by comparing performance to a benchmark. Within the singer, the role is often called the Inner Critic. It usually is alive and well and needs to be managed or balanced by other audience roles.
- **Spiritual Seekers**—are alive to their own "singer in the soul." They attend performances hoping to transcend the Critical Judge and even Appreciative Encourager, maybe hoping to reconnect with their own Inner Singer. The Spiritual Seeker can be an organizing principle in an audience, enabling the Critical Judge and Appreciative Encourager to join in a transcendent experience of the music.

HOW DOES A TEACHER ORIENT TO THIS RANGE OF ROLES?

Over time, teachers also develop a range of roles that enable them to be alive in the moment and bring vitality to the work. Figure 10-4 maps seven core roles required by singers and teachers within the partnership.

Teachers offer their particular strengths and gifts to the singer. The following are seven core roles—clusters of abilities that are central to the teaching and learning process.[15]

- **Inner Singer**—is the teacher's Inner Singer; is intuitive and insightful about the singer's existential issues and the meaning that singers attribute to their lives and work. The Inner Singer inspires and brings presence and unconditional regard to the teaching and learning partnership. It can be seen as the *organizing principle* within a holistic teaching and learning partnership.
- **Spiritual Champion**—holds a vision for the integrity of the Inner Singer and guards the singer from external threat; keeps watch over his or her own process to ensure it does not violate or damage; challenges threatening or compromising situations and passionately advocates for the singer, if necessary; knows when to step aside to support the singer's own Martial Artist.
- **Knowledgeable Teacher**—skilled in translating and applying knowledge and wisdom from experience to the teaching-learning situation; delights in providing technical knowledge and wisdom; understands how the whole person learns and facilitates the process; recognizes own limitations and when to connect singers

with other sources of expertise (e.g., vocal specialists, counselors, body-workers, agents).

- **Creative Midwife**—tracks and works with the singer's inner processes; aware of singer's emerging personal and career developments; encourages the new and draws forth inherent potential; looks out for the singer's well-being, waits and responds with impeccable timing in the "birthing" process; recognizes what is gained, lost and mourned.
- **Mentor Companion**—is a wise, compassionate fellow companion and journeyer. The Mentor Companion acts as mentor, focusing on success in the world; uses wisdom and sensitivity to share from own experience; knows when and how to listen, when to advise, and when to challenge; coaches the singer to challenge and deal with the sabotage of the Critical Judge; may befriend singer in life matters; gives support in different ways and celebrates successes together with the singer.
- **Truthful Mirror**—senses the singer's potential and helps to mirror it back. The essence is "clear, courageous seer" who is trustworthy and nonjudgmental in providing skilful feedback from a range of perspectives, including teacher, audience, management, or personal self. Truthful Mirror is unsentimental and can demonstrate "tough love" at the right moment.
- **Lifelong Learner**—loves learning and is curious about new ideas. Lifelong Learner continually seeks to learn from life and from those with relevant expertise; may join a multidisciplinary community of fellow travelers; is courageous in learning about self and developing capabilities. The Lifelong Learner reviews knowledge and practice for improvement.

IN SUMMARY

JC: *As I ponder about what I hope for my students and expect of myself, I feel somewhat awed. Three things occur to me which enable and support. First, I know that when I feel whole, singing and teaching are also simple. I move easily and without thought between roles because at that moment I am present to the situation and the singer. Second, it's not only up to me. The singer is on the team too . . . and there are other players to call on. I am part of a multidisciplinary team and depend on those contacts for help in areas in which I am not qualified. The framework helps me identify when I'm out of my depth and then I refer. Third, I continue to learn from others, and in unexpected circumstances including my own students. It's what I need in order to keep growing.*

3. THE H-RELATIONSHIP—DEVELOP A RELATIONSHIP TO CONTAIN AND SUPPORT THE PROCESS

The quality of the relationship between teacher and singer—the mutual capacity to give and take in the moment—creates the context for learning. This section focuses on trust, the foundation of a strong and resilient working relationship. Four facets of trust are explored under the headings:

- What is trust?
- Foundations for building trust—setting up clear roles and boundaries
- The rules of engagement—boundary issues
- Trusting yourself—clarifying your own purposes, values, and beliefs.

WHAT IS TRUST?

If the quality of the relationship between singer and teacher provides the container for learning, the heart of the relationship is trust—trust of self and trust between the singer and the teacher. One singer said that, *"This is a relationship where nothing is out of bounds."* Identity is at the core. A man who participated in the study reflected similar concerns of others when he wrote:

> My voice and I are intimately connected and I cannot be objective about it. It's one of the big problems I face, knowing that I can't trust how good or bad I am. I have asked others at the very top of their careers and they say the same, so finding someone who can give me feedback that I can trust is of immense importance.

Trust is the basis for all living,[16] the foundation on which all future hopes, expectations, and relationships (including with the self) rest. As the singer above indicates, learning how to trust the self is an ability that must, and can be, developed by all singers. However, many people carry scars from childhood that limit their ability to trust. Trust in childhood can be breached in many ways, for example, through abandonment by a significant person or through violating the integrity of a child's body, mind, or soul. If children have not developed a capacity for resilience, the results may show up in adulthood in many different ways, for example, in low self-esteem and confidence, inability to form lasting relationships, or maybe in a need for high levels of control. These scars of childhood may be revealed by the very act of singing and may present themselves as tension within the teaching and learning partnership.

JC: *When there is trust, almost anything can be achieved. Without trust, nothing, or even worse, damage. Whether we're working with the Master Technician, the Consummate Performer, or the Creative Artist, the singer needs to trust themselves to take personal risks—to be open to themselves, to feedback and correction. And they must also trust the teacher to lead them and have their best interests at heart. It's almost as tough for me as a teacher, for every time I make an intervention there's an implicit criticism and I must trust myself and the singer to handle it. This is a thoughtful feat that takes two mature adults who can patiently find a way to work together over time.*

Experience teaches us to invest trust wisely. It must be earned by the teacher, is likely to be tested often, and sometimes destroyed in a hapless moment. Therefore, it is critical that teachers are sensitive and educated in matters of trust, and take an early lead in setting up structures and processes that shape a safe and resilient container for learning.

FOUNDATIONS FOR BUILDING TRUST—SETTING UP CLEAR ROLES AND BOUNDARIES

The prerequisites for adults in building trust are a commitment on both parts to be respectful of one another, to accept differences, and risk transparent communications. When the stakes are high, it is dangerous to embark on the relationship without checking whether teacher and singer are both headed in the same direction and willing to be fellow travelers. The role of teacher bestows power, rank, and privilege,[17] so it is the teacher who must lead a conversation to gain shared understanding and equitable agreement. The purpose is to develop a map of the journey, be it for 5 sessions or 20, and temporarily agree on the destination.

What are our hopes and expectations for the journey? What does it mean for each of us to be a partner in this relationship? What do we expect of each other? What responsibilities do we have to each other? Who makes the decisions and how? In what situations might the "rules" change? How will we deal with conflict? What are the ethics and boundaries of our relationship? Where are we now on this journey? How will we know if things need to change? The exploration may be intense in the early stages of the relationship but the dialogue must continue as the relationship grows and changes. As milestones are reached and the terrain changes, the practice of reviewing the direction and quality of the journey together needs to be attended.

We asked participants in the study what they valued in a teacher. They were astute in their observations. Based on positive, as well as some very painful experiences as singers and teachers, they articulated clear expectations and knew what supported their learning. Singer/ teachers of the cohort expect that teachers:

- Hold a long and wide view.
- Recognize and develop their potential.
- Adopt a holistic approach; acknowledge and value the connections between mind, body, soul, and voice.
- Introduce new information skillfully, at the right time, and in achievable chunks.
- Ground their teaching in expert knowledge that is scientifically based.
- Make teaching relevant to their particular developmental needs and learning style.
- Remain objective; act as a trusted mirror; challenge and extend them, confront where required, and provide useful feedback skillfully.
- Nurture a sense of agency, empower, and tap into intrinsic motivation.
- Be a partner (50/50).
- Facilitate and engage in a mutual relationship that is characterized by qualities of love and commitment to singing and music, authenticity, respect for people, play, patience, honesty, and generosity of spirit.[18]

The singers hope that their unique needs will be addressed in a professional partnership, which is also a genuine relationship. They see themselves as collaborative partners in their own future, and at the same time, they want to be able to trust the teacher with their most prized possession—their voice. One said, *"I must be able to trust their expertise and wisdom to put myself in their hands."* Another said, *"The nature of singing means (the relationship) must be authentic, honest, and open. It's like having a best friend with whom I can discuss intimate matters."*

Ground rules support a clear process, but it is the willingness to risk personal disclosure that speaks of the trust at the heart of a holistic approach; for it is in revealing the self that the voice can be uncovered. To understand this is to cherish the gift of trust.

THE RULES OF ENGAGEMENT—BOUNDARY ISSUES

With the voice and identity linked, and much of the technique and artistry hidden from view, teachers monitor fine body movements and tiny variations in sound in order to track and engage with the inner world of the singer. This can be intimate and delicate work where boundaries unwittingly can be trampled or violated.

JC: *I feel very sensitive to people's personal space, and I endeavor to be careful to respect their boundaries because I know how hurt can so easily resonate to the core, and how hard it is to repair. If by mistake, I do stumble into the wrong territory I try to name this and apologize so that trust can be rebuilt. I can think back to many occasions in the past where I have failed and recognize, from doing personal psychotherapy, that boundaries were the very issue I needed to deal with.*

Boundaries define a teacher and singer's personal space in the relationship. Boundaries move constantly, contracting to reflect moments of intimate sharing, and widening to respect the need for distance at other times. They shift with a change in focus, from task (objective; focus on the singing and the song), to process (subjective; focus on the relationship). Although as human beings in social situations we unconsciously adjust our boundaries to suit the setting, teachers working with singers require intention, integrity, and conscious awareness in boundary work.

Sometimes, boundaries and perceptions become blurred and relationship issues get mired in the "murky depths." For example, this is evident in singers who seem to want a parent and not a teacher, or in teachers who see their own career mistakes in the singer. Sometimes, teachers make suggestions and singers hear nagging, or singers want to do it their own way and teachers feel rejected. The permutations are endless and without understanding and tools to assist, tension can lead to conflict, or even worse, silence, the basket labeled "undiscussable." These are the "hot spots" in the relationship.

> The point is this: difficult conversations are almost never about getting the facts right. They are about conflicting perceptions, interpretations, and values. They are not about what a contract states, they are about what a contract means. (Stone et al., 2000, p. 10)

In Goleman's terms (1995, 1998), high levels of EI (emotional intelligence) are required to address hot spots[19] and get the relationship back onto a sound working basis. In other words, what people feel about interactions, and the meaning they make of them, is as important as clarifying what happened. You are encouraged to read further and develop your abilities to address the hot spots in the relationship.[20]

TRUSTING YOURSELF: CLARIFYING YOUR OWN PURPOSES, VALUES, AND BELIEFS

Why do you teach, or sing? What is your core purpose in that pursuit? To earn a living? To make a difference to the lives of people? To have fun, or pass on your knowledge? To change the world, become rich, express your soul, "speak your truth?" To complete your own career?

Purposes connect us to our vision for the future and reflect the values to which we aspire, the "ideals that give significance to our lives" (Hall, 1994, p. 39). Values and beliefs shape mindsets—perceptions and assumptions about what is real and important, and these in turn, shape priorities, decisions, and practices.

Being aware of how our own mindsets shape the decisions we make is crucial for a teacher. It is an enlightening and possibly shocking experience to articulate and examine values and test the principles upheld against practice in the studio. An exercise to help explore and clarify vision, values, and beliefs can be found in Notes.[21]

4. THE H-TOOLBOX: CHOOSE TOOLS TO ENGAGE THE INNER SINGER AND CREATIVE ARTIST

The tools in a teacher's toolbox are carefully selected and acquired over time. The box will be filled with cherished models and skills that have been tested, crafted, and honed, ready for use in myriad situations. This section focuses on the qualities that teachers can bring to support a holistic approach, which especially involves the Inner Singer and Creative Artist. Three areas of exploration have been selected:

- Metaskills—the power of love, hope, and other qualities
- Imagination—the springboard for creativity
- H-factor: self as tool

METASKILLS—THE TRANSFORMATIVE POWER OF LOVE, HOPE, AND OTHER QUALITIES

It challenges social norms to name qualities such as love and spirituality in a scientific age where they cannot be easily measured. Where do qualities such as love, hope, faith, passion, optimism, honesty, openness, creativity, courage, respect, humility, inspiration, intuition, and wisdom belong in a holistic approach to teaching and learning? They create the conditions for growth. The Grail of the singer's journey is voice and performance, but singers cannot sustain their path without calling forth qualities such as these. Seligman (2002, p. 12) calls them signature strengths, positive emotions that "we may not know about until we are truly challenged." Happiness, joy, and ecstasy are positive emotions, which can be triggered by artificial means, but he says, "Positive emotions alienated from the exercise of character lead to emptiness, to inauthenticity, to depression, and, as we age, to the gnawing realization that we are fidgeting until we die." (p. 8).

How do teachers support and strengthen the qualities with which the singers/teachers in the cohort so strongly identify. Amy Mindell[22] calls them metaskills—feeling-attitudes with which singers or teachers approach situations, engage with (the music), and utilize techniques. Amy Mindell says, "They are the vehicles that animate our normal techniques and allow our deepest beliefs to take root" (1995, p. 19).[23] Mindell (1992, p. 59) provides the example of hammering a nail, "When I learn to hammer a nail, I have learned a skill, but the way in which I hold the hammer is a metaskill." For a teacher, communicating clearly is being skilful. Communicating clearly *and respectfully* changes the dynamics of communication, adds meaning and conveys core beliefs. This is using a metaskill. The decisive factor, then, lies in the orientation of the teacher toward the communication.

The teachers we spoke to say these qualities not only are desirable within the teaching and learning partnership, but that they are essential to singing. They can be developed. For instance, ask a student to imagine or remember a time when he or she was filled with fear, a common obstacle to singing well. Make it as vivid as you can and encourage them to notice what happens in the body—constriction of muscles in the throat and chest, cold sweat, state of suspension or cold, and so forth. Now do the same with the quality of love or hope, remembering a time and situation where it was a strong experience for them. Encourage them to pay attention and notice the subtle shifts in the body, the way it orients toward openness, warmth, relaxation. If they could remain in this state, how would they sing?[24]

IMAGINATION—THE SPRINGBOARD FOR CREATIVITY[25]

Imagination is the elixir of learning and the mechanism used by singers to form a *concept of that which is not actually present to the senses* or has never been experienced. Imagination also is active when images or ideas are combined to create something new, or to perceive the connections between disparate or unlikely things.

Ask a student, or try yourself to remember your Inner Singer, or if you prefer, Creative Artist, and draw a picture, sculpt your own body, or move your hand in a way to represent this by drawing in the air. Is there a sound or song, color, or perfume associated with this Inner Singer or Creative Artist? Give time to allow the imagination to unfold and the expression deepen and change. Write, sing, or draw what has been discovered. The process can deepen and enliven the connection.

Using active imagination to shape performance requires one to draw on all the senses, including intuition, allowing concepts be formed and reformed. The skill of teachers lies in stimulating the imagination and assisting singers to translate the singer's new understanding into action. For instance, a singer who is learning to express the potential beauty in the voice may be encouraged to enlist the imagination by thinking of someone who could do this, identifying the qualities the person brings to the sound, placing themselves in their shoes, and feeling how it is in all parts of the body to express such beautiful music. Alone, this is unlikely to enable the singer to make the sound, but it may enliven and recruit different intelligences into the learning process. Once the imagination is activated, it may become easier to make vocal adjustments that bring forth the sound.

H-FACTOR: SELF AS TOOL

Of all the H-factors, the teacher's own self is the most powerful.

JC: *There was a time when the word love was excluded from my professional vocabulary. When I was younger, I loved to sing. But I sang in order to be loved and that in itself was a roadblock to experiencing love as an artist—the love of being, of singing, and of creating.*

Now, as a teacher, I cannot afford to teach with anything but love.[26] It means having the capacity to trust, be open and fully present to the singer, the situation, and the moment, with all my resources on tap. Perhaps it's easier to talk about love's opposite—of fear, hate, and envy. I experienced that too as a singer, felt its effect from others, and for others. It contracts the body and cripples the spirit. As a young teacher, still grieving the diminution of my own singing career, I subconsciously guarded and held my negativity and sadness back because I didn't want to shower it on the students. But, in so doing, I also dammed up love and other positive feelings which are so essential to building a decent relationship with people. A couple of years with a good therapist helped me. That's a commitment to yourself that you need to make as a teacher—to keep growing.

> **Four elements that contribute to creating a teaching and learning partnership that fosters a holistic approach have been explored in this chapter:**
>
> - Learning is seen as synonymous with change. Howard Gardner's concept of *multiple intelligences* was briefly described as a structure for understanding the importance of making connections in learning; and special attention was paid to the development of emotional intelligence as an integral source of creative and artistic drive.
> - Singers require more than a fine technique. From their stories, it is evident that a wide range of roles and life-

skills are required to sustain a singer and a professional career. The roles required by a teacher are somewhat different and equally complex. The Inner Singer lies at the heart of both teacher and singer.

- Sound teaching and learning partnerships are relationships of mutual trust where both risk themselves in the learning. Where a singer's instrument and identity are so interconnected, the development of singing also invites the development of the singer. This section explores ways for teachers to establish norms that support learning; identify and work with boundary issues; and points out the need for self-knowledge through clarification of purposes and values.
- In a holistic framework, the teacher consciously engages with the Inner Singer and Creative Artist. This requires the ability to both engage and simultaneously maintain perspective. Fostering the imagination, maintaining awareness of self, being authentic and willing to share of the self are powerful tools for partnering and teaching. The concept of Metaskills is introduced within which qualities such as love, courage, empathy, and determination can be validated.

REFERENCES

Atkin, J. A. (1997). *Stimulating and integrating whole brain processing: Going beyond preference to capacity.* Paper delivered at national conference, "Using Your Brain," promoted by Hawker.

Dennison, P. E., & Dennison, G. E. (1989). *Brain gym* (Teacher's ed.). Ventura, CA: Brain Gym International/Educational Kinesiology Foundation.

Gardner, H. (1983). *Frames of mind: The theory of multiple intelligences.* New York, NY: Harper and Row

Gardner, H. (1987). *Developing the spectrum of human intelligences: Teaching in the Eighties: A need to change.* Cambridge, MA: Harvard Educational Review.

Glaser, B., & Strauss, A. (1967). *The discovery of grounded theory: Strategies for qualitative research.* Chicago, IL: Aldine.

Goleman. D. (1995). *Emotional intelligence. Why it can matter more than IQ.* London, UK: Bloomsbury.

Goleman, D. (1998). *Working with emotional intelligence.* New York, NY: Bantam Books

Hall, B. P. (1994). *Values shift: A guide to personal and organizational transformation.* Rockport, MA: Twin Lights.

Hulcup, C. (2004). *Opera training: Skill integration, philosophy and practice.* Thesis submitted for Master of Music Performance, School of Music, Victorian College of the Arts, University of Melbourne, Australia.

Mindell, Amy. (1995). *Metaskills: The spiritual art of therapy.* Portland, OR: Lao Tse Press.

Mindell, Arnold. (1992). *Leader as martial artist.* Portland, OR: Lao Tse Press.

Mindell, Arnold. (1995). *Sitting in the fire.* Portland, OR: Lao Tse Press.

Seligman, M. E. P. (2002). *Authentic happiness.* Sydney, Australia: Random House.

WEB SITES

http://www.pz.harvard.edu/PIs/HG_Larsen : Larsen, S.N. (2002) *HG Interview with Steen Nepper Larsen on January 30, 2002.*

http://www.workforce.com : *31 core competencies explained.*

http://www.eiconsortium.org : The Consortium for Research on Emotional Intelligence in Organizations—*The emotional competence framework.*

BIBLIOGRAPHY

Atkin, J. A (1996). *From values and beliefs about learning to principles and practice.* Seminar Series No 54, Melbourne, Australia: IARTV.

Bandler, R., & Grinder, J. (1973). *Frogs into princes—Neuro linguistic programming.* Moab, UT: Real People Press.

Belenky, M. S., Blythe, M., Clinchy, M., Goldberger, N. R., & Tarule, J. M. (1986). *Women's ways of knowing. The development of self, voice and mind.* New York, NY: Basic Books.

Brownlow at the World Trade Centre, Melbourne, Australia: January 1997.

Capra, F. (1997). *The web of life. A new synthesis of mind and matter.* London, UK: Flamingo/HarperCollins.

Clayton, M. (1993). *Living pictures of the self.* Melbourne, Australia: ICA Press.

Cripe, E. J., & Mansfield, R. S. (2002). *The value-added employee.* St. Peters, New South Wales, Australia: Butterworth-Heinemann.

de Mallet Burgess, T., & Skillbeck, N. (2000) *The singing and acting handbook.* London, UK: Routledge.

Department of Primary Industries & Resources South Australia. (2004). *PIRSA capabilities dictionary—June 2004.* Adelaide, South Australia: PIRSA.

Erikson, Erik H. (1950). *Childhood and society.* New York, NY: W. W. Norton.

Gage, N. L. (1989). The paradigm wars and their aftermath. A historical sketch of research on teaching since 1989. *Educational Researcher, 18*(7), 4–10.

Jacobi, J. (1973). *The psychology of C. G. Jung.* New Haven, CT: Yale University Press.

Langrehr, John. (1995) *Become a better thinker.* Victoria, Australia: Wrightbooks.

Lazear, D. (1991). *Seven ways of knowing: Teaching for multiple intelligences* (2nd ed.). Andover MA: Skylight.

McLeod, J. (2003). *An introduction to counselling* (3rd ed.). Buckingham-Philadelphia, PA: Open University Press.

Moreno, J. L. (1994) (4th ed.) *Psychodrama and group psychotherapy.* Princeton, NJ: American Society of Group Psychotherapy and Psychodrama.
Wilber, K. (1996). *A brief history of everything.* Melbourne, Australia: Hill of Content Publishing.
Brain Gym International/Educational Kinesiology.

NOTES

1. Questions and topics we addressed include:

- Describe situations in which you have experience satisfaction in working holistically
- Describe situations that have been unsatisfying and in which you learned something about working holistically
- What does the term holistic mean in the context of teaching and learning?
- What are the implications for you as a teacher?
- What are the implications for working this way?

2. The H-Factor: This model builds on the skills and practices of sound teaching and learning. Thus, one would assume teachers already had some understanding of learning theory and were skilled in communicating, giving and receiving feedback, managing conflict, and so forth.

3. This section was written in collaboration with Dr. John Langrehr who has contributed his expertise on multi-intelligence and learning styles.

4. The development of an intelligence is obviously limited by our opportunities and experiences, by personal interest, motivation, and self-belief, and by the consistency and effort of our practice. We each have a "supercomputer" at birth with incredible power if we want to use it.

5. These intelligences are located in different memory sites of the brain. For example:

- Logical-mathematical intelligence is centered in the frontal lobes of the brain.
- Visual-spatial intelligence is centered in the back of the brain in the occipital lobes.
- Interpersonal and intrapersonal intelligence (our emotional intelligences) are centered in the pair of amygdala and inner limbic parts of the brain.
- Verbal-linguistic intelligence is in the central semantic or word fact memory.
- Body-kinesthetic intelligence is in the cerebellum attached below the brain.

They link to the "fundamental disciplines" referred to by de Mallet Burgess and Skillbeck (2000, pp. 14–16) of relaxation, fitness, flexibility, and control, concentration, awareness, imagination, and spontaneity.

6. The critical factor for "hooking up memories" lies in activating the senses of sight, sound, taste, touch, and smell as well as intuition, and turning on the brain. Then learning can occur when people are engaged in the activities of gathering and thinking about information and facts; doing; feeling, acting out, or applying in different contexts.

7. High math-logical and verbal intelligences that dominate intelligence tests do not guarantee future success in life nor in singing. In fact, EQ—interpersonal (social) intelligence and intrapersonal (emotional) intelligence—is more important than IQ for predicting future success. There is compelling evidence to suggest that the qualities of a high EQ (a positive orientation including self-awareness, persistence, zeal, self-motivation, and empathy) mark those who excel in life.

8. NB: this is in no way intended to be a one-size-fits-all solution. Emotions are linked to memories. The path for people who have suffered violation, early trauma such as sexual or psychologic abuse, or loss of home and country can be tortuous. Memories charged with negative emotions such as fear, terror, or pain can be imprinted into the psyche and awakened by trigger events. For instance, a war veteran may relive the horror again in a situation where there are loud noises. This reaction can be relearned, but often only with professional help. Those who feel blocked by difficult memories may need the healing skills and support of another person such as a therapist or even a spiritual mentor. For the teacher, the critical factor is in recognizing when singers need other professional helpers.

9. See the dictionaries of *Core Capabilities for Singers* and *Core Capabilities for Teachers* (see Appendix 2). Capabilities are defined as the *ability to act skillfully and in congruence with inner qualities and values in a situation and context.*

10. As opposed to fixed, socially ascribed roles such as teacher, doctor, or nurse, J. L. Moreno (1972, p. 4) defines a role as the *"functioning form the individual assumes in the specific moment, (s)he reacts to a specific situation in which other persons or objects are involved."* He states that the *"role concept cuts across the sciences of man, physiology, psychology, sociology, anthropology and binds them together on a new plane."* Moreno notes that roles bring a human being into connection with other things and people, emerging from moment to moment in relation to the situation and environment. Moreno, a student of Freud and later an innovator in the field of psychotherapy in America, is the "father" of Psychodrama (drama of the soul) and Sociodrama (drama of the group), which he developed to help people change and grow. Psychodrama (sometimes called action methods) is currently used to assist people to grow and change in many fields throughout the world including psychotherapy, education, and theatre.

11. Actually, these are called role clusters. Within each cluster, a number of other roles are contained. For example, some of the roles within the cluster of Consummate Performer would be: Confident Actor; Masterful Technician; Courageous Risker; Spontaneous Creator; Engaging Provocateur; and Observant Monitor who maintains awareness of the whole, gauges the connection with the audience, and recommends changes to the singing and action. One would also expect Observant Monitor to be an active role within the other role clusters, and as in life, its shadow will be present as the Critical Judge or Inner Critic, attacking the sense of self, undermining confidence and courage.

12. Moreno (1972) links spontaneity with creativity which he recognizes as primary forces in human behavior. He asserts that every person has the potential for creative genius.

13. Spontaneity is a dynamic force, a kind of intelligence which operates in the here and now. Moreno defines spontaneity as an adequate response to a new situation or a novel response to an old situation (1972, p. xii).

14. The roles of the Singer have been described in behavioral terms in a dictionary of *Core Capabilities for Singers* (see Appendix 2). Capabilities are defined as the ability to act skillfully and in congruence with inner qualities and values in a situation and context.

15. See also a dictionary of *Core Capabilities for Teachers* in Appendix 2.

16. Erikson (1950) was a leader in defining developmental life stages. He defines the stages by articulating central dilemmas and tasks. The first four stages take place during childhood: trust versus mistrust; autonomy versus shame and doubt; initiative versus guilt; industry versus inferiority. The fifth stage, identity versus role diffusion, is linked to adolescence.

17. See Mindell, A. (1995). *Sitting in the fire.* Portland, OR: Lao Tse Press. 18. See Appendix 2 for an expanded description of core capabilities required by teachers.

19. Hotspots: a term used by Arnold Mindell to pinpoint the "undiscussable" moments that people tend to jump over when interacting in relationship. Hotspots are often not noticed at a conscious level, but people are often aware of levels of discomfort which they prefer to repress.

20. See Goleman (1995, 1998); Mindell, Arnold (1992, 1995); Seligman (2002); Stone et al. (2000);Yalom (2001).

21. Reflection for teachers. (Adapted from Atkin, 1996, p. 10)

PART 1
Remember and imagine a teaching-learning experience from your professional life in which you felt a high degree of satisfaction, a time in which it was obvious to you why you were teaching and why you wanted to teach.

1. Explore and note:
   - What inspired you; what you aspired to achieve
   - The things influencing the situation that made a difference
   - The qualities you demonstrated
   - The things you did to make a difference
   - What happened for the learners that made it so satisfying for them.
2. Write down some statements about your vision and values for teaching.

3. Use the following statements to explore your beliefs:
   - I believe that teachers are effective when they
   - I believe that teachers should be
   - I believe that singers learn best when they
   - I believe that singers need
   - I believe that singers need to be

4. Reflect on the extent to which your practice is consistent with your values and beliefs.

PART II

Remember a teaching-learning experience from your professional life in which you felt unsatisfied, a time in which you questioned why you were teaching.

1. Identify the key elements of the situation, the attitudes and behaviors you exhibited, and use your notes from Part 1 to examine and compare the situations.

2. What have you learned about yourself from this exercise?

22. Amy Mindell. (1995). *Metaskills: The spiritual art of therapy.* Portland, OR: Lao Tse Press.

23. Also see Arnold Mindell, *Leader as martial artist*, 1992, p. 49; and *Sitting in the fire*, 1995, pp.183–196. Arnold Mindell (1940–) is a physicist and a Jungian therapist. His work melds eastern and western philosophy and he has contributed to psychological theory and practice through the development of Process-Oriented Psychology (one-to-one and small group change), and World Work (large group change).

24. Metaskills have been incorporated into the dictionaries of core capabilities in Appendix 2.

25. Imagining: experiment with this technique by remembering and forming a concept of feeling about a relaxing day of an idyllic holiday. As you allow this, notice if you tend to see, feel, smell, or hear the memories of that day. Also be aware of the effect on your body as it relaxes, warms to the sun, and imagines drinking a cool lemonade. Here is an example of positive emotion changing a current state.

26. At the 2nd International Conference on Healthy Ageing and Longevity in Brisbane, March 2005, Professor Marc Cohen (RMIT) defined love as *something that makes you feel as if time has stopped still.* As distinct from romantic love, this is the experience of engaging with any activity like gardening, playing golf, painting, or singing that makes you forget to take lunch. There is often joy and exhilaration. Thus, love is a state of mind as much as a feeling. There is concentration and openness, focus and soft perspective, the whole and the part. Qualities such as hope, patience, respect, and courage can be seen as the faces of love, much as the facets of a crystal.

Chapter 11

VOCAL AND RESPIRATORY ANATOMY AND PHYSIOLOGY

John S. Rubin

𝒱ocal and respiratory anatomy and physiology can be a lifelong pursuit, not just the subject of this chapter. That said, whenever possible I endeavor to present concepts rather than go into details, and I try to avoid detailed literature references.

The physiology of voicing is far more than repetitive opening and closing of the vocal folds. It involves synchronized activity of much of the body. Thus, Wilbur J. (Jim) Gould, who I feel particularly fortunate to say was my mentor, considered the entire body as the "vocal organ." This chapter breaks down voicing into sections concerned with: (1) The "Bellows" (the entire mechanism involved with the creation of a volume of gas, in this case air, that is presented under some pressure up to the vocal folds, and thereby helps to develop "subglottic pressure"); (2) The "Vibratory unit" (a.k.a. the sound source; effectively the true vocal folds and the supporting musculature, and (3) the "Resonators" (everything "above" the true vocal folds). We approach this from the bottom up, starting with the Bellows.

BELLOWS

The Bellows are a biomechanical system—a biologic system (us) creating a mechanical output (air under pressure). Much of applied biomechanical literature relating to the voice has focused not on the bellows, but rather on the sound source. This is not unduly surprising as it is the vibrations of the vocal folds (previously called vocal cords, but now noted to be much more physiologically complex than just cords of tissue and thus now called folds) that create the sound source. For example, Hast's landmark study (1966) investigating the mechanical properties of the cricothyroid, one of the major joints involved with the sound source, is now 45 years old. In the voice literature, several other investigations have tried to study the biomechanics of the laryngeal muscles, comparing their myoelastic properties to vocal gestures (e.g., Cooper, 1993).

But what every singing teacher knows, and needs be remembered by the rest of us who are interested in researching the subject, is that the mass of muscle energy expenditure at the level of the sound source is tiny compared to that spent in the bellows for respiration. This chapter initially considers the mechanism of the bellows, those muscles and structures that support the sound source.

The mechanism of the bellows (Figure 11–1) consists of the rib cage, pleura, lungs, intercostal musculature, musculature of the abdominal wall and back, and the diaphragm. The key issue, perhaps, as discussed above, is the development of a volume of air under pressure that is then presented to the vocal folds.

Let us start with respiration. Quiet respiration is a reflex, predominantly under medullary control, heavily influenced by the level of carbon dioxide centrally.

On quiet inspiration the adductory muscles of the larynx (the muscles that bring the vocal folds together and tense them) tend to be at relative rest. On the other hand, the posterior cricoarytenoid muscles, the muscles that open (abduct) the vocal folds and permit us to breathe, are, of course, electrically active with consequent relative abduction/opening of the true vocal folds. That said, they do not open maximally as they do during the "sniff" maneuver. The phrenic nerve (C3, C4, C5) fires. The diaphragm contracts, thereby effectively enlarging the thoracic cavity. This leads to a reduction in lung pressure (versus atmospheric pressure, the pressure at which the air is taken from the outside), and thereby leads to negative pressure in the chest. Air then is sucked in correcting this relative vacuum back to atmospheric pressure (see Figure 4–2 in Chapter 4).

During quiet inspiration, the external intercostal muscles also may play a small role. In general, the amount of air inspired is approximately one-half of a liter, and the majority of quiet inspiration takes approxi-

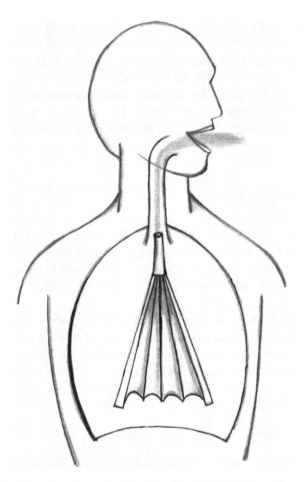

Figure 11–1. A drawing demonstrating the effect of the bellows. Copyright Richard Webber, 2005.

mately 1 second. As the chest "fills up" with air, the vagus nerve fibers involved in the "respiratory reflex" activate, thereby preventing further inspiration (Boileau Grant & Basmajian, 1965, p. 496.)

On quiet expiration, there is a general soft tissue and chest wall relaxation with expulsion of the air, following absorption of the oxygen. This occurs in tandem with diaphragm relaxation and reposition. In a healthy individual, this occurs approximately 12 to 18 times per minute, and goes on entirely unnoticed. Most people breathe in through the nose rather than the mouth during quiet respiration. This has the advantage of humidifying and warming (or cooling) the air so that it is at body temperature when it reaches the lungs. Nasal breathing has a further advantage of cleaning much of the ambient debris. In general, inspiration and expiration are of roughly equal time duration during quiet respiration.

During the act of speaking, and even more pronounced during the act of singing, there are gross alterations in the steady state noted during quiet respiration. It is not uncommon for airflow to occur through the mouth rather than the nose (thereby allowing for a continued raised palate position and facilitating performance (personal observation, J. Chapman, 2005). Inspirations tend to be brief and rapid. Expirations tend to be prolonged. Although this act of breathing still is predominantly unconscious, it can be brought to the conscious mind.

LUNGS AND PLEURA

The lungs share the thoracic cavity with, predominantly, the heart, the major vessels (in particular the aorta and vena cava), the trachea and esophagus, and lymphatics (Figure 11–2). The right lung is slightly larger than the left due to the position of the heart (Dickson & Maue-Dickson, 1982).

The lungs consist of a series of alveoli (air sacs) connected to the trachea via the bronchioles (a series of tubes). These are surrounded by smooth muscle (this is muscle that is controlled by the autonomic nervous system and greatly influenced by the relative levels of norepinephrine [adrenalinelike compound] in the system). There is an extremely rich

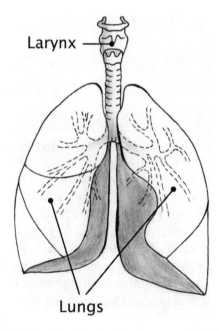

Figure 11–2. A drawing showing the lungs and their relation to the heart (not shown) and diaphragm. Copyright Richard Webber, 2005.

blood supply. This is crucial to allow the oxygen in the inspired air to be rapidly absorbed and transferred to the circulation and then the vital organs in the body. The nerves to the system are the thoracic sympathetics (the adrenergic group), and branches of the vagus (which carry the cholinergic supply). These nerves carry chemicals that constrict or dilate the muscles around the bronchioles. For example, many of the medications used by asthma sufferers act at this level to facilitate breathing.

The pleura is a membranous sac. It consists of two layers, one (visceral) that attaches directly onto the lungs, and the other (parietal) that attaches directly onto the chest wall. The visceral pleura actually envelops the lungs. The pleura is important to the bellows. It secretes a soaplike substance called surfactant that acts to reduce the surface tension between the lungs and rib cage. In essence it produces a material that acts like grease on ball bearings. The linkages of the pleurae to the rib cage and lungs not only reduce surface tension, they also have a direct effect on the elasticity of the system. When trying to envision the pleura, it helps to recall that it binds the lungs to the diaphragm as well as to the rib cage. This adherence is tight but elastic enough that any increase or decrease in the system will yield equivalent changes in lung volume.

RIB CAGE

The rib cage consists of 12 pairs of ribs (Figure 11–3). At birth, these ribs are basically horizontal and respiration is said to be abdominal, strictly controlled by the upward/downward plunging action of the diaphragm. By year 2, the ribs tend to adopt an oblique orientation and by year 7, respiration is said to become more thoracic in nature (Boileau Grant & Basmajian, 1965, p. 497). The ribs all articulate (insert) posteriorly with the vertebrae (spine). The first rib is the shortest and articulates directly anteriorly (is fused to) with the manubrium of the sternum (breastbone). The rib length increases through rib 7 then decreases through rib 12. Ribs 2 through 7 have a movable cartilaginous joint that connects the costal (rib) cartilages with the sternum.

Ribs 7 to 10 have a joint cartilaginous articulation that connects up to the sternum, ribs 8 to 10 attach to the cartilage of rib 7. Ribs 11 and 12 do not communicate with the sternum and have been described as "floating."

From the standpoint of rib movement, it is their orientation that controls their mobility. In general, ribs 1 to 5 have an oblique movement during inspiration, going from inferior posterior to anterior superior. They have been described by Meribeth Bunch Dayme as having a "pump-handle-like" motion. This is so, because each consecutive lateral rib border is located increasingly lower, in relation to both its vertebral

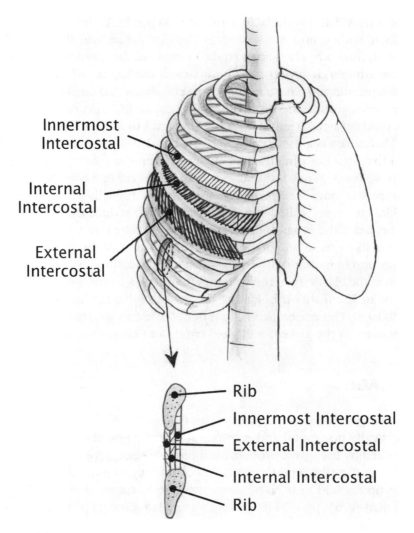

Innermost Intercostal

Internal Intercostal

External Intercostal

Rib

Innermost Intercostal

External Intercostal

Internal Intercostal

Rib

Figure 11–3. The twelve ribs comprising the rib cage. Note the three intercostal muscles demonstrated between two ribs. Copyright Richard Webber, 2005.

and /or sternal end. (Bunch, 1995, p. 34; Dickson & Maue-Dickson, 1982, p. 75). Ribs 5 to 7 tend to cause the chest wall to move in a lateral as well as in an anteroposterior fashion.

Ribs 7 to 10 have a flattish articulating surface where they attach to the spine. It allows the neck of the rib to slide superoposteriorly to anteroinferiorly. Ribs 8 to 10 have a particularly wide excursion due to the fact that they are not directly attached to the sternum. These ribs have been described by Meribeth Bunch Dayme as moving in a "bucket-handle" fashion. (Bunch, 1995, p. 35; Dickson & Maue-Dickson, 1982, p. 75). The increased movement of these lower ribs and their importance to singing is discussed in Chapter 4.

MUSCLES OF INSPIRATION

Muscles of inspiration (see Figure 4–2) are said to include the diaphragm, the external intercostals and the "accessory" muscles. The accessory muscles include the sternocleidomastoid, scalenes, pectoralis major, serratus anterior and posterior, and the levator costarum. These latter tend not to be used in normal respiration, but can be accessed during extreme inspiratory activity such as that associated with prolonged exercise or in individuals with abnormal states of health such as end-stage chronic obstructive pulmonary disease, severe asthma, and so forth (see section on Accent Method in Chapter 4 for further details).

Diaphragm

The diaphragm is the key muscle in inspiration (Figure 11–4). It consists of two large dome-shaped muscle masses that are rounded and cupola-shaped. It has a depressed median part on which the heart sits (Boileau Grant & Basmajian, 1965). In essence, the diaphragm separates the body into two halves, separating the lungs from the abdominal contents. Its muscles form the walls and floor of the thorax as well as attaching to the ribs. The nerve supply to the diaphragm is the phrenic nerve. It also receives sensory innervation from the lower intercostal nerves.

Contraction causes the domed muscles to flatten and straighten. This activity compresses the abdomen, lengthens the thorax, and causes

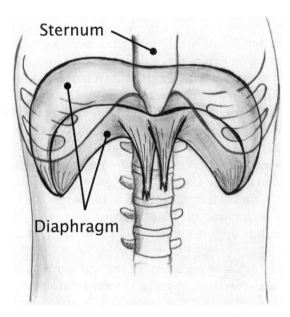

Figure 11–4. The diaphragm and its relation to the rib cage and lungs. Copyright Richard Webber, 2005.

the abdominal viscera to descend and the abdominal wall to yield. Due to the vertical aspect of the muscular fibers in the diaphragm, contraction also can result in elevation of the inferior margin of the rib cage (Dickson & Maue-Dickson, 1982, p. 127). Bunch (1995, p. 37) argues that in deep inspiration, the diaphragm alone accounts for 60 to 80% of increased lung volume.

Intercostal Muscles

The intercostal muscles consist of three layers (see Figure 11–3), the external, internal, and (incomplete) innermost. These muscles lie between the ribs, extending from the vertebral column to the costochondral junction, and their major function is chest wall stability.

The external intercostals are the most superficial, extending from the inferior margin of one rib to the superior margin of the next. Their orientation is oblique. This is thought (at least by Dickson) to exert its effect on the lower rib, and lift it. On EMG they have been identifiable as inspiratory muscles (Dickson & Maue-Dickson, 1982; Taylor, 1960).

The internal intercostals insert on the lower ribs and are believed to be active in expiration. Their function is thought to be reversed from the external intercostals because their upper attachment is more distant from the fulcrum than their lower attachment. Thus, they are believed to lower the upper rib.

EXPIRATION

As previously noted, there is a natural tendency to elastic recoil of the chest wall assisting in expiration. Passive expiration, brought about via such recoil, in particular of the lungs, transversus abdominis, and costal cartilages is satisfactory for quiet respiration. However, for controlled expiration, and in particular for increasing intensity or duration of sound, more expiratory muscular activity is necessary. This has been recognized for over 45 years (Agostini & Mead, 1964). The expiratory muscles are particularly important when exhalation continues below 35% of vital capacity (Dickson & Maue-Dickson, 1982, p. 86) (Figure 11–5).

Two general mechanisms, other than elastic recoil, assist in active expiration. These include the muscles that contract, alternatively to the diaphragm and support expiration and the muscles that lower the rib cage.

The former consist in particular of the abdominal wall musculature especially the transversus abdominis, external abdominal obliques, and internal abdominal obliques. These muscles, in synchrony, maintain the intra-abdominal pressure, and support the fascia overlying the abdominal viscera. That said, they also support expiration by working against a

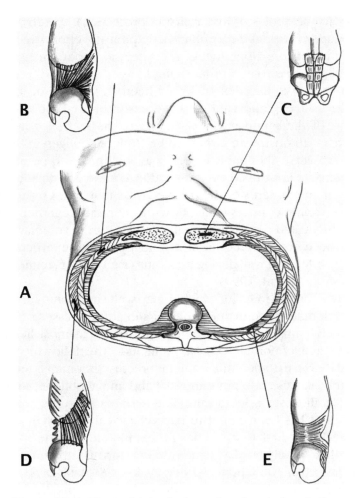

Figure 11–5. The periabdominal muscles of expiration: **A.** Cross-section of abdominal musculature. **B.** Cutaway demonstrating the internal oblique muscles. **C.** Cutaway demonstrating the rectus abdominis muscles. **D.** Cutaway demonstrating the external oblique muscles. **E.** Cutaway demonstrating the transversus abdominis muscles. Copyright Richard Webber, 2005.

relaxing diaphragm, in effect "pushing" the abdominal contents upward, and assisting in development of subglotttic pressure. (These muscles are discussed in Chapter 4.)

It must be remembered that the function of these muscles is not specifically for vocalizing, but rather for lifting, breath-holding, and raising intra-abdominal pressure. They are crucial in activities such as micturation, defecation, birthing, and so forth, and thus are essential to life. They also contract actively during sneezing and coughing (Boileau Grant & Basmajian, 1965, p. 208). Their role in voicing can be viewed as secondary (much as the role of the vocal folds for voicing can be viewed as secondary to their roles of lower airway protection), thereby "controlling" expiration during the prolonged expiratory efforts required in speaking and singing. Nonetheless, their central importance, as noted, ably underlines their role in primal sound.

In the past two decades, there has been an upsurge of interest in study of the main expiratory muscles of the ventrolateral abdominal wall, through use of ultrasound and EMG. This work has been spearheaded by, among others, an Australian group led be Hodges (Hodges, 1999).

The transverse abdominis muscle may well prove to be of particular importance to controlled expiration, due to its structural attachments to the costal components of the diaphragm as it attaches on to the distal ribs. For example, it has been shown to contract together with the external oblique and rectus abdominis muscles during voluntary efforts. It also has been noted to recruit preferentially to the superficial muscle layer of the abdominal wall during breathing (De Troyer, Estenne, Ninane, Van Gasbeke, & Gorini, 1990).

This work is still in its infancy but may well shed some further light on the development and maintenance of subglottic pressure.

In general, muscles that have been postulated as most likely to be involved in active/ forced exhalation include the following: internal intercostals, external abdominal oblique, rectus abdominis, transversus thoracis, transversus abdominis, internal abdominal oblique, subcostals, sacrospinals, iliocostalis lumborum, and serratus posterior inferior. Of these, the first has been noted to have electrical activity in conversational speech, the first four in effortful expiration, and the fifth, sixth, and seventh are likely to play some role in effortful expiration (Boileau Grant & Basmajian 1965; Bunch, 1995; Dickson & Maue-Dickson, 1982, p. 129) (see Figure 11–5). In this discussion, I have specifically left out the muscles of the pelvic floor, which act as a crucial counterbalance for many of our most basic postural activities. For more information, see Rolf (1989).

SUBGLOTTIC PRESSURE

This brings us to the final concept that we shall discuss in relation to the Bellows, that of subglottic pressure. Development of subglottic pressure is critical to vocalizing. It is created by flow of expired air against a partly closed glottis. Its importance is twofold: the control of airflow, and the achievement of a (more or less) constant sound intensity. In assisting this process, there are mechanoreceptors in the subglottic mucosa that are sensitive to changes in air pressure, which in turn cause reflex activity in the laryngeal musculature.

We have been looking at this section of phonation from a biomechanical basis. From such a perspective, phonation can be seen as the movement of the chest wall and diaphragm, thereby determining airflow and subglottic pressure. Singers require the ability to sustain the subglottic pressure. The intercostals are particularly helpful for this at high lung volumes, and together with the abdominal musculature work against a relaxing diaphragm.

Airflow tends to be in the 100 to 200 mL per second range. Subglottic pressure creating an audible result can range from approximately 2 to 60 cm water pressure (Proctor, 1980). A moderate tone requires around 10 cm water pressure; a crescendo around 50 to 60 cm water pressure. In quiet respiration, vital capacity is approximately 35 to 45% maximum, conversational speech uses between 35 to 60% vital capacity; and loud speech up to 80% vital capacity (Hixon, 1973).

Now, let us look at the other side of the biomechanical equation of phonation, the movement of the vocal folds and resonators, which helps determine pitch, loudness, and sound quality.

THE VIBRATORY UNIT

The vocal fold (Figure 11-6) and its musculature making up the vibratory unit is truly a remarkable mechanism. Its movements, together with the resonators, predominantly determine the pitch, loudness, and timbre of the sound. (The singer's ability to maintain the subglottic pressure, as previously noted, is mainly due to the abdominal wall musculature working against a relaxing diaphragm, and the internal intercostal muscles, and is also a feature in these qualities.)

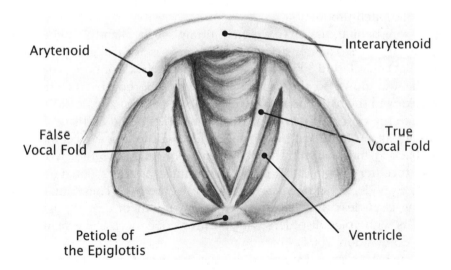

Figure 11-6. A drawing of the true vocal folds, as seen from above. Copyright Richard Webber, 2005.

The nerve innervation per unit muscle fiber in the laryngeal muscles is one of the greatest in the body, matched only by the periorbital muscles that move the globe of the eye. This undoubtedly due to the fact that the "true" role of the larynx is not production of sound, but rather the life-saving role of protecting the lungs from food and fluid particles as we swallow. The larynx also is intimately involved in lifting, coughing, and so forth, through its role in elevation of intrathoracic pressure. These features of the larynx are caused by its sphincteric pressure valving role, when it is closed and held together.

When we discuss the true vocal folds, first we need to have some understanding of where the larynx actually is in respect to the pharynx and neck. The true vocal folds are a part of the laryngeal structure, which in turn can be thought of as an "intrusion into the pharynx." It is predominantly an open tube suspended in the neck.

From above, the attachments of the larynx are muscular, from the hyoid bone (we shall consider this to be a part of the larynx for this discussion) to the mandible, tongue root, styloid process, and skull base. In essence, the larynx is "rooted" to these structures, but only by muscular attachments, albeit very powerful ones. These muscles are predominantly involved in swallowing. A simple test of placing one's fingers on the "Adam's apple" (midline protuberance of the thyroid lamina), and trying to prevent the larynx from rising during a swallow, will quickly show the reader just how powerful these muscles are.

From below, the larynx is "anchored" by the trachea through which air commutes up and back, to and from the lungs.

From in front, the larynx is connected to the hyoid bone above, by the thyrohyoid ligament, and to the sternum (breast bone) below by the "strap" muscles. These muscles are felt to have some secondary role in tone and pitch production.

From behind, the larynx is held firmly, albeit pliantly, by the constrictor muscles. The constrictor muscles are a powerful group of muscles that encircle and, in essence, shape the pharynx from the skull base all the way down to the esophagus. The middle constrictor attaches anteriorly to the hyoid bone. The inferior constrictor has a dense attachment to the posterior thyroid cartilage and the cricoid cartilage. These muscles attach from one side to the other, back to a heavy ligament in the back of the pharynx, the posterior raphe, and thus the two sides work together in concert. The constrictor muscles are essential to swallow, and under reflexogenic control (see Figure 6–2). Their impact on voicing is unclear (but Lieberman manipulates them directly in some patients with voice disorders with positive effects). (J. Lieberman, personal observation, 2004).

The reader immediately can see that the larynx is held in place predominantly by a series of muscles that frequently are in motion themselves. Thus, it will come as no surprise to the reader that many patients who present to the voice clinic with voicing problems are found to have increased tension, activity, contractility, or spasm of some of these muscles.

And, of course, immediately behind the larynx and pharynx is the spine together with the prevertebral muscles. The spine is not an immutable structure, but rather one that responds to movement and muscle stresses. It too has been noted in many patients who present with voicing problems to be held in certain inefficient patterns (Rubin, Blake, & Mathieson, 2007).

The next question to be posited is, what exactly comprises the superstructure of the larynx in which the true vocal folds are housed? From below upward, the larynx arguably can be classified as consisting of the cricoid cartilage, thyroid cartilage, arytenoid cartilages with the (rudimentary) corniculate and cuneiform cartilages, epiglottis, and hyoid bone. Embryologically, the hyoid bone comes from a separate anlage and thus is felt by many not to be a part of the larynx. It is so intricately incorporated in laryngeal physiology, however, that I feel it is beneficial to do so.

CRICOID CARTILAGE

The cricoid cartilage (Figure 11–7) is signet-shaped, narrow at front but broad and high in the back. It is the only circumferential structure in the larynx, and thus has been treated with particular respect by surgeons. Its inferior edge is firmly attached by ligamentous structure to the first ring of the trachea.

Anteriorly, the superior aspect of the cricoid is attached to the thyroid cartilage via a thin, avascular membrane, the anterior (median) cricothyroid ligament. This is the anterior border of the cricothyroid membrane. This cricothyroid membrane, in toto, extends up to the vocal ligament to which it attaches, as far posteriorly as the vocal process and inferior fossa of the arytenoid cartilage. The body on this membrane is known as the "conus elasticus" and is the supporting structure for the deeper structures of the vocal folds below the vocal ligament (Dickson & Maue-Dickson, 1982, p. 158).

Laterally on the cricoid cartilage, near the junction of the arch and the laminae, lie the paired cricothyroid articular facets into which the inferior horns of the thyroid cartilage insert. This joint is a plane synovial joint. The functional potential of this joint is limited, the obliquity of the joint precluding posterosuperior to anteroinferior motion. It is very important to voicing, however. Joint rotation is in a vertical direction, with limitation only by the cricothyroid ligament. Lieberman and Harris (Harris, Harris, Rubin, & Howard, 1998) refer to this mechanism as the "visor." Through an investigation on fresh human cadaver larynges, Dickson has identified correlative vocal fold changes in length through vertical

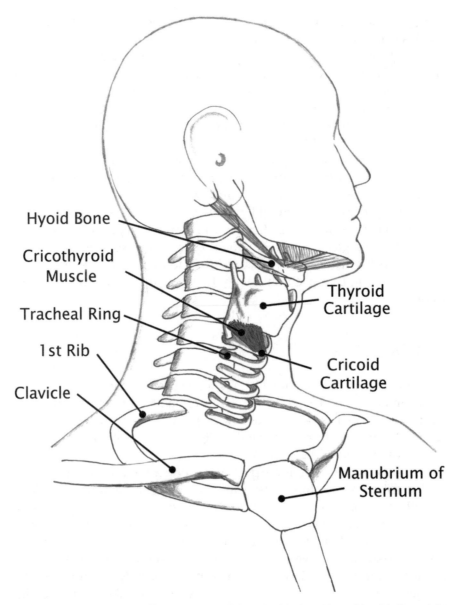

Hyoid Bone

Cricothyroid
Muscle

Tracheal Ring

1st Rib

Clavicle

Thyroid
Cartilage

Cricoid
Cartilage

Manubrium of
Sternum

Figure 11–7. A slightly off-center view of the cricoid, thyroid, and hyoid. Copyright Richard Webber, 2005.

movement of this joint of approximately 25% (Dickson & Maue-Dickson, 1982). Such lengthening of the vocal ligament leads to a thinning and stretching of the vocal fold with associated elevation in the pitch of the voice. This is further discussed in the section on the cricothyroid muscle, which "controls" this movement.

Posteriorly on the cricoid's superior rounded surface are two elliptical facets, each 6 mm in length. These facets slope laterally, downward and forward. In each facet sits the deeply grooved base of the arytenoid cartilage, with its long diameter set at right angles to that of the cricoid (Boileau Grant & Basmajian, 1965, p. 701) (see Arytenoid Cartilage below).

THYROID CARTILAGE

The thyroid cartilage is lacking posteriorly. Anteriorly, it is shaped like a shield. In the upper central portion, its two pentagonal laminae meet with a "bulge" which is more acute and noticeable in adult males (90 degrees, vs. adult females, 120 degrees) and is referred to as the Adam's apple. There are superior and inferior horns on the thyroid. The superior horns, as well as the entire superior edge of the thyroid cartilage, are connected by the thyrohyoid membrane to the hyoid bone. Laterally, the thyrohyoid membrane is pierced by the superior laryngeal nerve (internal branch) and vessels. In the lateral aspects of the two pentagonal laminae of the thyroid are the two oblique lines. These serve as the origin of the deep layers of the strap muscles (the thyrohyoid and sternothyroid muscles).

The inferior horns connect into the cricoid articular facets already discussed above. Externally, the thyroid cartilage is covered by heavy perichondrium; internally, it is covered by thinner perichondrium, which is dehiscent over a small prominence where the anterior commissure of the true vocal folds attaches.

ARYTENOID CARTILAGES

The paired arytenoid cartilages (Figure 11–8) articulate with the superior facets on the posterior cricoid cartilage, already referred to. Each arytenoid has a pyramidlike structure, and is crucial to positioning the true vocal fold. According to Dickson and Maue-Dickson (1982), the average height in adult males is 18 mm and in adult females 13 mm. A-P measurements respectively, are 14 mm and 10 mm. It has three pronounced angles: a sharp anterior angle, the vocal process (which makes up to 40% of vocal fold length in the adult); a blunt lateral angle, the muscular process; and a recurved superior angle, the apex (Boileau Grant & Basmajian, 1964, p. 700).

The muscular process is of particular importance, as many of the intrinsic laryngeal muscles attach therein. These muscles are discussed below. Just inferior to the muscular process is the deeply grooved base that articulates with the cricoid. The cricoarytenoid joint so formed is a true synovial joint. Motion of this joint is permitted by sliding along the long flat axis of the cricoid facet and rocking over the short convex axis. The movement is further controlled by two ligaments, the posterior cricoarytenoid ligament and the anterior (vocal) ligament. The former is contiguous with the joint, attaches to the superior rim of the cricoid lamina between the two cricoarytenoid facets, and extends anteriorly to

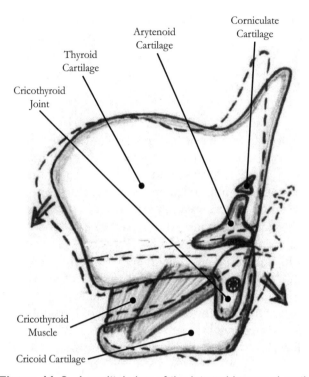

Figure 11–8. A sagittal view of the internal laryngeal cartilaginous structures. Note particularly the pyramidal-shaped
arytenoid cartilage and the effect on the vocal ligament
(*dashed horizontal line*) of the movement of the cricothyroid
joint, as brought about by contraction of the cricothyroid muscle. The epiglottis is omitted. Copyright Richard Webber, 2005.

the medial surface of the arytenoid cartilage. The latter attaches to the
vocal process and extends anteriorly to insert onto the thyroid cartilage.
Together with the vocalis portion of the thyroarytenoid muscle, it makes
up the bulk of the true vocal fold. There also is a tight fibrous articular
capsule enclosing the cricoarytenoid joint (Dickson & Maue-Dickson,
1984, p. 153).

Arytenoid motion is complex; it occurs in three directions. Anterior
and posterior movements and vertical movements are due to "revolving"
or "pitchlike" motion along the minor axis of the cricoid. The medial and
lateral motion is determined by the orientation of the cricoarytenoid
facet. During adduction, the outward angulation of the vocal process
away from the body of the arytenoid permits the length of the vocal
process to approximate at the proper vertical height. Overall, it is a bit
like sitting in a rotating and sliding rocking chair.

The corniculate and cuneiform cartilages are rudimentary bits of
elastic cartilage that do not appear to have any role in laryngeal function.
The corniculates are conical and sit atop the arytenoid cartilages.

EPIGLOTTIS

The epiglottis (Figure 11–9) is a large, leaf-shaped structure made up of fibroelastic cartilage. The petiole of the epiglottis attaches just above the insertion of the vocal ligament into the inner surface of the thyroid cartilage. The epiglottis extends superoposteriorly to the level of the base of the tongue where it overhangs the larynx. Its perichondrium is more tightly bound on its laryngeal than its lingual surface. Mucous glands are present on both surfaces although more are located on the laryngeal surface.

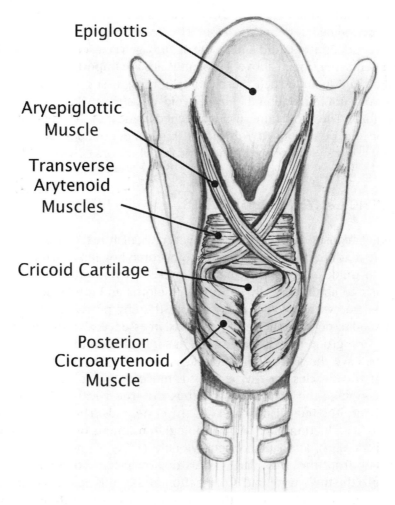

Figure 11–9. The larynx from the back, demonstrating the laryngeal intrinsic musculature. Note the relative large size of the posterior cricoarytenoid muscle in relation to the other demonstrated muscles. Note also the height of the cricoid from the back, and how the muscles shown insert into the muscular process of the arytenoids. The epiglottis is also seen from behind. Copyright Richard Webber, 2005.

Superiorly, above the level of the hyoid bone, the epiglottis forms the vallecula with the base of the tongue via a series of mucosal condensations. Inferiorly, it defines the laryngeal inlet, together with the arytenoid cartilages, via a series of mucosal folds (the aryepiglottic folds). As noted later in this chapter, a series of intrinsic laryngeal muscles insert into the epiglottis and are concerned mainly with laryngeal protection during swallowing.

HYOID BONE

The hyoid bone (see Figure 11-7) is a more or less horseshoe-shaped bone consisting of a central body and lateral greater and lesser cornua, the greater being inferior to the lesser. The hyoid bone attaches the larynx to the tongue musculature and to the skull base via a series of muscular attachments mentioned above. These muscles are important in laryngeal elevation and include such muscles as the myoglossus, hyoglossus, and geniohyoid, not to mention the myelohyoid, digastric muscles, stylohyoid, and so forth. The hyoid bone also is attached to most of the strap muscles (sternohyoid, omohyoid, thyrohyoid) that, upon contraction, act as laryngeal depressors (sternohyoid, omohyoid) or elevators (thyrohyoid).

INTRINSIC LARYNGEAL MUSCLES

As we next consider the intrinsic laryngeal musculature (see Figure 11-9), I believe that the crucial issue is not to become bogged down in detail, rather to think in general terms. The muscles overall have two broad functions: to sphincterically close the epiglottis and aryepiglottic folds over the true vocal folds during swallow, thereby protecting the lower airway; and to position the true vocal folds. In essence, all muscles providing the first group of activities attach in some fashion to the epiglottis, and thus have the word "epiglottis" as a part of their names. Thus, the aryepiglottic muscles, the thyroepiglottic muscles, and so forth. The muscles positioning the arytenoids and thus the true vocal folds insert, in general, into the muscular process of the arytenoids. These muscles are involved in adduction (medial positioning), tensioning, or abduction (lateral positioning). The lateral cricoarytenoid (LCA) is one such muscle. Extending from the muscular process downward and obliquely, it lies inferior to the thyroarytenoid. Contraction of this muscle leads to medial positioning and tensioning of the true vocal fold. It also thins the free edge of the vocal fold and lowers the position of the vocal fold.

The posterior cricoarytenoid muscle (PCA), is a large muscle extending from the posterior cricoid up laterally and forward over the cricoid and inserting into the muscular process of the arytenoids. Contraction of this muscle leads to abduction of the true vocal fold. The "sniff" maneuver causes maximal stimulation of this muscle and maximal abduction.

It is classically stated that the posterior cricoarytenoid muscle is the only muscle in the body to cause abduction of the true vocal fold. Harris (Harris et al., 1998) rather persuasively argues, however, that a three-quarters view of the larynx with the thyroid cartilage cut away, demonstrates the close interrelationship of the PCA and the LCA muscles. He believes that it is naïve to state that one muscle acts without the other in any of the activities of the larynx. Rather he suggests that muscle activity in the larynx should be considered from the standpoint of vectors of pull, and that the LCA, although a laryngeal tensor during one laryngeal activity, can also be a laryngeal abductor during another. This concept has yet to be widely accepted; that said, recent EMG studies have demonstrated activity of the LCA as well as the PCA during abduction, and a few surgeons have begun injecting botulinum toxin into the vicinity of the LCA rather than the PCA into selected patients with abductor spasmodic dysphonia with positive results (G. Brookes, personal communication, 2004).

For the student, all the muscles mentioned above are innervated by the recurrent laryngeal nerve. The interarytenoid muscle, due to its position crossing from one side of the larynx to the other, is innervated by the recurrent laryngeal nerve, but from both sides. Thus, it is in the special case that, when one recurrent laryngeal nerve has been damaged, this muscle will continue to work, thereby bringing the "paralyzed" vocal fold toward the midline.

There are two other muscles worthy of specific discussion, the thyroarytenoid with its specialized medial portion known as the vocalis, and the cricothyroid.

Thyroarytenoid Muscle

The thyroarytenoid muscles are adductors of the true vocal folds. They are innervated by the recurrent laryngeal nerve. These muscles also shorten the true vocal folds. The medial aspect of the thyroarytenoid muscle is known as the vocalis muscle. This "muscle" is attached to the vocal ligament. When it contracts, it causes bulking of the vocal fold and thereby changes its vibratory characteristics. EMG studies demonstrate that the thyroarytenoid muscle is electrically active in the lower portion of a singer or speaker's range, but less active in the upper register. Generally, contraction of the thyroarytenoid is associated with a lowering of pitch. It is thought to be the most important muscle for phonation. Sanders has studied the vocalis muscle from the standpoint of velocity of muscle fibers. He has found the medial aspect to have predominantly "slow-twitch" fibers and the more lateral portions to have predominantly "fast-twitch" fibers (as do the muscle fibers found in the portions of the TA in the false vocal fold, and the LCA). From the standpoint of phonatory control, he speculates that the human vocalis muscle has become highly subspecialized; that the "slow-twitch" fibers are more likely associated with phonation and the "fast-twitch" fibers associated with adduction. Although this is still speculative, it is fascinating (Sanders, in Rubin, Sataloff, & Korovin, 2003).

Cricothyroid Muscle

The cricothyroid muscles (see Figure 11–7) are believed by many authors to represent extrinsic, rather than intrinsic muscles of the larynx. This is so, due to their position and innervation. Each cricothyroid muscle is a large, (by laryngeal standard) muscle located on the exterior surface of the larynx. Each consists of two parts, a vertical and an oblique part. The vertical part arises from the anterior superior edge of the cricoid arch and inserts into the inferior border of the thyroid cartilage, whereas the oblique portion extends from the lateral surface of the cricoid to the posterolateral edge of the thyroid cartilage. The cricothyroid muscles are innervated by the external branch of the superior thyroid nerve. The action of the cricothyroid muscle is to tilt the larynx by approximating the cricoid and thyroid anteriorly. It has a significant effect on the vocal pitch. Contraction of the muscle leads to lengthening of the vocal ligament by up to one-third and lowering of the relative position of the true vocal fold within the larynx. It simultaneously augments the tension of the vocal fold, while decreasing its mass per unit length during pitch elevation. Because it stretches the vocal fold, it thins the vocal fold and sharpens its edge. On EMG studies, the cricothyroid activity has been noted to be moderate in chest and head, and high in falsetto. Generally, contraction of the cricothyroid is thought to be associated with pitch elevation.

CROSS-SECTIONAL ANATOMY

In a typical female primary schoolteacher, it has been stated that the vocal folds can vibrate up to 1 million times in a given day (Erkki Vilkman, unpublished observation, 1999). One interesting question is, how can we have such a high rate of repeated movement without causing damage? The answer is that we cannot, and that the larynx is likely undergoing degrees of damage much of the time, but it has a robust mechanism for repair, which is still only partially understood. We now will spend a little time and look at the cross-sectional anatomy of the larynx and potential effects of trauma therein.

From a cross-sectional perspective, the larynx is a multilayered structure (Figure 11–10). It consists of the epithelium, basement membrane

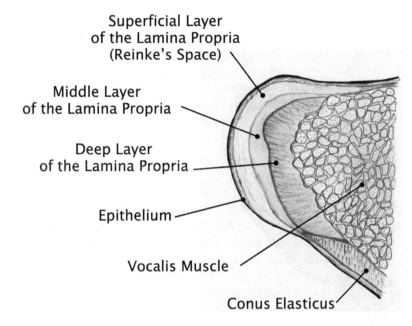

Figure 11–10. A coronal diagram of the complex layered structure of the true vocal fold, showing the epithelium, superficial layers of the lamina propria, vocal ligament consisting of middle and deep layer of the lamina propria, vocalis muscle, and conus elasticus. Copyright Richard Webber, 2005.

zone, superficial, intermediate, and deep layers of the lamina propria, and the vocalis muscle. The superficial layer of the lamina propria also is known as Reinke's space, or just as the SLLP. The intermediate and deep layers of the lamina propria make up the vocal ligament.

Epithelium

The epithelium consists of stratified squamous epithelium. It is the toughest epithelium in the body, and is found in other areas that are used frequently, for example, the palms and soles. It has six or seven layers. The deeper layers are cuboidal and nucleated and metabolically active. Nearer the surface, the cells flatten and lose their nuclei. At the surface of epithelial cells are microridges and microvilli. Lubrication is necessary for phonatory activity, and these villi and ridges are said to spread and help retain mucus created by the glands surrounding the larynx. It should be noted that, unlike respiratory epithelium, stratified epithelium do not have cilia or underlying glandular elements.

Basement Membrane Zone of the Epithelium

There has been considerable interest in the basement membrane zone of the epithelium in the last decade. It is an area that both provides physical support for and is essential for repair of the epithelium. It is composed of two zones, the lamina lucida and the lamina densa. The lamina densa is an area deep to the lucida that is composed of collagen type IV in a "chain mail"-like series of loops. Anchoring fibrils link it to the SLLP. Between the collagen are found interstitial proteins. This region has been found to be reduplicated in nodules, suggesting that repeated injury and repair takes place from voice overuse (and possibly use).

Superficial Layer of the Lamina Propria

This layer also is referred to as Reinke's space. It has significant importance in voicing, because of the degree of vibration that occurs here during phonation. Sato (Sato, in Rubin, 2003) has identified fibrillar proteins including reticular fibers and elastic fibers. Ground substance of glycoprotein and glucosaminoglycan is also present. These structures add to the viscoelasticity of the SLLP and are crucial, as the SLLP acts as a vibratory interface and shock absorber between the epithelium and the vocal ligament.

Vocal Ligament

The vocal ligament consists of the intermediate and deep layers of the lamina propria. Although there is collagen throughout the ligament, the intermediate layer consists primarily of mature elastin running parallel to the long axis of the vocal fold. The deep layer of the lamina propria consists primarily of collagen. The ligament is designed so that it can readily stretch and retract depending on the degree of tensioning from the various muscles.

Physiology of the Vibratory Vocal Folds

This is a complex area and deserves a full chapter. To briefly summarize (from R. C. Scherer, 2003, Laryngeal Function During Phonation; and Rubin, Korovin, and Epstein, 2003): Sound is produced only when the vocal folds are close together within what Scherer describes as "phonatory adductory range." Under these circumstances, during expiration, alternative buildup, and release of air pressure occurs at the vocal folds. The vocal folds then mechanically open and close in a below-to-above direction. The pressure differential created by a large volume of compressed air streaming through the small glottal space initiates vocal fold vibration. This is due, partly to the natural elasticity of the tissues, as well as Bernoulli's law. Bernoulli's law relates to the effects caused when an object partly blocks a stream of liquid or gas. An easy way to understand it is to visualize the effect that a small island has on the flow of water in an active current. Basically, by blocking flow, layers of stream are created. In the glottis, the middle layers of stream go through the vocal folds more or less undisturbed while the more lateral layers interact more directly with the vocal folds. Unlike the island described above, which is immutable, the vocal folds are soft bits of tissue, and the negative pressure created has the tendency to draw them together.

Thus, a "mucosal wave" is started, from below upward. As the vocal fold systematically opens and closes, each such cycle is known as the vocal cycle. This can be measured by a device that looks at impedance, in other words that looks at when the vocal folds are together, and when they are apart. The pulsatile stream of air opening and closing the glottis is translated into sound, the fundamental frequency (F_0) of the sound is directly related to the number of oscillations per second. This in turn is determined to a large extent on the tension placed on the vocal folds by the intrinsic and extrinsic laryngeal muscles, to some degree modified by the strength of the subglottic pressure. The sound wave created can vibrate at a wide frequency range (openings and closings per second). Modal (chest) register in untrained speakers can vary from 75 to 450 Hz in men and 130 to 520 Hz in women (Baken, 1997; Scherer, 2003).

A certain minimum amount of subglottic pressure is needed both to start the vocal folds vibrating and then to maintain them. The threshold level varies with F_0, ranging at low frequencies around 3-cm water to 6-cm water pressure for higher frequencies. As noted earlier in the chapter, subglottic pressure is critical to control of airflow and intensity. Pitch correlates, but in a nonlinear fashion, to fundamental frequency. It depends not only on the vocal fold length but also on the tension. Although the vocal folds do not vibrate like a string, some researchers have tried to use such a model to explain some aspects of vocal fold vibration. In a string model, pitch is directly related to the tension applied and inversely related to the mass (or thickness) and length of the string. Tension changes have been related to pitch variation. Increasing vocal fold length in modal register has been found to correlate to increased F_0; in falsetto, however, the vibrating length shortens as frequency increases. Vocal fold thickness or mass has been found to be, in modal range, of particular importance; an increase in length correlates with a decrease in mass and higher vibrating frequencies. This has caused some researchers to use a rubber band as a model for studying vocal fold vibration, even though the vocal fold does not really vibrate like a rubber band. In this model, after certain stretch, the thickness remains the same.

Loudness is the perceptual correlate to intensity. It is strongly related to subglottic pressure and the velocity of expiration. In other words, the faster air moves through the glottis, the greater the intensity in the sound. The rapidity at which the vocal folds "snap" shut also appears to have some influence on loudness. This can be measured, again using impedance measurements, as described above.

The sound that is created at the level of the vocal folds has a buzz quality, but contains a complete set of harmonic partials, which are mathematic repetitions of energy. Thus, a sound created with a fundamental frequency of 150 hertz (in other words that was created by the vocal folds opening and closing 150 times per second,) would contain within it harmonics at 300 hertz, 450 hertz, 600 hertz, ad infinitum. These harmonic bundles of energy are then altered by the structures through which they travel.

RESONATORS

The structures in which the sound travels are known as the resonators (Figure 11-11). In the larynx, these consists of the mucous membranes of the supraglottic vocal tract. Above the larynx, the pharyngeal muscles, the tongue base and tip, the lips, teeth, jaw, postnasal space, nose, and so forth, to some degree, all can have an impact on the sound that is produced. In the last two decades, there has been particular interest

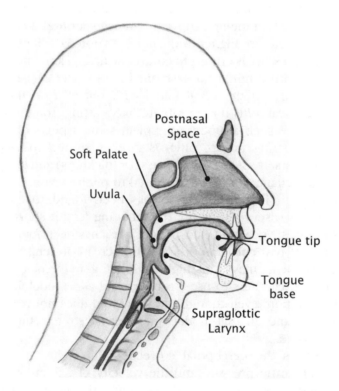

Figure 11-11. A sagittal view demonstrating some of the resonators. Note the supraglottic larynx, tongue base and tip, uvula and soft palate, and postnasal space; choanae of the nose are not shown. Copyright Richard Webber 2005.

in the impact of the sound bouncing off the epiglottis. This interest was kindled by the observations of Jo Estill that certain laryngeal positions that can be taught, have a characterizable and characteristic effect on the quality of the sound produced. As all our resonators are coated with mucus to one degree or another, the level of hydration and the nature of the mucus probably also have some impact on sound quality. Research into this area is still in its infancy.

To a varying degree, the harmonics available in the sound created at the glottis are damped (absorbed, and lost), maintained, or even amplified by certain of these structures. Ultimately, these sounds are shaped (or at least frequently are) into sounds recognizable as language, particularly by the tongue, palate, and lips. As noted, certain of these harmonics are amplified by the resonators. Such regions of amplified acoustic energy, as demonstrable on a spectrogram as a "peak," are known as "formants." The adult male vocal tract has been noted by Sundberg (1997) to be approximately 17 to 20 cm in length and to have recognizable formants at roughly 500 hertz, 1500 hertz, 2500 hertz, and 3500 hertz. The adult female formants are about 15% higher. The first formant seems to be particular to the shape of the base of the tongue, the second formant to the shape and position of the mid-tongue, and both the second and third to the position of the tongue tip. To create understandable speech by moving our articulators, we constantly are changing the actual spectrographic location of these formants.

SUMMARY

To summarize, voice is produced by a power source causing the oscillator to vibrate, thereby producing a sound that subsequently is shaped by the resonators and articulators.

This chapter reviewed and highlighted the various parts of the body responsible for the creation of sound. It has only scratched the surface, and has been somewhat arbitrary. Entire areas, for example, the neural aspects of vocalizing, have been left out, and others, for example, the physics behind pulmonary or vocal physiology, have been shortened mercilessly. That said, it is designed to give the reader an introduction into voice production, via the concept of the bellows, the vibratory unit, and the resonators.

REFERENCES

Agostini, E., & Mead, J. (1964). Status of the respiratory system. In W. O. Fenn & H. Rahn (Eds.), *Handbook of physiology, section 3: Respiration, Vol. 1*. Washington, DC: American Physiological Society.

Baken, R. J. (1997). An overview of laryngeal function for voice production. In R. T. Sataloff (Ed.), *Professional voice, The science and art of clinical care* (2nd ed., pp. 147–166), San Diego, CA: Singular.

Boileau Grant, J. C., & Basmajian, J. V. (1965). *Grant's method of anatomy* (7th ed.). Baltimore, MD: Williams & Wilkins.

Bunch, M. A. (1995). *Dynamics of the singing voice* (3rd ed.). Wien, Germany: Springer-Verlag.

Campbell, E. J. M., Agostini, E., & Newsom Davis, J. (1970). *The respiratory muscles: Mechanics and neural control* (2nd ed.). London, UK: Lloyd-Luke.

Cooper D, (1993). Muscle energetics. In I. R. Titze (Ed.), *Vocal fold physiology, Frontiers in basic science*. San Diego, CA: Singular.

Cutler, A. G. (Managing Ed.). (1972). *Stedman's medical dictionary* (22nd ed.). Baltimore, MD: Williams & Wilkins.

De Troyer, A., Estenne, M., Ninane, V., Van Gansbeke, D., & Gorini, M. (1990). Transversus abdominis muscle function in humans. *Journal of Applied Physiology, 68,* 1010–1016.

Dickson, D. R., & Maue-Dickson, W. (1982). *Anatomical and physiological bases of speech*. Boston, MA: Little, Brown.

Harris, T., Harris, S., Rubin, J. S., & Howard, D. (1998). *The voice clinic handbook*. London, UK: Whurr.

Hast, M. H., (1966) Physiological mechanisms of phonation: Tension of the vocal fold muscle. *Acta Otolaryngologica, 62*(4), 309–318.

Hixon, T. J. (1973). Respiratory function in speech. In F. D. Minifie, T. J. Hixon, & F. Williams (Eds.), *Normal aspects of speech, hearing and language*. Englewood Cliffs, NJ: Prentice-Hall.

Hodges, P. W. (1999). Is there a role for transverse abdominis in lumbo-sacral stability? *Manual Therapy, 4*(4), 74–86.

Proctor, D. F. (1980). *Breathing, speech and song*. Wien, Germany: Springer-Verlag.

Rolf, I. P. (1989). *Rolfing: Re-establishing the natural alignment and structural integration of the human body for vitality and well-being*. Rochester, VT: Healing Arts Press.

Rubin, J. S., Blake, E., & Mathieson, L. (2007) Musculoskeletal patterns in patients with voice disorders. *Journal of Voice, 21*(4), 477–484.

Rubin, J. S., Sataloff, R. T., & Korovin, G. S. (2003). *Diagnosis and treatment of voice disorders* (2nd ed.). Clifton Park, NY: Thomson.

Scherer, R. C., (2003). Laryngeal function during phonation. In J. S. Rubin, R. T. Sataloff, & G. S. Korovin, *Diagnosis and treatment of voice disorders* (2nd ed.). Clifton Park, NY: Thomson.

Sundberg, J. (1997). Vocal tract resonance. In R. T. Sataloff (Ed.), *Professional voice: The science and art of clinical care* (2nd ed, pp.167–184). San Diego, CA: Singular.

Taylor, A. (1960). The contribution of the intercostal muscles to the effort of respiration in man. *Journal of Physiology, 151,* 390–702.

Chapter 12

VOICE AND THE BRAIN

Pamela Davis

Listen and attend with the ear of your heart.

Saint Benedict

Evolution does not produce systems from scratch nor does it discard a functional system. It "tinkers with odds and ends" by changing an existing system to give it a new function, or combining systems to produce a more complex one (Darwin, 1859). The lung and larynx evolved together about 300 million years ago in primitive fish able to breathe in the water using their gills as well as breathe air using a primitive lung. From these fish evolved amphibians, and ultimately mammals. Muscles around the opening of the primitive lung evolved into a larynx and were important to keep water out of the lungs when submerged. The larynx, then, has had a key embryonic and developmental role in regulating the flow of fluid (in an embryo) or air in and out of the lungs. The neural control of the primitive larynx-lung enabled a functional system that let air enter the lung when the system opened, for that air to be expelled and to prevent water entering the lung when the animal submerged. The larynx-lung structure shown in Figure 12-1 is that which I believe should be studied and taught, instead of the top few centimeters of the organ (i.e., the isolated larynx), which humans have dissected away from its associated structures.

Darwin's theory of evolution was that genetic variation of behavior which conferred advantages with respect to survival were more likely to be reproduced (Darwin, 1859). Features of the human voice may be

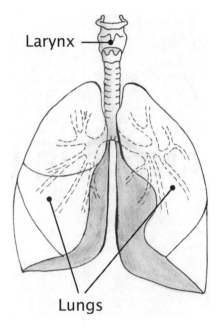

Figure 12–1. Drawing of larynx and lungs showing hyoid bone, thyroid cartilage and cricoid carilage, trachea, and bronchi. (Copyright Richard Webber, 2005.)

essential for survival if they evoke responses in listeners that lead to effective coping strategies. This is almost certainly true, both for an individual as well as the group. For example, when a baby is extremely distressed, such as when in pain, the cry contains vibrato. Is it possible that a cry which includes vibrato has an emotional effect on the caregiver, convincing one of the genuine nature of the baby's pain? In addition to vibrato, other voice features are likely to have emotional responses. Do certain musical features have a strong emotional effect on listeners because they tap into primitive emotional responses? Does the "goose bump factor" that sells seats in theaters have a primitive root in responding to a loved one's emotion or distress?

THE NERVOUS SYSTEM

The human nervous system is divided into the central nervous system comprising the brain and spinal cord and the peripheral nervous system. A friendly tutorial of the complex system of the brain and spinal cord is available at http://faculty.washington.edu/chudler/neurok.html .

The brain is divided into two halves, or cerebral hemispheres, covered by the cerebral cortex, sitting atop the brainstem, a swollen area at the top of the spinal cord (Figure 12–2). Central neurons (interneurons)

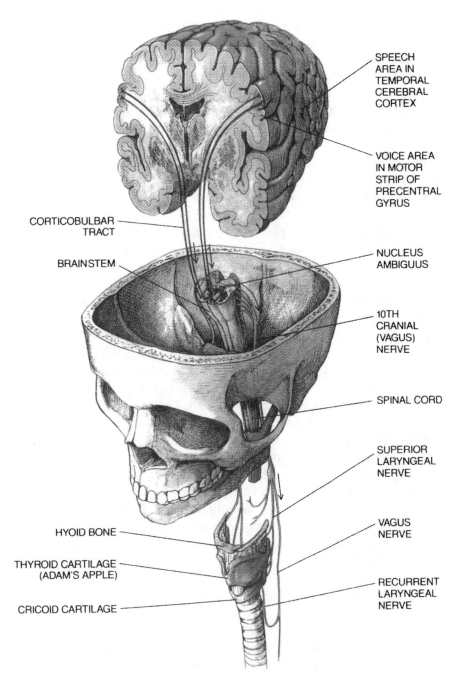

Figure 12–2. How the voice is produced. (Reproduced from Sataloff, RT, *Vocal Health and Pedagogy* [1992]. San Diego, CA: Singular Publishing Group, Inc., with permission.)

send out processes, or an axon and dendrites to connect to different interneurons in other parts of the brain and clusters of neurons are called nuclei. There are about 100 billion neurons in the human brain.

The cerebral cortex is folded into many grooves and makes up the outer layer of the brain: the gray matter is the cell bodies of the neurons and the white matter is the myelinated processes of these neurons. The neocortex is subdivided into many functional distinct areas such as motor, sensory, and association areas. This area has evolved to a larger size and capability in primates, especially humans, with its memory stores and interconnections and with it, more complex functioning—reason, thinking, sensory perception, language, artistry, as well as voluntary movement. In terms of evolutionary development from reptiles to humans, this neo (or new) cortex is essentially a "new brain" laid down on top of older evolutionary brains by evolution and necessarily linked to these older areas. A way of thinking of it might be that instead of renovating, the evolutionary tinkerer places a new house on top of older houses, without removing the older ones, and the new "house" (or neocortex) is connected up to the existing (subcortical) services by neural pathways.

There are many important subcortical structures. The brain usually is divided into forebrain, midbrain, and hindbrain. The forebrain consists of the cerebral cortex, thalamus, hypothalamus, basal ganglia, and the limbic system. The thalamus relays information from the environment to the neocortex. This includes changes to the environment outside our body, such as visual or auditory signals that might trigger the fight or flight response, as well as to changes in our internal environment such as the way our body reacts to pain or injury. The hypothalamus regulates thirst and body temperature as well as blood pressure and heart rate and it stimulates hormonal activity. Emotional experiences and expression include many brain structures usually referred to as the limbic system, which includes structures such as the prefrontal and cingulate cortex as well as deeper structures including the hippocampus and the amygdala, structures where emotions are thought to be generated, perceived, and remembered. The midbrain forms connections between the hindbrain and forebrain and receives sensory input from auditory and visual receptors. The hindbrain consists of the pons and the medulla containing neural networks for breathing and cardiovascular regulation and the cerebellum, which is concerned with balance, equilibrium, and voluntary muscle coordination.

Motor neurons have their cell body in the brain and send their long process, or axon, outside the brain to fire or innervate the muscles. Sensory neurons transmit signals from receptors in the periphery, such as the hair cells in the inner ear, to the brain via their axon. Neurons to or from a similar site collectively are called nerves and the system of these nerves is called the peripheral nervous system.

The medulla contains the cell bodies of the nerves to the larynx (Davis & Nail, 1984) and lung in a long nucleus called the nucleus ambiguus, called so because the borders of this important nucleus with its many scattered motor neuronal cell bodies are ambiguous to define.

Cell bodies to the heart, lung, gastrointestinal tract, and the pharynx also are contained within this nucleus. The processes of all these cell bodies leave the brain as the vagus nerve.

Some neurons fire muscles that we can move voluntarily, for example, as we can voluntarily move our hands, and this part of the peripheral nervous system is called the voluntary or somatic motor system. This includes the laryngeal and breathing muscles, although many of these muscles are controlled involuntarily as part of a pattern, such as the swallowing, coughing, or vocal pattern, and we do not have the same fine level of voluntary control over individual muscles that we have over a finger or tongue tip, for example.

We lack conscious or voluntary control over many other muscles, the so-called smooth muscle, which lines our heart, lungs, gut, and blood vessels. This system is called the autonomic nervous system and is responsible for the body's essential functioning such as keeping the air moving in and out of our lungs, even when we sleep, keeping the blood pumping around our body, and preparing our body for fight or flight or to recover from such active states. Nerves from this system travel from the brain and spinal cord to the viscera, blood vessels, irises, glands, and other involuntary structures, such as the smooth muscle surrounding the hairs on our body. There are sympathetic and parasympathetic parts: the sympathetic nerves generally increasing in action and the latter decreasing it. Control over the autonomic nervous system is carried out by networks of neurons in the brainstem.

EMOTIONAL EXPRESSION—THE "EMOTIONAL MOTOR SYSTEM"

Emotions are expressed and communicated through changes in the autonomic, voluntary motor, and endocrine systems. Darwin (1965) made a detailed study of the universal way that emotions are expressed. The term "emotional motor system" was introduced by Holstege (1992). Examples of the changes induced by emotion include changes in heart rate, blood pressure, urination, piloerection, and sweating as well as changes in breathing, facial expression, vocalization, body posture, and movement.

Most photographers know that to coax someone to smile genuinely by telling a joke will produce a different facial muscle pattern than just telling their subject to impose a smile. There are two pathways for many acts such as smiling, the voluntary motor pathway and the emotional or autonomic pathway, and these can be differentially impaired such as shown in Figure 12–3. The woman pictured has a lesion in the voluntary motor pathway to the facial muscles but is able to smile involuntarily in response to hearing a joke and then uses all her oral muscles, including those paralyzed to voluntary control (Holstege & Ehling, 1996). Other

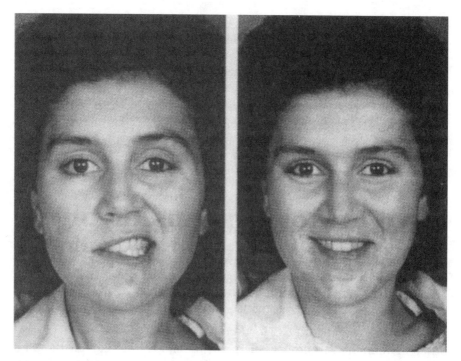

Figure 12–3. Two motor systems involved in speech. (From G. Holstege and T. Ehling [1996]. In *Controlling Complexity and Chaos*, N. Fletcher and P. Davis [Eds.], San Diego, CA: Singular Publishing Group Inc., pp. 137–153. Copyright © 1996 Delmar Learning, a part of Cengage Learning, Inc. Reproduced by permission.)

forms of brain damage prevent emotional expression but leave voluntary control intact.

This has important implications for singing if the same dichotomy is present in the laryngorespiratory system which is far more complex than the facial motor system. It appears that the emotional motor system, which is responsible for the genuine laugh or cry, has access to a different combination of muscles than is available to the voluntary motor system. It may be that certain singers and actors are able to use the emotion of the words of the song or speech to produce a different and coordinated pattern—including how they take air in, as well as how they use their abdominal, intercostal, laryngeal, pharyngeal, tongue, palate, lips, jaw, and facial muscles.

It is thought that a structure in the midbrain, the periaqueductal gray (PAG), plays a major role in emotional expression (Bandler et al., 1996; Bandler & Shipley, 1994). The PAG region comprises discrete longitudinal columns of neurons, which coordinate distinct coping strategies that are triggered by different types of stimuli in the environment. One set of behavioral changes that can be evoked from the lateral PAG enables an animal to confront a threatening stimulus and "fight": including piloerection (body hair erection), arching of the back, and vocalization, as well as increased blood pressure and heart rate and a redistribution of the blood flow to the face. In contrast, excitation of other parts of the PAG evokes other behavioral patterns, such as "flight" or passive immobility. It is important to note that stimulation of the PAG produces complex integrated patterns of involuntary changes in blood pressure and heart rate, as well as changes in the activity of muscles under voluntary control, including the breathing, laryngeal, facial, and oral muscles, which are always activated simultaneously in a coordinated manner and may be accompanied by body movement. In addition to the different somatic and autonomic responses, excitation of different PAG columns evokes analgesia or relief from pain.

INNERVATION OF THE LARYNX AND RESPIRATORY SYSTEM

MOTOR (EFFERENT) INNERVATION

The motor innervation of the larynx is considered in conjunction with that of the respiratory system as a whole—in almost all activities, the nerve impulses to the larynx are coordinated with the respiratory muscles. During every inspiration, the diaphragm and the posterior cricoarytenoid muscle, which dilates the glottis or opening between the vocal folds, are always active (well, almost always); the nerve impulses to the posterior cricoarytenoid muscle arrive slightly ahead of those to the diaphragm.

During nonvoiced expiration, the muscles of the abdomen, rib cage, and larynx may be silent (passive expiration). If they are active, the abdominal muscles (e.g., internal oblique) and the internal intercostal muscles will be recruited: the laryngeal adductor muscles (thyroarytenoid and lateral cricoarytenoid) may be slightly active or silent in nonphonated expiration. The interarytenoid muscle is silent. During voiced expirations, instead of the glottic dilator posterior cricoarytenoid being active, the glottic constrictor or adductor muscles are active, namely, thyroarytenoid, lateral cricoarytenoid, and interarytenoid muscles. Some extrinsic laryngeal muscles also are active in inspiration and voiced expiration

The main nerve to the larynx and lung is the vagus nerve, arising from cell bodies in the nucleus ambiguus in the medulla (see Figure 12–2). There are two major branches of this nerve to the larynx and trachea: the recurrent laryngeal nerve (RLN) and the internal laryngeal nerve (ILN) with its branch, the external laryngeal nerve (ELN). The RLN contains from 1,000 to 4,000 neurons in humans (depending on the level at which the count is made). As seen in Figure 12–2, the RLN loops back up to the larynx after traveling down into the chest. This nerve is called "recurrent" because the nerves to the larynx develop with the nerves to the heart (also supplied by the vagus nerve) and the right RLN loops around the right aortic arch and so when the heart descends and the neck elongates during embryonic development, the right RLN is dragged down with the heart vessels.

The RLN provides motor innervation to most of the laryngeal muscles as well as sympathetic and parasympathetic nerves to the glands and smooth muscle of the trachea. It also supplies sensory innervation below the level of the vocal folds. The RLN innervates the internal laryngeal muscles that either dilate or constrict the glottic airway: the posterior cricoarytenoid, thyroarytenoid, lateral cricoarytenoid, and interarytenoid muscles. In the embryo, these muscles develop with the cartilages of the larynx from the fifth or sixth brachial arch, derived from the gill arches of our fishy ancestors.

The superior laryngeal nerve arises from the vagus nerve above the level of the larynx and a branch, the ILN travels down to pierce the thyroid lamina and enter the interior of the larynx. Prior to the ILN piercing the thyroid lamina, a tiny branch, the ELN is given off to innervate the cricothyroid muscle and it also has a small number of sensory fibres. This muscle develops from the fourth brachial arch like the pharyngeal muscles (and epiglottis) and, in this respect, differs from the internal laryngeal muscles whose chief function is to move the vocal folds. That the cricothyroid muscle and its innervation arise from different embryonic structures suggests that the neural control of the cricothyroid muscle may share more similarities with the neural control of the muscles of the oropharynx.

The bronchi and lung are supplied by cardiac and pulmonary branches of the vagus nerve. Activation of this parasympathetic pathway produces constriction of the bronchi, an increase in pulmonary secretion, and a decrease in heart rate. Sympathetic nerve fibers act in the opposite manner on smooth muscle and glands.

The respiratory muscles are supplied by the phrenic nerve (to the diaphragm) and by branches of the 12 thoracic spinal nerves to the intercostal muscles. The 7th to 12th nerves are special in that they supply the abdominal muscle wall as well as the lower five thoracic intercostal muscles and (the 12th or subcostal nerve) parts of the transverse, oblique, and rectus muscles.

SENSORY (AFFERENT) INNERVATION

It is important to note that not all *afferent* nerves have associated *sensory* perception—some of the sensory nerve endings in the larynx trigger important reflexes, which do not depend on conscious perception. More correctly then, the nerves that conveys nerve signals from the periphery to the brain should be called "afferent" rather than sensory.

Hearing one's own voice is essential for the production of voice. This is particularly evident in humans and some other animals, such as bats which adjust the sound quality of their calls by monitoring the characteristics of the returning echo signals. It is noteworthy that there is no evidence that the human auditory neural pathway, via the auditory nerve, has become specialized for speech or song perception.

What sensations can be felt from the larynx? There is some evidence that pain and temperature can be perceived and touch is likely to be perceived if the person could attend to it as the touch will elicit some powerful reflexes, such as coughing, that they are going to be overpowering. Proprioceptive control, or the awareness of a part of the body, is noticeably absent from the larynx. Your vocal folds move slightly open as you breathe in and close slightly as you breathe out—can you perceive these movements at the level of your larynx? The answer is "no" although you can, of course, perceive whether you are breathing in or out. The diaphragm also is poorly supplied by proprioceptive nerve fibers. Perhaps the brain has evolved so that the structures that are essential for breathing and life, the larynx and the diaphragm, are "protected" by not being able to be brought to conscious perception and potentially voluntary intervention.

The lower intercostals and the abdominal muscles are richly supplied with proprioceptive nerve fibers. There are two ways of controlling our breathing: behavioral control such as in speech and song and metabolic or automatic control such as when we are asleep. At a voluntary level, we can hold our breath until the build-up of carbon dioxide forces us to take a new breath; or we can sustain a sung sound or speech sound for as long as air remains in the lungs. We also can initiate a new breath whenever we wish and we can alter the rate and depth of breathing on a breath-by-breath basis or maintain a level of contraction of various muscle groups, such as by holding in the tummy or releasing the abdomen. We achieve this via cortical (voluntary) projections to the individual muscles (Macefield, Gandevia, McKenzie, & Butler, 1996). Any voluntary alteration of the respiratory pattern continues only as long as we maintain conscious awareness, although postural changes may result in more sustained changes and it is possible to "unlearn" inappropriate voluntary effort such as recruitment of the neck and shoulder muscles during inspiration.

All the nerves to the larynx, the RLN, the ELN, and the ILN contain sensory fibers, but by far the nerve containing the most sensory axons or nerve fibers is the ILN. This nerve is the major sensory nerve of the laryngeal structures above the level of the vocal folds and in contrast to the sensory innervation by the RLN, the number and exquisite sensitivity of ILN mucosal receptors is remarkable (Davis & Nail, 1987). The reason is a lifesaving one: the supraglottic laryngeal mucosa, and that overlying the arytenoid cartilages and the base of the epiglottis, is linked to many protective reflexes designed to prevent foreign bodies from entering the lung. This was the first function of the larynx in the early fish and these reflexes are well developed. The extent to which signals from the ILN are used for proprioception in voice is unknown: ILN axons can fire at several hundred cycles per second, which is important for detecting the movement of a foreign body into the larynx. However, whether these signals are also used to monitor vocalization is unknown although there is no evidence that the reflex sensitivity is reduced during vocalization; an inhaled crumb will still elicit powerful coughing reflexes even if one is vocalizing.

Afferents that are crucial in control of breathing are those from the lung and airways that travel in the vagus nerve. These afferent nerve endings signal lung pressure/volume, inhaled irritants and other chemicals, and pain. There is evidence that signals from the pulmonary stretch receptors signaling airway pressure/lung volume (and, of course, subglottic pressure during vocalization) are crucial in initiating and sustaining vocalization (see below).

CENTRAL NERVOUS SYSTEM CONTROL OF VOICE

Vaughan Williams (1955) describes the voice as the perfect instrument on the basis that there is a minimum of mechanism between the performer's will and the result. So, which part of our brain do we use when we speak or sing? Recent research has established that language functions are distributed between the cerebral hemispheres: the left hemisphere is concerned primarily with processing the linguistic aspects such as words and syntax, whereas the right hemisphere is concerned with processing prosody, gestures, and complex linguistic relations. But language is not voice; the sound that underlines the words that we speak or sing is part of the way that we express emotion.

As well as singing, humans make nonbiological sounds such as beating drums or blowing into a pipe and are unique in that they listen to music for pleasure. This suggests that our brain has evolved in ways that facilitate singing. These skills have developed because of an enlarged human brain experimenting with instruments and tools, perceiving, remembering, developing artistically, and recreating pleasing sounds.

However, the key factor that led to speech and song was unquestionably the development of intention—or voluntary control and the vast development of memory. "May not some unusually wise apelike animal have begun to use emotional outcries intentionally and so have taken the first step towards the development of true speech?" (Darwin, 1859). Darwin developed his own theory of the origin of speech, namely, that it started as singing to woo sexual partners. An interesting theory! Humans can voluntarily control their breathing within limits set by the brain. Significantly for singing, they also can voluntarily inhibit emotional expression if required and can re-create an emotional experience from memory. Such voluntary control skills are not seen in any other species. Even for other primates such as the chimpanzee, vocal sounds always are emotional in nature and rarely can be inhibited, even if this is to the detriment of the individual by alerting others to its location. The brain mechanisms of vocalization for these so-called "lower" primates then are similar to those of the human newborn.

It always has been assumed that vocalization during human speech and song was something that depended on different brain regions and pathways, reflecting the sophisticated human vocal control. With the exception of Darwin, the prevailing scientific wisdom has been, and continues to be, that the processes must be governed by the "higher" brain, the cerebral cortex, the part of the brain that is so different in humans compared to the "lower" species. (It is noteworthy that this theory fails to take into account the very sophisticated vocal mechanism of many bats and birds. It also fails to take into account that the larynx is not the vocal organ, which requires the coordination of the larynx and the lung as discussed earlier.) As shown in Figure 12–2, it is thought that human voluntary motor control of voice is associated with nerve pathways from a prefrontal strip of gray matter containing neurons connected to the nucleus ambiguus, a nuclear group of motor neurons in the brainstem that control the laryngeal muscles. However, the evidence for this direct pathway to the laryngeal motor neurons is sketchy (Kuypers, 1958), which is not surprising as we do not have voluntary control over the internal muscles of the larynx; for example, we can open our larynx but only in synchrony with our respiratory muscles and the same applies for vocalization, effort closure, and other activities. This suggests that the voluntary vocal control is to some motor "pattern generator" not to the individual laryngeal motor units controlling the glottis. There are, however, much more clearly defined nerve pathways from the motor cortex to the motor neurons for the orofacial articulatory muscles (Kuypers, 1958) and indeed we do have a much finer control of some of the orofacial organs in isolation, that is, you can move your tongue alone, not just as part of a swallowing pattern. This corticobulbar (i.e., cortex to medulla) pathway and its connections undoubtedly play a key role with respect to many aspects of the initiation and expression of human language and precise articulation of speech sounds.

There is evidence for additional neural vocal pathways. The limbic system and motor pathways through the basal ganglia, the extrapyramidal pathway, are undoubtedly involved in both human and primate vocal output. In addition, there is now evidence that a very primitive and unconscious part of our brain that is involved in emotional expression, and which is probably responsible for the unconscious sounds that we make, may also play a role in the motor control of voice for speech and song (Davis, Winkworth, Zhang, & Bandler, 1995, Davis, Zhang, & Bandler, 1996a, 1996b; Zhang, Davis, Bandler, & Carrive, 1994).

Recent data have demonstrated striking and detailed similarities in the laryngeal muscle patterns for PAG-evoked vocalization in animals compared to that for human speech during consonants and vowels (Zhang et al., 1994). We proposed that PAG does not mediate just emotional vocalization, but that indeed, all sound production was critically dependent on the lateral PAG and its output pathway. If so, this may help to explain the extent to which emotion is so closely aligned to speech and singing if both are governed, in part, by the PAG. The lateral PAG is associated with vocalization in animals and possibly some human emotional utterances, such as primitive cries of pain or distress or the newborn's cry. In support of this latter hypothesis are the observations that when anencephalic newborns are born with little or no forebrain, but an intact midbrain, they vocalize in a manner that is relatively similar to that of normal infants (André-Thomas, 1954). Recently, on the basis of PAG recording studies (Larson, 1991), Bandler, Keay, Vaughan, and Shipley (1996) proposed that the PAG may play a critical role in speech and song by setting a necessary state of readiness for voiced and voiceless sound production, rather than controlling the motor patterns directly.

Of importance here is the fact that the PAG output is necessarily linked to the sensory input from the respiratory system and the larynx. The PAG receives afferent information related to the volume/pressure of air in the lungs and this information is used in planning the motor pattern for vocalization (Davis et al., 1993; Nakazawaa et al., 1997). It appears that, unless the PAG receives a signal that sufficient lung (and subglottic) pressure is available for voice, the muscle activity and the sound, is terminated and a new inspiration occurs. This coordination ensures that a new breath is taken naturally as the lung volume decreases during sound production. The same may apply to human speech and song. Possibly related is the finding that the depth of inspirations in human spontaneous speech was related to the length of what the speakers intended to say (Winkworth, Davis, Ellis, & Adams, 1995). Of significance is that we cannot modify the activity of the respiratory network deep in the brainstem medulla and there has been a failure to find evidence for anatomic connections from the voluntary part of the brain (motor cortex) to the (unconscious) respiratory network, specifically to the nucleus retroambiguus where the expiratory coordination of the laryngeal and respiratory muscles for voice appears to take place. However, it is known that PAG output for vocalization connects to the nucleus retroambiguus, a finding that supports the idea that PAG may facilitate the breath-voice coordination for human speech and song (Zhang et al., 1996).

In addition to this crucial signal that there is sufficient air volume/pressure to vocalize, the PAG receives motivation-controlling input from limbic structures and auditory, visual, and somatosensory input from diverse sensory-processing structures. Whether the PAG is able to signal readiness or controls the motor patterns for vocalization directly still is unknown, but it is likely that the PAG and the emotional motor system play a key role.

How does the central nervous system control voice? How is voice coordinated with respiration and articulation? It is difficult to jump from animal models (that give us clues about how the human system may have evolved) to human models of vocalization. However, most agree that the midbrain PAG as well as the mediofrontal cortex (anterior cingulated cortex and supplementary and presupplementary motor area) are crucial for the production of voluntary vocalization (Jürgens, 2003).

Then, we might speculate that the evolutionary tinkerer might have combined:

- A primitive sound production system—over 300 million years old—with a breathing system and a larynx that became capable of making sounds varying in pitch and intensity;
- A primitive oral system capable of varying that sound by altering the positions of the pharynx, tongue, jaw, and lips;
- Primitive unconscious brain control with emotional vocal expression, emotional responses to sounds and voice coordinated with breathing—the vocal component of the emotional motor system;
- More recently developed neocortical brain development: language, memory, perception, music, and some voluntary control of breathing and emotional expression—the ability to remember a feeling and express it again, memory of events, inhibition of emotional expression; and
- Pitch discrimination and hearing to help make sense of the environment—ability to reproduce sounds that are concordant.

VOLUNTARY VOCAL CONTROL

What voluntary control do we have of the vocal folds, with sound and without sound? This question was the one that led to my study of the nervous system, 25 years ago. I still do not have the answer but I know that humans have exquisite control of the sound that they can produce.

Imagery of the voluntary movement of a particular limb activates the motor areas of the cerebral cortex (Ehrsson, Geyer, & Naito, 2003) and thus it appears that the brain "simulates" the movement that the person imagines that they are performing. This is dependent on the difficulty of the movement and posture. There is additional evidence that, when we observe facial expressions associated with strong emotion, the observer simulates the expression and that this influences the observer's autonomic system (Levenson, Ekman, & Friesen, 1990). This occurs even when the stimulus is presented subliminally, without conscious recognition.

In the case of singing, we are dealing with one of the most complex human (and avian) motor skills. The singers can tell us if they are able to internally simulate sounds they hear, not only by supraglottic, that is, oropharyngeal and respiratory muscle changes, over which there appears to be a greater degree of voluntary control, but also by laryngeal glottic adjustments. Pitch control is very fine, but as inferred above, the cricothy-roid muscle shares its development with the musculature of the pharynx as do the muscles that move the epiglottis. The question that follows is whether a listener is convinced of the genuine quality of a singer's expression by unconscious simulation of the sound in the listener's voluntary and autonomic nervous systems. The joy of music is the pleasure that this gives an audience, regardless of what might happen subconsciously.

As a neuroscientist, it seems to me that many descriptions of the voice and the brain ignore what we know intuitively—that our voice is inexorably linked to our emotional state and that we often can sense how someone else is feeling from his or her voice. When we hear some singers, our bodies can react as if the emotional expression is genuine: the hairs on our bodies stand up and we feel tingles that are related to changes in the blood flow throughout our body. These are all part of the neural control of voice that has evolved over many millions of years. This chapter reviews the neural control of the voice: the voluntary and involuntary or emotional control of the various systems that are principal in producing sound. It then discusses some relevant issues in this very complex area.

REFERENCES

André-Thomas, J. (1954). Le nouveau-né normal et l'anencéphale. *Presse Médicin, 62*, 885–886.

Bandler, R., Keay, K., Vaughan, C., & Shipley, M. T. (1996). Columnar organization of PAG neurons regulating emotional and vocal expression: In N. Fletcher & P. Davis (Eds.), *Controlling complexity and chaos* (pp. 137–153). San Diego, CA: Singular.

Bandler, R., & Shipley, M. T. (1994). Columnar organization in the midbrain peri-aqueductal gray: Modules for emotional expression? *Trends in Neuroscience, 17*, 379–389.

Darwin, C. (1859). *On the origin of species* (Facsimilie ed. 1964). Cambridge, MA: Harvard University Press.

Darwin, C. (1965). *The expression of the emotions in man and animals.* Chicago, IL: University of Chicago Press.

Davis, P., & Nail, B. S. (1984). On the localization of laryngeal motoneurons in the cat and rabbit. *Journal of Comparative Neurology, 230,* 13-22.

Davis, P., & Nail, B. S. (1987). Quantitative analysis of laryngeal mechanosensitivity in the cat and rabbit. *Journal of Physiology (London), 388,* 467-485.

Davis, P., Winkworth, A., Zhang, S. P., & Bandler, R. (1995). The neural control of vocalization: Respiratory and emotional influences. *Journal of Voice, 10,* 23-38.

Davis, P., Zhang, S. P., & Bandler, R. (1993). Pulmonary and upper airway afferent influences on the motor pattern of vocalization evoked by excitation of the midbrain periaqueductal gray of the cat. *Brain Research, 607,* 61-80.

Davis, P. J., Zhang, S. P., & Bandler, R. (1996a) Midbrain and medullary regulation of vocalization. In N. Fletcher & P. Davis (Eds.), *Controlling complexity and chaos* (pp. 121-136). San Diego CA: Singular.

Davis, P. J., Zhang, S. P., & Bandler, R. (1996b) Midbrain and medullary control of respiration and vocalization. *Progress in Brain Research, 107,* 315-325.

Ehrsson, H. H., Geyer, S., & Naito, E. (2003). Imagery of voluntary movement of fingers, toes, and tongue activates corresponding body-part-specific motor representations. *Journal of Neurophysiology, 90,* 3304-3316.

Holstege, G. (1992). The emotional motor system. *European Journal of Morphology, 30,* 67-79.

Holstege, G., & Ehling, T. (1996). Two motor systems involved in speech. In N. Fletcher & P. Davis (Eds.), *Controlling complexity and chaos* (pp. 137-153). San Diego, CA: Singular.

Jürgens, U. (2003). Neural pathways underlying vocal control, 1. *Neuroscience Letters, 340,* 111-114.

Kuypers, H. G. J. (1958). Corticobulbar connections to the pons and lower brain stem in man: An anatomical study. *Brain, 81,* 364-388.

Larson, C. R. (1991). Activity of PAG neurons during conditioned vocalization in the macaque monkey, In A. Depaulis & R. Bandler (Eds.), *The midbrain periaqueductal gray matter: Functional, anatomical and neurochemical organization* (pp. 23-40), New York, NY: Plenum.

Levenson, R. W., Ekman, P., & Friesen, W. V. (1990). Voluntary facial action generates emotion-specific autonomic nervous system activity. *Psychophysiology, 27,* 363-384.

Macefield, V., Gandevia, S., McKenzie, D., & Butler J. (1996). Cortical and reflex control of human respiratory muscles, In N. Fletcher & P. Davis (Eds.), *Controlling complexity and chaos* (pp. 219-235). San Diego, CA: Singular.

Nakazawaa, K., Shibaa, K., Satoha, I., Yoshidaa, K., Nakajimab, Y., & Konnoa, A. (1997). Role of pulmonary afferent inputs in vocal on-switch in the cat. *Neuroscience Research, 29,* 49-54.

Vaughan Williams, R. (1955). *The making of music.* Westport, CT: Greenwood Press.

Winkworth, A. L., Davis, P., Ellis, E., & Adams, R. (1995). Lung volumes and breath placement during spontaneous speech. *Journal of Speech and Hearing Research, 38,* 124-144.

Zhang, S. P., Bandler, R., & Davis, P. (1996). Integration of vocalization: The medullary nucleus retroambigualis. *Journal of Neurophysiology, 74*, 2500–2512.

Zhang, S. P., Davis, P. J., Bandler, R., & Carrive, P. (1994). Brain stem integration of vocalization: Role of the midbrain periaqueductal gray. *Journal of Neurophysiology, 72*, 1337–1356.

Chapter 13

HEARING AND SINGING

Adrian Fourcin

INTRODUCTION

This chapter was written in response to Janice Chapman's request that someone working in the area of Speech Sciences should contribute a brief overview of the ways in which hearing and singing might interact. I hesitated before agreeing to embark on the work; the subject area is immense in scope and profound in its links with the way that we have evolved. In consequence, I have concentrated on only a few aspects of possible answers to a very small number of salient questions and arranged the discussion into four overlapping parts:

1. HEARING THE PITCH OF THE SINGING AND SPEAKING VOICES
   - Is it likely that we listen differently to song than we do to speech?
   - Is voice production controlled auditorily differently in singing than in speech?
2. HEARING ONESELF
   - Do we hear other voices differently from the way in which we hear our own?
3. SINGING AND THE BRAIN
   - Is hearing in the singer's brain likely to be organized differently from that of an ordinary person?

4. SINGING AND LANGUAGE
■ Are there language differences that might possibly predispose their hearers to make special use of the singing voice?

1. HEARING THE PITCH OF THE SINGING AND SPEAKING VOICES

For most practical purposes, the really important, dominant, dimension in hearing voice is pitch. Classically, pure tones provide a basic reference for the pitch of the singing voice and also for both the definition and perceptual investigation of the pitch percept itself. Subjective psychophysical data have been stably established over many years on the basis of the use of pure tones. Maximum discriminability in the sense of just being able to hear pitch differences is reached between 1 kHz, C6, near the top of the soprano register, and an octave above with an average best just noticeable difference, (JND), of about 0.7% at 200 Hz and 0.4% or 4 Hz in the region of 1 kHz (Nelson, Stanton, & Freeman, 1983; Vance, 1914). Individual listener's sensitivities may be as low as 0.1%. Auditory pitch detection for the frequency ranges of the speaking and singing voice appear to employ mechanisms that operate, at least in part, on the basis of temporal processing (Moore, Glasberg, & Peters, 1985). This level of pitch discrimination implies an ability to detect **average** temporal differences between successive periods of about 4 microseconds (μs) and, for some individual listeners, 1 μs. This temporal signal-processing ability for pitch perception is paralleled in the ability to detect changes between left and right positioning of a sound source, auditory lateralization, where interaural time differences of about 2 μs to 10 μs are detectable.

In singing and speaking, the ability to detect changes in pitch may be even greater in the young adult. For steady complex tones and vowels in the fundamental frequency range of conversational speech, the pitch discriminations are even smaller than those obtained with pure tones. Wier, Jesteadt, and Green (1977) and Moore et al. (1985), for example, within the range 200 to 600 Hz, reported values from about 0.15% to 0.3%.

For vowel-like sounds with simple changing fundamental frequency contours, however, a listener's ability to perceive differences in fundamental frequency is drastically reduced and may be 8% at about 100 Hz (Klatt, 1973). This increase in, and magnitude of, JND also has been found for whole word utterances with simple intonation contours, the JND here never being less than 6%. When more complex contours are used, the differences needed to achieve reliable detection may be as great as 20% (Hart, Collier, & Cohen, 1990). The subjective results for these sound types are not as well-established as for sustained sounds and there is a dependence on the duration of the tone. There is, however, a good working consensus between a large number of reported observations

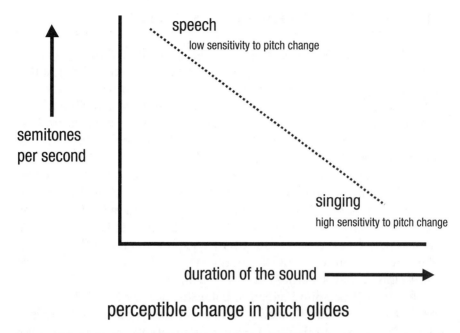

Figure 13–1. Pitch related to stimulus duration. Vertically the graph line spans the range from one-hundredth of a semitone/second to 100 semitones/second and the corresponding durations are 60 milliseconds and 5 seconds (Reprinted with permission from Hart, J., Collier, R., Cohen, A., 1990. *A perceptual study of intonation: An experimental phonetic approach.* Cambridge: Cambridge University Press).

(Hart et al., 1990). Figure 13-1 gives a simple overview of results of pitch perceptual experiments that have made use of both voice and psychophysical test stimuli. This average graph is based on listeners' abilities to perceive pitch changes in a gliding tone as a function of its duration.

The practical implication of these observations for singers is that, for the operatic voice where sustained notes are typical, the control of pitch is capable of being maintained with a variability of far less than an eighth of a tone whereas any rapidly variable speechlike intonation can only be associated with auditory control at the level of a tone.

2. HEARING ONESELF

We are all used to the "sound of our own voices" and it often comes as a shock when we hear, for the very first time, the replay of a recording. The sound from the loud speaker or headphone is not what we are used to hearing when we sing or speak, and in some cases, it's unrecognizable and even unwelcome. Physically, three principal effects or, more precisely, three different sound transmission environments, are responsible to different degrees for the discrepancy.

IN THE AIR—FROM MOUTH AND NOSE TO EAR

Acoustic energy in both speaking and singing is radiated primarily from the nose and lips. The radiation is quite directional; there is a big difference, for example, between the sound levels in front of the face and those at the back of the head and at the level of the chest. At a meter distance, at frequencies from C4 to C5, the intensity of the sound at the ears is less by half than that directly at the front of the mouth. For sound components around C7 to C8, the region of the singer's formant (Figure 13–2), the sound at a meter in front of the mouth is twice as loud as that at one meter from either ear (Chu & Warnock, 2001; Dunn & Farnsworth, 1939) because bone conduction in this frequency region is not as important as air-conducted sound (Pörschmann, 2000) . This difference in loudness between the low and higher frequencies in the acoustic signal makes the self-monitoring of the energy in the singer's formant more difficult (Cabrera, Davis, Barnes, Jacobs, & Bell, 2002).

Relatively little sound radiation comes from the neck and head and other parts of the body. However, this energy has to travel to the ears in order to be heard and there is no single straight-line airborne path. For example, from the mouth to the left ear, energy both travels around the left cheek and also by the side of the right cheek all round the back of the head. These are two instances of an infinite number of paths around the head from the radiating sound sources at the mouth and nose to the two external ears and an infinite number of possibilities for the acoustic waves to interact, in ways that depend on the size and shape of the speaker/listener's head. These interactions give a coloration to the perceived sound of one's voice that is not present in the neutral presentation that comes from replaying a recording that has been made with an omnidirectional pressure-sensitive microphone.

The recording will be characterized by an essentially flat transfer function, room acoustics apart, whereas the frequency response of the self-monitoring paths to the ear will both have humps (for an adult male around 2 kHz and 4 kHz) and troughs (around 1 and 3 kHz) and a very large tail off by about 20 dB at 10 kHz (Pörschmann, 2000). This is very different from what we are supposed to seek when buying a hi-fi system —but only the first of the three main sources of discrepancy between what the singer hears and what the singer produces.

IN THE ENCLOSURE

From anechoic room to concert hall and cathedral, each enclosure has its own acoustic characteristics that are imposed on any sound source it contains. We are used to hearing the sound of our surroundings and if, in the extreme case of the anechoic room, the enclosure has no sound

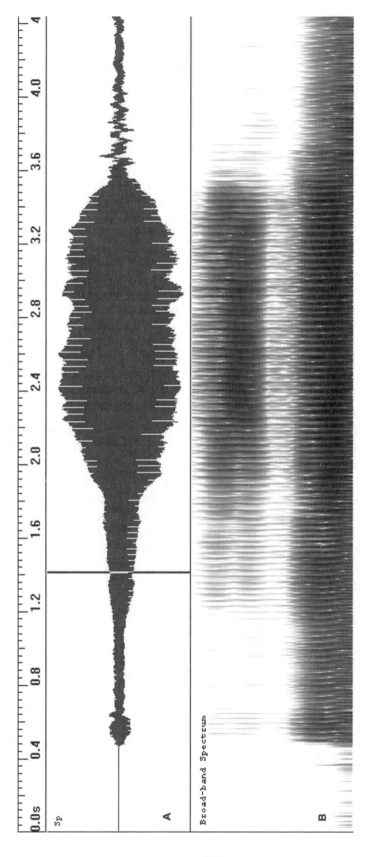

Figure 13–2. Singer's formant. **A.** shows the way that the singer has gradually increased the acoustic pressure by the control of his vocal fold vibration. **B.** is a spectrogram analysis of the evolution of formant grouping as timbre is enhanced and reduced (0 to 4 kHz). (Original voice recording produced and kindly supplied by Professor David Howard.)

237

of its own, we feel that our ears are muffled. A single smart hand clap awakens the "voice" of any live enclosure and tells a story about its nature, size, and intrinsic makeup. In its paths from the source to the listener acoustic energy is shaped in loudness, timbre, and timing by the enclosure. As a consequence, the sound produced by a singer or speaker is not the sound that will be heard by the distant listener. Nor, indeed, is it the sound that will be heard by the original source, the singer or listener. Energy may, by design or accident, be directed so that the audience hears well and the performer hears with difficulty. Quite small changes in reflector positioning or the provision of personal monitors can make major changes to self-perception. An important aspect of concert hall design is to ensure that, for any part of the auditorium, a listener will hear the primary sound that comes from the singer fused with the secondary reflections that come from surrounding surfaces. Haas (1951) found that, if the secondary reflection arrived more than 50 ms after the primary, there would be a marked reduction in intelligibility. For an effective fusion of the primary and secondary sounds that enable the sound source to be accurately localized, the delay between the two must be less than about 10 ms (this is an example of the precedence effect, Litovsky, Rakerd, Yin, & Hartmann, 1999), the sound then appears to come from a single source.

For singers the primary sound comes from their own voice production but in some acoustic environments a special difficulty arises when the lack of adequate reflecting surfaces results in an inadequate level of secondary sound to provide a sufficient basis for auditory feedback. This is the opposite of the effect where sung or spoken levels are increased to overcome the influence of ambient noise (Lombard, 1911), and although the trained voice may not be susceptible to masking noise (Weiss, 1993), the lack of feedback could be disturbing. The provision of a performer's reflecting surface can solve this problem and entirely transform the feeling of "presence."

IN THE HEAD

In addition to traveling externally through the air to the ear, sound energy also travels through the head itself. Acoustic energy in the vocal tract is coupled into the bony structure of the skull, soft tissues, and cerebrospinal fluid of the brain. The energy propagated via these transmission paths leads to movements of the ossicular chains of each ear relative to their cochleae and in turn leads to consequent vibratile excitation of inner ear structures. Von Békésy (1948) reported that these internal paths of acoustic energy transmission were responsible for about half of the self-perceived loudness of the speaking, and by implication the singing, voice.

Loudness, however, is only one aspect of the percept; timbre is equally important and these internal head transmission paths give a coloration to the sound of one's voice that is quite different from the coloration that arises from external airborne paths around the head and within room and concert hall enclosures. They can introduce additional resonances to those of the vocal tract itself (Howell & Powell, 1984). The difference is easily demonstrated. Speak or sing with the forefingers pressing the tragus of each ear (the fleshy part of each of the pinnae, adjacent to the auditory meatus) into the ear canal so as to close off external sound. The resulting sensation of one's voice essentially is due only to internal head-borne transmission. It is biased toward the lower frequencies. Internal head acoustic transmission typically has a very prominent peak (adult males again) around 1 kHz and is reduced by approximately 20 dB at 10 kHz. In the region of the peak at 1 kHz, internal head transmission is greater than externally airborne energy (Hansen & Stinson, 1998; Pörschmann, 2000). This head transmission appears mostly to be due to brain/fluid-based paths (Sohmer, Freeman, Geal-Dor, Adelman, & Savion, 2000) but skull resonances may also contribute and could do so in ways, and degrees, that may be very different from one individual to another (Fourcin & West, 1973). The notion in singing teaching that voice is associated with nasal, frontal, or other head resonances could come from percepts associated with internal head transmission paths. Although these paths are not linked to external acoustic radiation, they might have an impact on the overall sensation and monitoring of the voice, and provide useful internal references—that may well, however, differ from person to person.

Self-monitoring with the aid of external reflecting surfaces provides another method of voice control. One particular technique uses ellipsoid reflectors mounted on either side of the mouth so as to give preferential higher frequency feedback (Laukkanen et al., 2004). This approach does give measurable results and, for some singers, has been shown to lead to better vocal fold closure in terms of both rapidity and duration when electroglottographic/electrolaryngographic waveforms are examined. In practice Laukkanen et al. say that it may be of value for choral singers.

3. SINGING AND THE BRAIN

Specialized areas of the brain that, although differing in precise location from person to person (Rorden & Brett, 2000), correspond to essential aspects of speech production, language organization, and hearing have been progressively better defined and understood for over a hundred years. The first classical phase of this work gave particular prominence to the left hemisphere in regard to speech and language (Broca, 1861; Wernicke, 1874). The more recent advent of methods for the noninvasive detection of cortical activity has led to an enormous wealth of experimental results that link cortical areas and sensory and motor function and given a better understanding of the division of responsibilities between the left and right hemispheres with regard to the singing voice.

It is difficult for workers in this area to arrive at very clear-cut demonstrations of specialization partly because of the intrinsic interrelated complexities of cerebral information processing related to language, speech, and singing and partly because of the difficulty of defining tasks that enable clear contrasts to be made. One approach involves the study of speaking and singing where only one hemisphere is operating as the result of stroke. An interesting study involved only the left brain (Hébert, Racette, Gagnon, & Peretz, 2003) and here the abilities to sing and speak were comparable, showing that there is not a total division of function. Developmental studies where cortical function is not finally established provide another means of experimental control and one especially interesting result of this approach shows that, using cerebral blood flow measures, in the first two to three years of life, the right brain is likely to be dominant (Chiron et al., 1997); linking, by infererence, the age-associated development of laryngeal control, intonation, and prespeech sustained vocalization. Another experimental method involves controlling the complexity of the task. Chanting in a monotone and imitating a given melody both were found to be linked to a right hemisphere bias; but complex singing involving harmonization brought in a purely right hemisphere activity, indicating a real right brain singing specialization (Brown et al., 2004).

An especially clear experimental demonstration of right brain dominance in a singing task (Jeffries, Fritz, & Braun, 2003) made use of a familiar text that was both read and sung (Figure 13-3). Quite clear

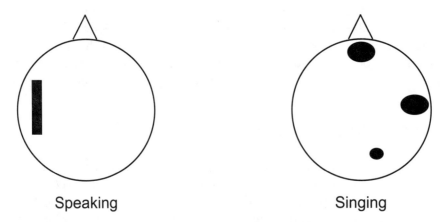

Speaking   Singing

Figure 13–3. Diagrammatic illustration of cortical activity when trained singers spoke the words of a very familiar song, on the left, and sang the same words to a familiar melody on the right (left hemisphere to the left in each diagram). These very simple sketches are based on in-depth work by K. J. Jeffries, J. B. Fritz, & A.R. Braun, (2003) *NeuroReport, 14*, 749–754.

increases in the activity of the right brain were found for singing as opposed to reading. It is beginning to appear that not only the perception of pitch and the physical structure of temporal organization are special to singing but that so also is the central processing by the brain of the production of song.

4. SINGING AND LANGUAGE

We hear different spoken languages as being both dissimilar from our own and as having their own rather special auditory characteristics. It seems logical in consequence to suppose that the use of voice in singing might be assisted preferentially by one language environment over another —both perhaps in the way that voice skills are acquired by the developing child and also by the way that they can be applied by the professional singer. Figure 13-4 gives an example of the ways in which speech sounds are organized in terms of their phonetic inventories for two exemplar languages: English, and Italian.

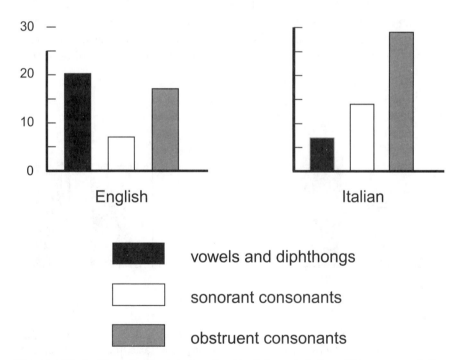

Figure 13–4. Phonetic inventories for English and Italian. This representation shows the number of sound types in each of three primary categories. Although it conveys the essential phonetic sound groupings for the two languages neither inventory corresponds to what we can hear in a casual appraisal of the overall "sound" of the two languages. The number of vowel categories is smaller and the number of obstruent consonants greater in Italian than it is for English, but the "sound stream" for Italian appears, informally, to be less broken up than English.

The difference is striking and counterintuitive. Italian has a smaller vowel inventory and a larger number of obstruent consonants than English. Ordinarily one would suppose that a larger proportion of obstruents in Italian would increase the number of occasions when voice is interrupted in fluent speaking and singing and, in consequence, reduce the "smooth flow" of voice production. This, however, is not the impression received when listening to fluent Italian. Another possible basis for the perception of voicing in fluent speech is shown in Figure 13-5. Here, the relative durations are shown for the time spent in producing voiced sounds and in producing no voice at all. If Italian owes its apparent smooth flow to the greater proportional use of voicing, then the Italian distribution should be associated with an appreciable difference between the voice and "no voice" percentages. There is, however, no marked difference between the two language samples in this respect (and indeed there is no marked difference found when the same analysis is applied to two- to three-minute native speaker samples of spoken French, German, Portuguese, American English, and Cantonese and Putongua).

A possible main source of the perceptual difference between the languages is shown in Figure 13-6 where the detailed use of voice in the same two recorded speech samples is analyzed. English in Figure 13-6 tends to have voiced consonantal durations that are much shorter than those found in Italian. Remembering that pitch is not readily heard for periodic sounds whose durations are less than about 30 milliseconds

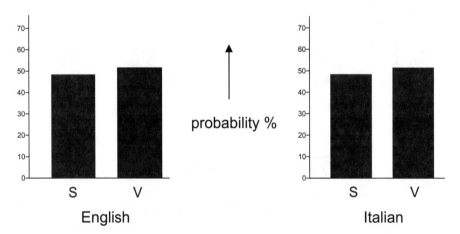

Figure 13–5. Relative durations of voiced sounds, **V**, and unvoiced sounds plus silence, **S**. The plots show the results of analyzing read texts; respectively for English and Italian. **S** represents the relative duration of the combination of all the silences together with all the voiceless fricatives. **V** represents the relative duration of all the voiced sounds in the read text. Voicing here is defined by the presence of vocal fold vibrational contact. Only two female speakers are involved here but very similar results are obtained from other speakers (both male and female and, in fact, other languages).

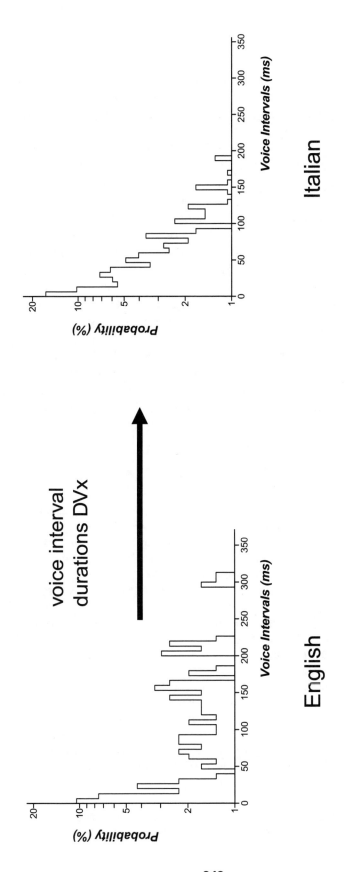

Figure 13–6. Voice interval distributions for two-minute samples of spoken English and spoken Italian. Although the overall relative durations of voicing in the two spoken language samples are essentially the same, the detailed use of voice timing, shown in this figure, in the two languages is very different. The voiced consonants of English tend to have much shorter durations than the voiced consonants in Italian. The ear of the listener can follow the pitch of the Italian consonants in running speech much more readily than is feasible for English. (These analyses are based on the use of two-channel recording derived from an omnidirectional pressure-sensitive microphone and an electrolaryngograph.)

243

(see Figure 13-1), one can see that the Italian distribution gives much better pitch carrying temporal representation for sound durations up to 90 milliseconds than the English distribution. Returning to Figure 13-4, the apparent paradox is explained when one realizes that many Italian obstruent consonants are increased in regard to their use of voice duration by the process of gemination (see, for example, Chapallaz, 1979). This enhancement of the probability of finding voice samples in running speech that enable pitch to be better defined for the consonantal range of sounds, is even greater for tone languages, such as Cantonese and Putonghua (Mandarin Chinese). It must be emphasized that, although these observations are very likely to stand the test of time, they are only the first indicators of much more important possible future developments. The child before birth, for example, is preferentially exposed to the sound of its mother's voice rather than to the voiceless sounds of its language environment, and it could be that this type of language difference is of crucial importance in the development of voice pitch processing ability, especially when mother-infant voice interaction takes place after birth. Similarly, to extend the speculation, contrastive communicative development in the first year of life may be facilitated in the tone language environment by the prior establishment of pitch perceptual skills, and these in turn may help in the development of the singing voice.

REFERENCES

Békésy, G. v., (1948). Vibration of the head in a sound field and its role in hearing by bone conduction. *Journal of the Acoustical Society of America*, *20*, 749-760.

Broca, P. (1861). Nouvelle observation d'aphémie produite par une lésion de la moitié postérieure des deuxième et troisième circonvolution frontales gauches. *Bulletin de la Société Anatomique*, *36*, 398-407.

Brown, S., Martinez, M. J., Hodges, D. A., Fox, P. T., & Parsons, L. M. (2004). The song system of the human brain. *Cognition Brain Research*, *20*, 363-375.

Cabrera, D., Davis, P., Barnes, J., Jacobs, M., & Bell, D. (2002). Recording the operatic voice for acoustic analysis. *Acoustics Australia*, *30*(3), 103-108.

Chapallaz, M. (1979). *The pronunciation of Italian: a practical introduction*. London, UK: Bell and Hyman.

Chiron, C., Jamaque, I., Nabout, R., Lounes, R., Syrota, A., & Dulac, O. (1997). The right brain is dominant in human infants. *Brain*, *120*, 1057-1065.

Chu, W. T., & Warnock, A. C. C. (2001, September). *Detailed directivity of sound fields around human talkers*. Research Report RR-104. Montreal, Canada: Institute for Research in Construction, National Research Council of Canada.

Dunn, H. K., & Farnsworth D. W. (1939), Exploration of pressure field around the human head during speech. *Journal of the Acoustical Society of America*, *10*, 184-199.

Fourcin, A., & West, J. (1973). Unpublished data. *Forehead to mastoid bone conduction frequency responses for eight subjects*.

Haas, H. (1951). Über den Einfluss eines Einfachechos auf die Hörsamkeit von Sprache. *Acustica, 1*, 49-58.

Hansen, M. O., & Stinson, M. R. (1998) Air conducted and body conducted sound produced by own voice. *Canadian Acoustics, 26*, 11-19.

Hart, T. J., Collier, R., & Cohen, A. (1990). *A perceptual study of intonation: An experimental phonetic approach.* Cambridge, UK: Cambridge University Press.

Hébert, S., Racette, A., Gagnon, L., & Peretz, I. (2003). Revisiting the disassociation between singing and speaking in expressive aphasia. *Brain, 126*, 1838-1850.

Howell, P., & Powell, D. J. (1984). Hearing your voice through bone and air: Implications for explaining stuttering behaviour from studies of normal speakers. *Journal of Fluency Disorders, 9*, 247-264.

Jeffries, K. J., Fritz J. B., & Braun, A. B. (2003). Words in melody: an H_2^{15} PET study of brain activation during singing and speaking. *NeuroReport, 14*, 749-754.

Klatt, D. H. (1973). Discrimination of fundamental frequency contours in synthetic speech: Implications for models of pitch perception, *Journal of the Acoustical Society of America, 53*, 8-16

Laukkanen, A. M., Mickelson, N. P., Laitala, M., Syrja, T., Salo, A., & Sihvo, M. (2004). Effects of HearFones on speaking and singing voice quality. *Journal of Voice, 18*(4), 475-487.

Litovsky, R. Y., Rakerd, B., Yin, T. C. T., & Hartmann, W. M. (1997). Psychophysical and physiological evidence for a precedence effect in the median sagittal plane. *Journal of Neurophysiology, 77*(4), 2223-2226.

Lombard, E. (1911). Le signe de l'elevation de la voix. *Annals Maladies Oreille Larynx, 37*, 101-119.

Moore, B. C. J., Glasberg, B. R., & Peters, R. W. (1985). Relative dominance of individual partials in determining the pitch of complex tones. *Journal of the Acoustical Society of America, 75*, 550-561.

Nelson, D. A., Stanton, M. E., & Freyman R. L. (1983). A general equation describing frequency discrimination as function of frequency and sensation level. *Journal of the Acoustical Society of America, 73*, 2117-2123.

Pörschmann C. (2000). Influences of bone conduction and air conduction on the sound of one's own voice. *Acustica, 86*, 1038-1045.

Rorden, C., & Brett, H. M. (2000). Stereotaxic display of human brain lesions. *Behavioural Neurology, 12*, 191-196.

Sohmer, H., Freeman, S., Geal-Dor, M., Adelman C., & Savion, I. (2000). Bone conduction experiments in humans—a fluid pathway from bone to ear. *Hearing Research, 146*, 81-88.

Vance, T. F. (1942). In E. G. Boring, *Sensation and perception in the history of experimental psychology* (p. 340). New York, NY: Appleton-Century-Crofts (original work published in 1914).

Weiss, W. (1993). The vanished Lombard effect. *Journal of the Acoustical Society of America, 93*, 2393-2394.

Wernicke, C. (1874). *Der Aphasische Symptomencomplex.* Breslau, Germany: Cohn and Weigert.

Wier, C. C., Jesteadt, W., & Green, D. M. (1977). Frequency discrimination as a function of frequency and sensation level. *Journal of the Acoustical Society of America, 61*, 178-184.

Chapter 14

WORKING WITH THE PROFESSIONAL SINGER

Janice Chapman

My work with professional singers tends to be with three distinct types of client.

- Those who have been my students for many years and attained their professional status during this time.
- Singers who have already achieved professional careers and have sought lessons from me at a later stage.
- Professional singers who have experienced vocal problems mid-career, some having been referred by an ENT surgeon or speech and language therapist.

MAINTENANCE OF MY OWN STUDENTS

The lifestyle of these singers is nearly always one of their prime challenges. They can be away from home for months at a time, and then when they return need to prepare for their next job (often in a hurry), while still recovering from their last spate of performances. In a typical lesson, we usually spend some time with a vocal debriefing from their last job before moving on to the next project. I usually find the opportunity to check them over physically while they are singing to make sure that all their vocal support systems are functioning efficiently, while listening for any sounds of mechanical unease in their voice production. If there are areas needing correction or "fine-tuning," this will be done using the basic model (see Chapter 1) as necessary. These singers usually are very self-aware and able to self-correct during their engagements away. Sometimes they call up for a telephone session and because our language is physiologic we often are able to diagnose and correct any problems as they occur, using a sort of checklist menu.

When I know a singer very well I sometimes can predict what he or she might be doing; for example, sometimes a singer might have a sensitivity to criticism aligned with a tendency to grip with the tongue root, especially when upset. It might only take a couple of adverse comments in a press review to provoke this particular problem. The corrective exercises are very easily accessed under these circumstances along with encouragement and reassurance if needed.

At all times, my work with singers at the top level must be tailored individually. In the past, I have traveled abroad to hear some of them and am able to give feedback as needed, but this sort of "service" is costly in many respects (money, energy, and time away from other students). However, it is highly satisfying as there is an implicit trust in the relationship born of many years of working together toward a common end, that is, their continuing improvement and professional advancement and "on site" corrections can be highly effective and valuable to the artist.

Gordon: A Case Study

Gordon is a baritone on the international operatic circuit. He comes for a checkup or to prepare new repertoire vocally whenever he is at home in London. He also works with two main repertoire coaches who deal with languages and musical/vocal issues. He has been studying with me for over 10 years. When we started, he was singing all over the country for very small fees, while still working in another industry during the day. Once his vocal technique was fully developed, his career went forward very quickly and he was "thrown in at the deep end" in a major opera house. During this time, I attended rehearsals and performances whenever possible to monitor his singing and to evaluate how he was sounding in the theatre. I feel that this was a very important part of working with him. He is highly intelligent and motivated and something of a perfectionist, which means that he constantly strives to improve his singing and his performances. If he has one fault, it is that he is inclined to meddle with things that are already right, sometimes

> making them complicated and less good as a result. We have dis-
> cussed this, and one of my jobs now in working with him is to help
> him maintain a healthy balance. Perhaps the most important part
> of my work for this client is to attend performances from time to
> time and give him good clear feedback.

PROFESSIONAL SINGERS MIDCAREER WHO CHANGE FROM ANOTHER TEACHER OR HAVE NOT HAD LESSONS WITH ANYONE FOR SOME TIME

Working with professional singers who have transferred from other
teachers or not had any recent lessons can be quite tricky. When these
singers first approach me for a consultation, I take a history and then try
to ascertain what changes they wish to make, and why they want my
help. I then ask them to sing.

During the consultation, I first will ensure that they are grounded
in their strengths by reflecting back to them their positive attributes,
before describing the areas where I think they may have room for
improvement. I then try to demonstrate how I might go about making
corrections to their singing, so that they can get a "feel" for me and my
methods of working. By the end of the consultation, I will have a "gut"
feeling about whether I want to take the singer on. It is based on a number of criteria:

1. If I feel that I have a reasonable chance of working successfully with
   a singer,
2. If I believe that there is a match in their potential and their ambi-
   tions, and
3. If I feel they will be able to authentically engage with me in the
   teaching/learning process.
4. If I have room in my studio to give them the time they might need.

I probably will offer them lessons (perhaps a short course of six sessions
followed by a mutual review). I then suggest that they go away and think
about whether or not they wish to take up my offer before committing
themselves. I will give them a tape or minidisk recording of their consultation so that they can evaluate after the event and then come to a deci-
sion without feeling pressured.

Nearly always with these singers there is an inadequately taught or
understood breathing/support issue at the root of their problems, which
may manifest itself as a phonation, resonance, or articulation defect.
Needless to say, it is "back to the model" yet again.

THE WORKING PROFESSIONAL SINGER IN TROUBLE

This sort of work is altogether more stressful and demanding. Although I might have heard this singer perform, I may not know him or her personally at all. It takes considerable courage for professional singers to first admit that they need help, and even more to seek it. If they are in vocal trouble, especially if a pathology has resulted, they will be feeling terrified and dispossessed of their talent. Every case must be treated individually, but nevertheless I find myself adhering to the basic teaching model in the way I address their vocal problems. My experience both as a singer and teacher has been that one of the main antidotes to terror lies in good vocal technique. Changes to vocal technique are made incrementally so that they are manageable both physically and psychologically. I find it important to use positive feedback and enthusiasm tempered with as much honesty as I judge the singer can cope with (usually in inverse proportions to their level of terror).

In extreme cases where basic changes are required, it may be necessary to ask a singer to cancel some immediate professional engagements. In the short term, it will be easier for them to accommodate new technical information and to have time to recover their performing persona. This must be balanced against their need to earn money and maintain their contracted performances. If the problems are superficial (not involving the core components), it usually is possible for the singer to continue performing while making technical changes.

IN GENERAL

When a singer has achieved a "connected up" state, it is possible for him or her to sing in what seems to the singer to be a rather workmanlike way, but their imagination, emotions, and musicality still carry their intentions to the listeners. Some of them seem to find it difficult to trust this process and they often make comments which reflect their feelings that "they aren't doing anything." I think that it has much to do with the full circle expressed in my teaching model of Primal Sound, through all the components, to the Performance and Artistry segment, which is in itself a "finessed primacy of utterance." As primal sound recruits whole networks of systems within the performer, this can affect posture, movement, and musical and dramatic expression, at the same time as the vocal utterance is taking place. Vocal technique becomes fully subservient to the performance/artistry activity, as it should. Simplicity within this "zone" is experienced by the performer, but after their struggle to attain all the parts of the picture, it is not surprising that they have trouble trusting it and need much reassurance.

GENERAL FITNESS AND "SINGER FITNESS"

"Ho-jo-to-ho! Four hours singing and once more round the ramparts! Phew!" Copyright Simon Pearsall, 2005.

There is no question that it is necessary for performers to be as physically fit as possible. Aerobic fitness and general core stability (strength and endurance) are very important and most singers I work with pay attention to their general condition. I recommend fast walking, running, swimming, and regular visits to the gym, but do not advocate the use of weights or stomach-cruncher exercises which would be likely to produce "six-pack" muscles. The holistic approach to singing includes full body fitness. Care should be taken not to overwork the pectoralis major and upper trapezius muscle sets. However, the muscles of the back and the lower back (latissimus dorsi, the lower trapezius, and the deep abdominal muscles) can be safely strengthened. General physical fitness strengthens the immune system and helps stave off illness, and without wanting singers to become hypochondriacs, they certainly need to treat themselves as "walking musical instruments." For further information on health issues including practical advice on pharmacology, I recommend *Vocal*

Health and Pedagogy by Robert Thayer Sataloff, published by Singular Publishing Group. "Singer fitness" is what the rest of this book is about. A fully "connected up" singer who sings every day will maintain "singer fitness" just by singing well. Building this commodity in young/developing or disconnected singers is part of the responsibility of singing teachers.

SINGERS' WEIGHT

There also is the question of the weight of singers. Although I believe that the public goes to the opera and the concert hall to hear wonderful singing and many of the great voices come in large packages, I do feel strongly that all singers, including those with large bodies, need to be fit.

A TYPICAL "M.O.T. (Vehicle Road-Worthiness Test) AND OIL CHANGE" LESSON FOR AN ELITE SINGER

After a brief warm-up using rolled "rr"s and breath release exercises, I will ask the singer what he or she wants from the session. If they have specific areas of technical work they wish to address, then we will concentrate on some exercises that are pertinent to the relevant area of their vocal technique. When I have had a long relationship with a singer, we have built up a sort of code language, which can shortcut this process. Quite often singers prefer to work on their current repertoire but ask me to listen for the particular problem they are concerned about. If there has been a long gap between lessons (say 2 months or more), I also will be listening to them carefully monitoring for the signs of any vocal mannerisms or habits, which might be creeping into their singing, and of which they themselves are unaware. I will be as tactful as possible in making my own suggestions for improvements.

Another area of my work might be to help a singer cope with moving between the different types of role within their fach. An example would be for a lyric tenor who has been singing Rodolpho in "La Boheme," and then moves on to his next engagement which might be Manrico in "Il Trovatore." The vocal setup for these two roles is different and one or two lessons are needed to "reset" the fine tuning of the vocal instrument. Moving between languages also can be tricky. Singers often comment that singing a lot in English can upset their vocal setting. They often do not have the time they need between engagements, and I advise them to use the basic Italian "arie antiche" to revisit their optimal vocal setup whenever possible.

Generally speaking, my teaching model is revisited in all its aspects but with fine tuning and finesse. These singers also like to discuss with me some of the feedback they have from conductors and coaches and check out their responses for validity.

PSYCHOLOGY OF WORKING WITH THE "HIGH-FLYER" PROFESSIONAL SINGER

When elite singers come to a vocal studio for a session, they can feel that they are putting themselves into a position of lesser power. This requires much courage and trust on their part, and they often feel uncomfortably vulnerable in this situation. As a singer myself, I remember well this sort of dichotomy. I needed to feel supremely confident in order to do my job on the operatic stage, but also be capable of becoming a "student" in order to improve. This required an opening up to the vulnerability of being corrected. This subject is explored more fully in Chapters 9 and 10.

There also is a misbelief that the elite singers know how good they are and do not need to be told. Even though they appear to be very confident in their abilities, many are not and often need a list of what seems to be so obvious, that is, their strengths, before a teacher tackles any areas needing improvement.

Every singer is different and so is every teacher. It is important for both parties to feel that they are trusted within their working relationship. This is especially important at the elite level. Sometimes when a singer is resistant to change, it can mean that he or she is not emotionally ready to cope with it at that point in time. I have experienced this many times, and especially when the singer is under performance pressure, I have found that the best way to deal with it is to be prepared to back off and revisit the problem at a later time. Having flagged it helps prepare the way for subsequent change.

ACCOMPANISTS AND COACHES

I have a policy of employing very good pianists/accompanists/repetiteurs in my studio each day. Not only are they supportive in the studio, but they develop the sort of listening and diagnostic skills that can help them coach singers more effectively. It is especially useful for advanced singers to employ coaches who are already alert to a particular way of working with voice. When they have access to the same vocal language, they can make effective shortcuts. I also enjoy the positive energy coming from the pianist during a singing lesson. Singers can listen to me talking about something I feel they need to change, then just raise an eyebrow toward the pianist for confirmation. Here, I value the contributions that can be made by the pianists as they often confirm the point for the singer but can add the bonus of something else from their experience as an instrumentalist.

When I teach, I constantly consult my own "inner singer" on a subconscious level (see Chapter 10). Some vocal and repertoire coaches also have experience of their own "inner singer" to call on when coaching. This interior knowledge makes their work with singers more effective.

TRAVELING TO HEAR SINGERS IN PERFORMANCE

I undertake to do this whenever possible. The experience of hearing and seeing a singer in a theatre or concert hall performance can be very different from that contained within the voice studio, and the teacher gets a holistic view of the product they work with. I find this experience to be very important indeed, especially in judging where a singer is in his or her development, what needs further attention, and how he or she is coping psychologically, vocally, and physically with the stresses and strains of a very demanding professional life.

VISITING OLD REPERTOIRE

When a singer has changed vocal technique, especially if those changes involve the breath/support cycle, he or she probably will need to revisit all the old repertoire and make vocal changes within that particular music. Sometimes old repertoire can carry not only inefficient muscle patterns for technical reasons, but also the singer can be carrying a memory of fear or anxiety with that particular piece of music.

Fear, in my experience, needs to be named and consciously addressed by the singer, with the teacher's support. This subject is covered in more detail in Chapters 9 and 10 (The Teaching and Learning Partnership). For the singer, unrecognized fear can feel like panic and can become vocally debilitating. Merely naming and confronting fear may seem to be superficial, but sometimes this is all that is required. Music has great power over the psyche with strong links into the feelings of well-being for the singer. It can be evocative in a similar way to the sense of smell, and the presence of fear attached to particular repertoire is common in singers.

Not only does a singer need a rock-solid vocal technique, he also needs to perceive that he owns it. I believe that singers need to have knowledge about their instrument and the way it functions and behaves, which allows them to cope in times of stress and to make their own diagnosis and self-correction. When singers are away from their supporting home team of coach, teacher, therapist, and so forth, it is valuable for them to have at their disposal a sort of menu of what might go wrong and how to deal with any vocal problems or anomalies. It is easy to pick up a telephone and chat with a teacher (even in the middle of the night) about a vocal glitch, and when there is a common language between teacher and singer, the telephone lesson can be quite effective as a short-term solution. Obviously, they arrange to have an "MOT and oil change" lesson as soon as they are back in the country. Their physical health and their emotional state come into the equation, and the more vocal self-knowledge they have the better.

TO "MARK" OR NOT TO "MARK," THAT IS THE QUESTION

One of the biggest skills a singer learns is how to survive the rigors of the rehearsal period prior to performances. Tiredness of body, mind, and voice are major factors in the tricky negotiation of the preperformance period and no matter how much teachers try to warn young singers about this minefield, they do have to experience it for themselves before they realize what they are up against. One of the strategies commonly used especially during opera rehearsals is "marking." But how to do it safely is the question.

In rehearsal, what is required is that the singer is able to indicate to her colleagues, the conductor, the producer, and the repetiteurs or orchestra exactly how she intends to perform vocally and dramatically but without incurring wear and tear on the vocal folds. This means being able to "fake" the singing while not compromising the intonation, rhythm, phrasing, and dramatic intent.

The technical problems with "marking" are to do with the inevitable reduction in abdominal support and compromise in breathing patterns, which can easily occur when the voicing is lighter than usual, that is, the lighter the vocal attack, the less likely the body is to work well, except in very experienced singers who have probably found out the hard way. My advice to young singers about marking is unequivocal "You are not permitted to 'mark' in rehearsals unless you use full support." They usually come back to me with, "If I'm going to use full support then I might just as well sing out, as it's just as tiring." And this, in my view, is the crux of the issue. "Marking" at pitch must be fully "on the body" in just the same way as singing out fully. The other way to lighten the load is to sing the high-lying passages down the octave, but once again on the support. Once the singer's body is well tuned to his vocal tasks, it becomes easier to use "marking" safely and efficiently and in a way that does serve the purpose of lightening the vocal loading.

An easy way to help singers find this balance of abdominal support and lightened vocal load is to employ the "puffy cheeks" technique at the start of phrases when marking.

ADVANCED "TWEAKING"

Up-and-coming singers often ask why they need to see a vocal coach or singing teacher once they are underway in their careers. The very idea of needing a singing teacher when one is as famous as Pavarotti seems strange, but it is only the same as the top golf professional who is accompanied to matches by his trusted coach, who no doubt watches out for any signs of mannerism or change which might need early detection and "tweaking" back into line.

It is this sort of process that takes place in the studios of the singing teachers who work with elite professional singers. Very rarely is there need for major change. These singers know their own voices well and have very good interior knowledge of how they do it. But their ears and eyes usually are not at their own disposal during performances.

Here is a short list of the most common "tweaks."

1. *Postural asymmetry.* Singers slip very easily into physical asymmetry, slightly leaning their head toward their favorite shoulder. The reason for this is probably that a certain amount of aural feedback might be coming from this subtle change of posture. Remedial action involves awareness and working with a mirror.

2. *Focus of tone in the upper passagio.* It is very easy to slip into a spread tone in the upper passagio when not monitored by someone else. I use the French /y/ exercise (see exercise in Appendix 1).

3. *Articulatory mannerisms.* Singers are always being exhorted to "spit out the text" so that the words may be heard at the back of the theatre or concert hall. In trying to oblige, they easily can overuse the jaw (especially if they are English or German speakers). This fault needs to be nipped in the bud. The articulatory clarity so sought by producers and music staff is the product of a very fine interaction between the tongue, lips, teeth, and the vocal tract. (See Chapter 7 on Articulation.)

4. *Head/neck alignment.* The workload of the operatic voice sometimes pulls the neck forward producing a "singers' hump" at the level of cervical vertebrae 6 to 7. If the problem is not serious, I make some small adjustments to a singer's alignment, but when necessary I will refer them to an appropriate professional (physiotherapist, osteopath, or massage therapist).

5. *Loss of support in the lower middle voice.* When a singer is physically exhausted, she may lose her support under the lower middle

register. The tone will lose strength and focus, and if left unattended, this problem can develop into wide and unstable vibrato, or sometimes constriction of the root of the tongue, affecting both tonal clarity and audibility of both voice and articulation.

> **Professional singers are people who have committed to a difficult and often treacherously vulnerable lifestyle. They need and deserve support from their teachers and coaches and often it is the "positive energy" that has to be rekindled in a singing lesson. In the face of the demands made by the professional life, described in Chapters 9 and 10 by many of the singers in the study, singing teachers carry a great responsibility when they interact as a buffer between the hostility of the outside world and the sensitivity of the artist. Teachers deserve to feel proud when their students achieve success.**

REFERENCE

Sataloff, R. T. (1998). *Vocal health and pedagogy.* San Diego, CA: Singular Publishing Group.

Chapter 15

FROM PERFORMER TO PEDAGOGUE: A MULTIDISCIPLINARY ROUTE

Janice Chapman

What I set out to write at the beginning of this book is not quite what I ended up with. It has been a truly creative process, and although the writing itself was sometimes challenging and difficult, it was also enormously educative, exciting, and liberating to tease out and quantify what it is that I really do and why. The input from my colleagues has been pivotal for me—it has given me a chance for some further awakenings, especially in relation to the holistic nature of singing and teaching, and I have found that my methodology in the studio has been subtly changing as a result. Some of my murky past as a singer now seems to make more sense and my love of singing and teaching is put into a new perspective. I have offered my pedagogy in its present condition (warts and all), which can be used and explored creatively, criticized, and undoubtedly changed as needed.

One of the major issues to emerge for me from this writing process has been my concern for the future of our singing/teaching profession. In-service training and development programs are essential, especially for teachers who have changed profession, that is, from performer to pedagogue. The current system is based on a past model, which has been adapted but I believe not yet sufficiently changed to meet today's needs. A brief historical perspective is offered by Gordon Stewart, who writes:

> Exactly what the training of singers was in the past, and how it achieved its successes without the benefit of later scientific knowledge, is a project for major research. It might also reveal how many failures there were, using the same teaching methods. The best old teachers (Porpora, Lamperti, and such) must have had finely tuned ears, which provided a constant monitoring system. It was most likely combined with various rules of thumb (probably taking the form of imagery like *inhalare la voce*, and *appoggio*) and enforced with the strict discipline of never allowing a bad sound to go unremarked. Praise may well have played little part in the training, if there is a general truth behind the story of the castrato Cafarelli, who was confined to one page of exercises for a period of years, and never told what they were about, or how he was doing. It's known that teachers used sticks, as in dancing classes, to correct mistakes, probably of posture—in circumstances where modern teachers would use a hands-on approach. One suspects that they had other uses.
>
> It was normal for teachers to put their pupils under contract, not collecting money from them until they started earning. This must have sharpened the need to hand-pick pupils and get things right, and it probably affected the day-to-day working. It was a practice that continued into the 20th century: Benjamino Gigli is supposed to have been one of the last of these apprenticeship contract pupils. Who knows whether it still exists?
>
> Adopting your pupil was possible, and being regarded as a parent was quite common. Or a deputy one—*in loco parentis*. Until modern music colleges came to be the norm, even conservatoire students lived in the house belonging to their teachers, and could come downstairs for a lesson after a shout from a window.
>
> It seems very possible that the tradition of classical singing—what is sometimes called *bel canto*, a term which was invented, probably for commercial reasons, in the latter part of the 19th century—must owe its roots to the castrato voice. This was the voice which initially had serious training, uninterrupted by adolescent changes in muscles and psychology. Women weren't allowed to sing in church, and for years not in proper opera. A commentator in 1663 specified what a woman needed for a career: beauty, rich clothes, attractive singing, appropriate acting—in that order—rather than dazzling technical feats.
>
> Castration wasn't as fearsomely abhorrent in the 17th century as it is now—apparently the sexual activity that it was likely to exclude wasn't placed as high on the lists of human achievement—and deciding on it could be part of the teacher's responsibility—some

teachers paid for their pupils to be castrated. A conservative estimate in Rome in 1694 put the number of castrati earning a living at something like a hundred.

How the musculature worked for grown men with boys' voices isn't easy to get from books and not much castration goes on nowadays in our profession to enable research in this area. Training was exhaustive, and from early in the 17th century included trills and coloratura and practice before a mirror.

Descriptions of singing from that time on talk about the tone, the brilliance of the divisions (his or her throat was very flexible, they said), and the speed and accuracy of the shakes or trills. Lengthy breathing patterns were hugely admired, and probably still are.

Interpreting the contemporary literature, both from teachers and from commentators, probably involves what I would call sympathetic conjecture and imagination. (Personal communication, Gordon Stewart, 2005).

THE USE OF IMAGERY

For many years, singing teachers have used visual images as a way of helping singers use their instrument. Who has not had a singing lesson where they were given such instruction as "Imagine you are a ballet dancer on points" (when trying to sing high notes)? Indeed, one of my students told me that a previous teacher had explained how to sing high notes in the following terms. "Imagine you are walking across a bridge made of clingfilm (plastic wrap) in very high stiletto heels." This could be interpreted as singing high notes in a light and effortless way, but it also could easily produce the opposite effect to that desired by creating fear and constriction in the vocal tract. A singer needs to remain in good contact with the ground when singing high pitches and produce excellent airflow from well-recruited abdominal muscles (difficult when teetering on stiletto heels on clingfilm!). Images such as this, which are not physiologically based, can be interpreted by a student in many ways.

Another type of imagery commonly used has been "sniff a rose" (on inhalation, or as you are about to sing). With this type of imagery, the body may respond in an appropriate way to bring about a diaphragmatic intake of air, simultaneous onset of tone, and the opening/excitation of the nasopharynx. When such an instruction emanates from the teacher's understanding of the physiologic responses to "sniff a rose," the image may be powerful and unambiguous. If appropriate, the teacher then may choose to share this understanding to empower the student.

Here is an example of imagery based on body experience: "Imagine you are suppressing a giggle." The reality (from the Estill retraction figure) is that the vocal tract widens and the false folds retract creating a cleaner and fuller sound. With the assistance of the flexible nasoendoscope it has been possible to verify this "reality." The process follows approximately like this:

- The singer's imagination is used to find the sensation.
- The teacher reinforces that the sound quality is better.
- The singer registers the changes, both kinesthetic and aural.
- The singer practices the maneuver.
- Added to this is a visual stimulus in the Estill system, of holding the hands together with fingers interlocked and retracting the thumbs. Singers and teachers use this visual stimulus to save time.
- The muscle memory takes over from the conscious control and automaticity kicks in.

There is much to be said for the creative and skillful use of imagery in the teaching of singing. Imagery can be very useful if it is consistent with the science and the situation, the receptiveness of the student, and if it is very skillfully applied. However, if it is unskillful and stands as a substitute for informed teaching, I feel that it can be ambiguous, confusing, or even destructive for the student.

With an understanding of the vocal machinery (the whole body not just the vocal tract), different analogies are used to illuminate and enliven the learning. The diagnoses of vocal problems and faults can be much more precise and the recipe for their correction much easier to communicate. I do not use much scientific language in the studio. If a singer asks for an explanation of why a corrective instruction works, I try to explain in a way I think meaningful to the student, or I might encourage them to take the next available Estill course, Vocal Profile Analysis course, or another very useful legacy from our speech therapy colleagues "Accent Method" course. I also recommend Meribeth Bunch's book, *The Dynamics of the Singing Voice*, which is both accurate and easy to understand, *The Science of the Singing Voice* by Johann Sundberg, and *Singing—the Mechanism and the Technic* by William Vennard. (Revised ed., Carl Fischer, 1967). Two newer texts I have found helpful are *Respiratory Function in Singing—A Primer for Singers and Singing Teachers* by Thomas J. Hixon and *What Every Singer Needs to Know About the Body* by Malde, Allen, and Zeller.

THE ESTILL VOICECRAFT SYSTEM

The Voice Research Society and the British Voice Association brought the American researcher Jo Estill to London a number of times to give courses and workshops.

Jo Estill was first a singer and a singing teacher, and then in her middle age she became a researcher while doing a master's degree at Syracuse University, in the United States. With her own interior knowledge as a singer and using the scientific tools around her, she was able to develop a system of gaining relative isolation of the various moving parts of the vocal tract and exercising independent control over them, for example, raising and lowering the larynx (something every singer knows how to do on a subconscious level), opening and closing the velar port (the door to the nose), using the vocal folds on the thick edge or the thin edge, and closing and opening the cricothyroid visor to raise and lower pitch. In all, she has developed and researched a practical system that she called "Compulsory Figures," treating the practice of these individual exercises in the same way as skaters do their compulsory figures in preparation for putting them all together in performance. In the same way as the skaters' figures lead to better artistic performance in their free skating programs, so do the Estill figures lead to a much greater freedom and flexibility in the demanding work of the singer and actor.

In my opinion the Voicecraft system has some limitations particularly in terms of use of abdominal support for the breath flow. Personally, I am doubtful about some of the uses of "anchoring" (consciously engaging specific muscles in the neck and torso prior to singing) for classical singing, but have found that my own breathing/support/postural alignment paradigm (see Chapter 3, Postural Alignment and Chapter 4, Breathing and Support) works extremely well when underpinning the Estill system figures.

SCIENCE AND TECHNOLOGY

During the past 15 years, I have had the opportunity to work at the National Voice Centre, University of Sydney, and I also have spent time in the voice laboratories at the Groningen University in Holland, University College London, and at the University of York. This experience has brought me into contact with current technology including real-time spectrum analysis programs for analyzing vocal signals, which I think may become standard equipment in the singing studio of the 21st century. These programs are able to give singers and teachers much visual information about certain aspects of their singing, for example, the acoustic patterns of the vowels, the vibrato rate and amplitude, the presence or absence of the singer's formant, and much more. I feel that the next generation of highly computer-literate singers probably will be able to use these systems to advantage. My own ears, however, tell me things about someone's singing that do not appear at all on the screen. I feel interested and excited when a voice scientist comes into my studio with this equipment and hope that in the future the programs will improve to a point where they offer singing teachers and singers more than they can at present. However, in my opinion, you cannot learn to sing by looking at a screen. The teacher's whole craft is required to make changes to a vocal technique, which could then be fed back to the student's eyes via the computer program for affirmation.

There also is a problem with the limited time in the studio. One hour for a singing lesson passes all too quickly and, for me, using the technology would require much more time. However, many university and conservatorium voice departments have access to the latest computer technology in their voice laboratories. Students are encouraged to use the facilities and, for them, it can be a natural extension of the computer games they have grown up with. Certainly, I belong to a generation of teachers for whom the whole prospect of dealing with such a fast growing technology is daunting; however, the student singers and some of the teachers exposed to these facilities are excited and enthusiastic and possibly will help encourage a new generation of computer-wizard singing teachers.

However, I know that these tools will never replace the finely tuned ears of an expert teacher. So much of the art of teaching is dependent on the personal interaction between teacher and student, and singing is such a holistic expression that technology cannot cope with its magnitude. Machinery can only ever be a tool as good as the hands that hold it.

My goal is to enable singers to develop and use their vocal technique in a way that serves music through the art of singing. Vocal technique is never an end in itself but, at its best, becomes subconscious and fully in the service of the artistic imagination of the performer. Even when things are going really well, there is always the security in the background of the singer's consciousness that should things go wrong they will be able to get help or sort it out for themselves.

However, there are questions we must ask ourselves. As singing teachers in the 21st century have we not a responsibility and a duty to take on board the fact that our art of teaching is now underpinned by a relatively new and exciting science? It will be many years before there is a body of knowledge that is unchallengeable. For example, I feel personally critical of many of the research studies that are being undertaken using singers described as "trained." Such a vague generic term is meaningless, and to my mind, the results and conclusions of such research must also be questionable. In 2000, Meribeth Bunch and I produced a paper published in the *Journal of Voice* entitled, "Taxonomy of Singers Used as Subjects in Scientific Research" where we suggested a system where scientific research related to singing could be based on a quantifiable singing standard.

A MULTIDISCIPLINARY APPROACH TO SINGING AND TEACHING SINGING

I believe that one of the major factors shaping the future of singing and the teaching of singing is the emergence of multidisciplinary education in voice. Medicine, science, therapies, and performance in both spoken and sung voice all have input into the general pool of knowledge. Although each discipline has developed new knowledge in its specific field, it is the interaction between the disciplines that has changed the way we think about, understand, use, evaluate, and work with voice.

In the 21st century, singing teachers no longer have to work in isolation. Other professions with an interest in voice are able to provide information and support to the teacher as well as working with the student directly should the teacher wish to refer them. If asked to list other professions who could help them, most singing teachers immediately think of the staff of a typical voice clinic, which would involve laryngologists and speech and language therapists. However, in a truly multidisciplinary team, the input of other manual therapists such as physiotherapists, massage therapists, and osteopaths is seen as increasingly valuable in the management of vocal problems. In some cases, referral to psychotherapists, psychologists, and counselors also can greatly assist overall vocal management.

My ideal multidisciplinary team (in no particular order) would consist of:

- Otolaryngologist
- Speech and language therapist
- Manual therapists (physiotherapist, massage therapist, osteopath)
- Singing teacher
- Psychotherapist, counselor, hypnotherapist, psychiatrist, psychologist
- Music coach
- Repertoire and language coach
- Movement and/or drama teacher

The history of the multidisciplinary movement in the United Kingdom is part of my own story. In 1985, The Voice Research Society, a strange hybrid group made up of assorted voice professionals was formed in the living room of an otolaryngologist in South London. The first committee included laryngologists, singers and singing teachers, speech and language therapists, voice and drama teachers, and an acoustic scientist.

For the first year the meetings were semichaotic—because of the talking. It was tremendously exciting to find a whole world of knowledge *about our mutual interest opening up from different directions, sometimes using peculiar terminology and with different emphases, but with **voice** as the central theme.*

Awareness of the different disciplines and their terminologies was a starting point in setting up one of the first multidisciplinary symposia in London in 1986. In advance of this meeting, I was asked to do a small study and write a paper on terminology used by the singing teachers. The brief was, "find out what words they use and what they think they mean by these words." In my state of blissful naiveté, I thought that this would be easy and set about the task with great enthusiasm. Fortunately, I was due to attend a conference of singing teachers and produced a questionnaire that could be handed out and filled in on the spot during the conference. This way I managed to trap a good-sized sample. The paper was duly presented and published in the Conference Proceedings and in a subsequent magazine issue of the Association of Teachers of Singing. The outcome was that a list now existed of the most common descriptions and their definitions which could be referred to by other professions to help translate English type "singing teacher" language.

Others from the different professions also have made presentations on their terminologies, but of course this was only a starting point for the sharing of knowledge between us. At this stage, our awareness of each other as potential sources of education was very new in the United Kingdom, and what we could contribute was unknown territory too. I was encouraged to attend international multidisciplinary meetings such as the "Care of the Professional Voice" in Philadelphia and felt quite overwhelmed at first by the barrage of information being delivered from the podium. At first I thought that everything being presented was fact. Later, it appeared that some of it was not, that is, that I had to learn enough to be able to sift out the wheat from the chaff. Growing up in Australia, I had been educated as a typical 1950s female, namely, the arts plus office skills and no sciences. I was, therefore, quite lost when anything even vaguely mathematical or scientific appeared and the world of acoustics was a total nightmare. The otolaryngologist, Tom Harris, kindly and wisely gave me good advice —"Janice, just sit there—don't even try to understand everything at this stage, but let it wash over and into you. Later on some of it will start to make sense." He was right but it took effort as well as time.

Two or three years into this process, we had the great Japanese surgeon and voice researcher, Minoru Hirano in London to give an address at Guy's Hospital. At this stage, I was helping on the committee of the Voice Research Society and for this reason had to attend what I would not have thought initially was a meeting for me. Although the subject was microsurgery and the gathering almost entirely doctors, I found that I understood what he was saying and was enrap-

tured by seeing his wonderful slides of the vocal fold physiology. He was showing very clearly why, in operating on the vocal folds to remove a nodule, that they should not be stripped of their mucosal epithelium by surgeons (still common practice for the correction of vocal nodules and polyps in the 1980s), but demonstrating how the vocal folds healed easily and recovered their full usage when only the superficial layers were cut during the operation. This knowledge was crucial for me to have in the care of the professional singer, and his presentation was so clear. I had the opportunity to speak with him later at a dinner and thanked him for presenting in a way that allowed a singing teacher to understand. He told me that he had a great teacher as professor when he was a medical student who had given him the advice, "When you have a choice of words, always use the simplest one": advice he had followed all his life. He loved to sing himself and had a tenor voice of quality. In the absence of anyone who could play the piano, I ended up busking an accompaniment to "Santa Lucia" for him (poor man!).

Although much has been done toward standardizing terminology both within and between professions, many problems still are not solved. Debate still rages about such terms as "support" and "registers," and will continue to do so for years to come. There also is an international factor in this as the terminology we use in the United Kingdom may perhaps be different from that in the United States or Sweden, for example.

After five years The Voice Research Society evolved into its present form, The British Voice Association. Since that time there have been courses, one-day workshops, annual symposia, lectures, and conferences on a wide variety of voice-related topics such as "The effects of the hormonal cycle on the female voice" to "Safe singing in pop and rock styles." This cross-fertilization has given all the disciplines a wider and more comprehensive understanding of voice, its function, and care, while educating individuals within the various disciplines. The medical and therapy professions have reported that they too have learned much from the interaction with the performing professions, for example, "A singer's view of surviving a vocal crisis," and "Practical strategies for coping with eight shows a week on the West End stage."

Special interest subgroups have been formed, for example, one of the early initiatives was a Voice Care Network for school teachers run by Roz and David Comins, which became a separate organization. Others arose from our Estill Voicecraft workshops and operate in close association with the BVA.

Through the growth of the multidisciplinary associations, there have been changes in the way all the related professions approach voice training and care. This process has been evolving over the last 15 years and has influenced my own teaching in many ways.

Harriet: A Case Study

Harriet, a young soprano, came for a consultation after attending a BVA multidisciplinary workshop on breathing and support. She had been studying singing under a number of teachers over a period of about seven years and was in a state of confusion. My vocal diagnosis was that she had resonance and articulatory deficiencies, inadequate posture, and breathing and support problems resulting in compensatory use of the tongue root. She was singing habitually with pressed phonation and constriction. Following an initial series of sessions concentrating on the core components of the model, she mentioned that she was "tongue tied" and asked if it could be affecting her singing. Spoken vowels were clear and normal but resonance on sung vowels was greatly disturbed. On examination of her tongue, she could not protrude it past her bottom lip and indeed the tongue bifurcated on protrusion attempts. I agreed with her that this adversely impact her singing and referred her to an otolaryngologist for help.

We continued to work on the core components of the model while she was waiting for a frenulum release operation. This included work on Accent Method breathing and postural realignment. After the surgery, there was an immediate improvement in both resonance and ease of singing. Tongue exercises were instigated under the supervision of a speech and language therapist to encourage her newfound flexibility into full use. These exercises were modified for use into her singing voice. By now, her core components were functioning well and it was possible to address resonance issues directly. It took a few months for her to process this new kinesthetic experience of singing. Her joy in singing and her new connection to her vocal talent has been most satisfying and has led to a flowering of new skills in all areas of her vocalization. It would have been impossible for this singer to achieve these results without the input from a multidisciplinary team working in close consultation.

Stuart: A Case Study

I was approached by a colleague who was involved in music education for a London borough. She described one of her staff as a "very unhappy young man who was seemingly bereft of his singing voice." He arranged to come for a consultation.

He had fallen in love with singing while a teenager at high school and sung as a bass at the early age of 16, gaining much from his natural talent and the attention he received as a result of being able to make such a good sound so young. Within his family, there had been a cultural pressure to be "macho" and singing was viewed with disdain as being "for nancy-boys." In defiance of pressure to take up a "man's" job, he got a place at a music college and commenced his study. Not surprisingly, he failed to thrive and after two years dropped out, with his singing voice clearly mirroring his intense unhappiness.

The story so far was not presented at the first consultation: what was, presented was, "I don't know if I am a tenor or a bass," "My throat hurts when I sing," "I feel desperate to find myself as a person." It had been 10 years since he had left college and in this time he had worked in the computer technology field where he was able to utilize his formidable intellect. He had married and had two children, undertaken a course of psychotherapy, and more recently taken on the role of house-husband and child carer while also teaching singing and working part time in education. His wife had a good job and was fully supportive of his efforts to regain his ability to sing himself.

At the consultation I decided that I would try to help even though there was not much evidence of vocal talent at that stage. His pain and desperation convinced me to give it a try. I could not start him off immediately as I was going to be away for a few weeks and so recommended that he see a physiotherapist who I knew was an absolute ace at vocal manual therapy. By the time I got back and we had our first singing lesson, Stuart had been three times to see the physiotherapist, who had begun a process of manually loosening up the strap muscles which were holding the larynx very high and tight. These sessions were described by Stuart as causing him to weep—not because of the pain so much as because of the feelings that were released as the muscles loosened up.

I asked him if he felt he needed to go back into psychotherapy, but he felt that he could handle this process. He was writing journals throughout and these served as a sort of therapeutic outpouring. The effect on his voice was quite staggering; as constriction eased over the weeks, the voice got deeper and the fundamental frequency and timbre more basslike. If he had had a stressful week, his vocal timbre would revert, to sound more like a dysfunctional tenor. After a few months where Stuart juggled singing lessons and manual therapy sessions, his voice became increasingly more settled into a baritone with a nice low extension into the bass range.

My method of teaching him was to do only what I felt he could deal with at any given time—two steps forward and one back quite often, but overall following the model as described in Chapter 1.

Stuart's speaking voice has dropped and become naturally richer in harmonics throughout this process. I had considered suggesting speech therapy for him, but there were financial limitations. As it turned out, his speaking voice improved in tandem along with his singing. He has begun to sing small "gigs" to get some performing experience and I believe he probably will make a singing career. There is a big talent there, which was invisible at the start. The psychotherapy he had already undergone had paved the way for his vocal development to take place, and the manual therapy, which is ongoing but not so frequent, in tandem with the singing lessons were all part of the whole process of learning. He now is ready to have some repertoire coaching sessions and is accepting small local engagements to get himself back into the pleasure of performing.

Twenty years ago, I would have tried to deal with these two young singers on my own, maybe even with some limited success. But by knowing that the responsibility for their care could be shared with experts in related fields, I feel that I have been able to do more for them in a holistic way.

SINGING: FULL CIRCLE

In Chapter 1, I described singing as "emotional musical vocalization with or without text," but it is so much more than that. We, as human animals, have begun to lose touch with just how important this part of our human expression is. Placing the term "classical" in front of the word "singing" can have the effect of distancing people from something that has become an activity for the "few" or the "elite." The recording industry is guilty of helping to make it a perfectionist art form bearing little resemblance to its real power and value in society—communicating ideas and passions and music through the medium of another human or group of humans. It is a very big idea: that singing enhances and balances lives and can be so powerful a force that people without it feel bereft and diminished.

Singing is not a cultural additive. It is a birthright we are in danger of losing or devaluing. It is part of every known human culture and at best has the power to change lives. It can become a rare and wonderful art form, and at the same time, it also can be a way of drawing commu-

nities together towards a common goal (for example, at sporting fix-
tures, in churches, and at pop concerts). Our children and grandchildren
deserve to have this part of their heritage kept intact. Educators need to
recognize its importance.

> **My goal has been to raise awareness of the primal nature of
> this very basic human communication, and offer explana-
> tions leading to a better understanding of the connections
> between this primal activity and its highly finessed art forms.
> In the journey undertaken in writing this vocal pedagogy,
> I personally have gained much and enjoyed every facet of
> the experience. I sincerely thank my fellow travelers, contrib-
> utors, and readers.**

REFERENCES

Bunch, M. (1997). *The dynamics of the singing voice.* Wien, Germany: Springer-
   Verlag.
Bunch, M., & Chapman, J. (2000). Taxonomy of singers used as subjects in sci-
   entific research. *Journal of Voice, 14*(3), 363–369.
Hixon, T. J. (2006). *Respiratory function in singing—A primer for singers and
   singing teachers.* Tucson, AZ: Redington Brown.
Malde, M., Allen, M., & Zeller, K. (2009). *What every singer needs to know
   about the body.* San Diego, CA: Plural Publishing.
Sundberg, J. (1987). *The science of the singing voice.* Dekalb, IL: Northern Illi-
   nois University Press.
Vennard, W. (1967). *Singing—The mechanism and the technic* (Rev. ed.). New
   York, NY: Carl Fisher.

USEFUL WEB SITES

The British Voice Association. Web site: http://www.british-voice-association
   .com . E-mail: bva@dircon.co.uk or telephone: 44 0207 713 0064.
The Voice-Care Network. Web site: http://www.voicecare.org.uk .

Appendix 1

EXERCISES

Janice Chapman

I firmly believe that no one can learn to sing just from reading a book. However, I also believe that a few pages of exercises handed to a student with instructions to go home and practice them daily is a waste of time and energy.

The exercises I am describing in this Appendix are not numerous but can be used as basic templates which can be changed and developed creatively by singers and teachers. In my studio, I find that I design specific exercises on the spot, often with variations for a singer's particular problems and needs. The exercises I offer here are physiological and incremental in that they contain strategies for voice development as well as correction of vocal faults. These exercises need to be regularly supervised and are constantly being monitored and adjusted within the lesson to produce more layers of finesse.

Student singers can be rather dismissive of exercises unless they understand the reason for doing them. With the physiological and incremental approach, it is desirable to explain and demonstrate the reason behind each exercise, after which the students can then practice effectively. I often say, "Please do not practice unless you have your brain engaged because mindless practice is not beneficial and can even be detrimental." It is quite amazing how quickly a singer can exchange poor habits for good ones. My responsibility is to diagnose accurately and suggest the appropriate strategy. If they then apply themselves fully to each task, much can be achieved quickly.

1. "IN-BREATH" EXERCISE

RATIONALE

Singers need to develop their respiratory system flexibility to Olympic standards. It is, however, vital to always follow the body's natural instincts for respiration. We know from respiratory physiology that when the diaphragm descends it also exerts a force which encourages the lower ribs to expand. This is related to good posture and alignment in that the diaphragm and ribs need freedom for full movement. Postural slouching, for example, will inhibit this freedom. Likewise, overmilitary type of posture tends to lock the torso, also inhibiting these movements.

In my pedagogy the "out-breath" receives attention first because the "in-breath" is based on an automatic recoil action. However, sometimes in singers who use a different breath-management system, or in young and developing singers, I feel the need to also address the "in-breath" directly.

Use of the Alexander technique, particularly when accompanied by Accent Method breathing, usually is sufficient to take singers forward; however, in the studio I also employ the following:

1. Adopt monkeylike posture and breathe out maximally.
2. Hold the tension for 3 to 5 seconds.
3. Release the abdominal tension (SPLAT) and allow the lungs to fill, noticing how much the lower ribs at the back expand naturally. Be aware that the waistband muscles (the lateral abdominal junction) must not be part of this expansion, and the waistband must return to a neutral position during the "in-breath."
4. Repeat three times.
5. Stand straight in good alignment and repeat, noticing the full all-round expansion of the rib cage synchronized with the SPLAT (release) of the abdominal muscles while maintaining the posture in the upper chest.
6. Repeat as necessary.

2. ACCENT METHOD SIMPLIFIED

RATIONALE

It has proved very useful for singers to have an exercise paradigm which does not initially involve vocalization, so that they can practice the tidal movements involved in the natural ebb and flow of the breath. This leads the body back to the abdominodiaphragmatic breathing system preferred for singing. Pictures and figures illustrating the following exercises can be found in Chapter 4.

Exercise

1. The singer lies semisupine with maximum connection of their back to the floor, and allowing breath to ebb and flow as though during sleep. (Belly wall will rise on inhalation and relax toward the floor on exhalation.)
2. More active and energized use of the same tidal belly wall movement (up on inhalation and down toward the floor on expiration) with the use of breathy tone and fricative consonants, rhythmically using an up beat and a main beat as follows: ss-SS /s/, sh-SH /ʃ/, zh-ZH /ʒ/, zz-ZZ /z/, ff-FF /f/, vv-VV /v/, th-TH (voiceless and voiced) /θ,ð/, whoo-WHOO /wu/.
3. These sounds are repeated until an element of boredom sets in. This is usually when the conscious control gives way to the subconscious.
4. This exercise is then repeated lying on the side with the hand on the belly wall. Singers notice that they need to be a little more proactive with the belly wall in this position. In this position the acquisition of a SPLAT-breath is easier as gravity can assist the abdominal wall to release tension on inhalation.
5. The standing version of this exercise is with student and teacher paired like skaters, one foot ahead of the other, preferably in front of a mirror. They place their hands so that contact is maintained with the back of the hand on each other's belly wall. Then a gently forward and backward rocking movement is added, raising the front toe and then the back heel in turn. This rocking movement coordinates with the movement of the belly wall, that is, belly out as the body moves forward, and belly back as the body moves back, but not disturbing the general posture. The up beat and main beat fricatives/vowels sequence is used to gain access to the voicing.

Step 5 may not be used until the previous 4 are well-established and easy for the student. The singer then places his or her own hands in turn on the muscle support junctions as described and repeats step 4, noticing the muscle activation that occurs naturally following an Accent Method (or SPLAT) in-breath.

Ideally, it is the deepest layer of the abdominal girdle, namely the transverse abdominis muscle, that leads the movement, allowing the oblique muscles to follow. The transverse abdominis muscle has some interdigitation with the diaphragm, so activating it assists the singer to gain braking control. The bracing/tensing of the rectus abdominis muscle should be avoided as it can easily reduce airflow.

3. THE "HEY-HA" EXERCISE

RATIONALE

This exercise works well in raising awareness of the abdominal girdle as an air compressor and braking system all in one. The muscles are fired by primal sound initially then this exercise is used to give them practice under conscious control followed by acquisition of gradual automaticity.

Exercise

1. Stand well with hands firmly on waistband muscle junctions.
2. Shout "hey" as if to someone across the street noticing the bulking up of the muscle junction.
3. Sing "hey-ha" on single pitch repeated though a comfortable range checking for full release between each sung note. (i.e., the waistband muscles must disengage).

"Hey-Ha" exercise

Hey,   Ha,   Hey,   Ha,   Hey

4. Sing up a major scale "hey" (release) "ha" (release). On the ascending scale, each note of the scale activates the support and each rest indicates the release. On the descending scale the support is maintained under a single "hah" with the release after the end of the phonation (see Figure 4–4).

Hey, ha, hey, ha, hey, ha, hey   ha_____

NOTE: The impulse for the engagement of this muscle junction must be the movement of the belly wall toward the spine, as occurs in primal sound-making (see Chapter 4 on Breathing and Support). It is possible for singers to consciously "flare" the waistband muscles, but this can become a counterproductive maneuver if it is not allied to breath flow.

5. Repeat step 4, but add as many scales on the legato "ha" as the student has air for. This trains the system to achieve more strength and flexibility.

To extend supported air

Hey,   ha,   hey,   ha,   hey,   ha   hey,   ha_____

3   and so on

Pitch range for all voices: starting on a comfortable low note
and not rising above the upper passagio pivot note at the top.

Because the student's own hands on the waist may produce an artificial
shoulder girdle setting, it is a good idea for the teacher's hands to be
employed from time to time. The teacher can then monitor the student's
use of the muscles and also help raise the student's kinesthetic awareness.

Starting and finishing notes for voice types:

Baritones and basses start on Bb2 and finish on Eb3.

Tenors start on C3 and finish on F3.

Countertenors, Contraltos and Mezzos start on Bb3 and finish on E4.

Sopranos start on C4 and finish on F4.

Light/stratospheric sopranos start on D4 and finish on G4.

4. SEMIOCCLUDED VOCAL TRACT EXERCISES

ROLLED "r"

RATIONALE

This exercise can be used for all singers. It assists in the development of
the core skills directly. The rolled "r" providing as it does a secondary
valve produces back pressure in the mouth promoting easy phonation
at the vocal fold edges. The rolled "r" itself places an insistent demand
on the airflow and support. For example, singers with a locked abdominal wall often find it impossible to maintain even and steady vibration of
the tongue due to poor breath support and reduced airflow. They also
find the extremes of their vocal range to be limited. These features may
be associated with increased tension in the tongue and constriction of
the pharynx.

Sequence and Rationale of Teaching

1. Unvoiced trilled "r" on a single sustained breath:
   This should be a light unvoiced tongue flutter without phonation being engaged. This promotes airflow and tongue flexibility.
2. Add modal voice with easy glides:
   The goal is to have similar airflow and tongue flexibility with phonation engaged. Singers with excessive tension in the the speaking voice or in the articulators may find this stage difficult. Deficits in airflow and tongue flexibility should be addressed at this point with additional work on support. For singers who appear to have physical articulatory restriction the opinion of a speech therapist should be sought.
3. Scale of an octave + 1 (9th scale):
   Starting at the bottom of the vocal range sing scales of an octave +1 up and down while maintaining the "lightness" of tongue use and easy phonation.

   - Tongue root and floor of mouth tension should be checked by a thumb under the chin. There should be no downward pressure of the floor of the mouth.
   - Phonation should be easy and free. Pressed phonation must be avoided.
   - Support must be engaged throughout the exercise. Particular emphasis should be placed on the downward scale as support is more likely to disengage in this portion of the exercise.
   - The abdominal wall should be soft and flexible throughout.
   - The mouth and the muscles of facial expression (especially the obicularis oris) must be free of tension. Tension in the face and lips can refer through to the floor of the mouth and then into the base of the tongue and the larynx creating a bottled tone.

   Rolled "r" scale

   rr_____

   Full pitch range all voices.
   Gradually extended up to 4 or 5 scales in one breath over time.

4. Sing the scales with the tonic ascending in semitones.
   These scales can be taken upward safely into the extreme top of the range.
5. To extend the strength and endurance in the support muscles add more scales on a single breath. (In order to "trick" a singer into tak-

ing only a SPLAT-breath and utilizing their residual air rather than overbreathing, I will say the number of scales to be sung after they have inhaled but before they start the scale.) In developing singers I build this up gradually as they are able to encompass more and more repeats.

■ It is important to remember that this exercise cannot hurt the voice. The constant airflow and relaxed phonation allow the vocal folds to operate in the best possible environment. The voice can then be safely and gently stretched over its whole compass. Laryngeal tilt is also encouraged by the airflow and tongue position.

6. Addition of "sob" or "collar connection":
Sob can be usefully added to the start of phonation as it appears to widen the laryngopharynx. This engages the "collar connection." The collar connection can also be seen as the upper border of the support system.

■ The collar connection is an interface between subglottal air pressure and laryngopharyngeal width, and is dependent on good alignment of the head, neck, and torso.
■ To access collar connection I suggest the use of a "sob" maneuver which is thought to engage the sternothyroid muscles. This assists the widening of the laryngopharynx. Subglottal air pressure is demanded by this maneuver.
■ Externally the base of the neck at the level of the sternal notch inflates (rather like a frog or a bird). This can easily be felt with thumb and forefinger stretched wide like a necklace. Once this is active the singer can also easily see it in a mirror.
■ Teachers need to monitor the set of the head, neck, and jaw to maintain appropriate alignment.
■ When this is working correctly there is almost no kinesthetic awareness of the collar itself.

7. Addition of "collar" to the whole exercise:
"Collar" through the whole exercise promotes width and stability of the vocal tract allowing for efficient phonation.

■ The sternothyroid muscle (being a true depressor of the larynx) appears to act as a vocal stabilizer. The collar connection helps maintain appropriate laryngeal setting for the task in hand.
■ Maintenance of width and stability in the vocal tract is a resonance issue as it promotes expansion of the supralaryngeal area known as the epilarynx. The epilarynx is now thought to be a primary resonator site in the vocal tract.

- Posture and alignment must remain adequate and appropriate throughout the scale, otherwise the collar connection could be lost or inadequate.
- The tongue trill must continue evenly through the whole scale. If the tongue trill stops, airflow and support problems are the most common cause. Slow development and patience will be needed if there are problems in maintaining the trill. A combination of airflow and support work may be needed to assist in this development.
- There appears to be a connection between the abdominal wall and tongue flexibility. Singers with locked, rigid abdominal walls find this exercise particularly difficult. Accent Method breathing instruction may be required before this exercise can progress.

8. Use of the lip trill:
The exercise given above can also be performed using a lip trill. This promotes facial muscle relaxation and prevents tension in the lips and floor of the mouth.

   - Airflow needs to be high to cause sufficient vibration of the lips. If airflow is a problem and the lips cannot be readily inflated, use of "puffy" cheeks with extra air in the oral cavity will help promote steady, even vibration. Fingers placed on either side of the lips may also assist the development of good steady vibration.
   - Development of skill in this exercise may be slow, and patient persistence may be required before the singer is able to perform it properly.

9. Advanced level use:
A synchronization of both tongue and lip trills can be performed. Start with the lip trill and add the tongue trill to it. This leads to complete facial and lingual freedom, by developing into a vibration of the articulatory structures in sympathy with phonation.

   - Trying too hard is actually counterproductive to performing this exercise successfully. Singers must be encouraged to do these exercises in an easy almost carefree way to prevent tension developing. They can be done at various nonsinging times of the day while washing up or even in the shower.

10. Exercise as a whole-range warm-up:
Properly done the lip and/or tongue trill can be used as a whole-range warm-up as it promotes the core skills of postural alignment, support, and airflow with articulatory flexibility.

This exercise acts to promote a synchronization of body and larynx. The addition of the collar connection provides a platform on which the larynx can tilt easily and efficiently. The large muscles of the torso, if properly engaged, maintain postural integrity which allows the small muscles of the larynx and pharynx to perform discrete movements that enhance phonation and resonance. These fine-motor controls ultimately can give a singer access to a full range of artistic expression which is synchronized subconsciously in their singing at the bidding of their imagination.

- This exercise must be carefully monitored while it is being learned, to ensure correct synchronization of breath and voice. Ease of pitch attainment is the most salient monitor for both the teacher and the singer. Once kinesthetic patterns have been established the singer can practice alone.

THE PUFFY CHEEKS EXERCISE

RATIONALE

Singing teachers have used semioccluded vocal tract exercises over centuries, for example, the rolled "r," the lip trill, and voiced fricative consonants such as /v/ and /z/. I have developed a simple technique using puffy cheeks with a small /w/ shaped lip opening (like the aspirated /w/ in "which" and "when" as spoken by a Scot!). The puffy cheeks component makes it different to other semioccluded sounds in that it provides additional back pressure, which helps lift the soft palate and widen the pharynx, as well as general release of facial muscles. The puffy cheeks also provides access to other benefits known about the SOVT postures, such as increased vocal fold contact efficiency, improved thyroid tilt, more acoustic reinforcement from the vocal tract (narrowing of the epilarynx), and improved breath management (consciousness of abdominal support is raised). Scientific study continues into these SOVT postures following the pioneering work of Ingo Titze into singing through drinking straws.

In my studio, I find the following exercises very valuable for such problems as pressed phonation where the effort levels in the larynx are very high, excessive nasality due to the soft palate being too low, resonance imbalances where the pharynx width and/or vocal tract length is inadequate, and registration difficulties.

Setting Up the Oral Posture

- Gently inflate the cheeks and form a small /w/ opening
- Blow air gently through the opening maintaining air in the cheeks and in front of the teeth.

■ Vocalize while maintaining this gentle airflow (check by placing a finger in front of the lips and notice the airstream).

Exercises

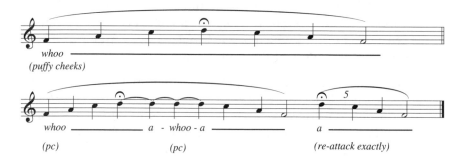

whoo
(puffy cheeks)

whoo _____ a - whoo - a _____ a _____

(pc)   (pc)   (re-attack exactly)

All voices :
Use pitch range from comfortable middle voice up to above the upper passaggio.
Notice the lightening of the vocal loading at the higher pitches.

To carry over the benefits of this exercise into repertoire, it is very helpful to sing the melody with the puffy cheeks vocalization followed by a combination of puffy cheeks and text. Clearly, the consonants will be compromised but the tongue will be making excursions in the mouth approximating the final text positions. Once this has been practiced, it is easy to make the transition to full singing maintaining the puffy cheek benefits. It is worth noting that undesired tensions in the jaw are automatically reduced via this exercise.

Raspberry Puff (No, not a pastry recipe!)

This is a modification of the puffy cheeks exercise specially designed for singers who have a recalcitrant tongue-root problem. These singers still are able to engage tongue-root tension during the puffy cheeks exercise, which negates many of its benefits. Set up the oral posture for puffy cheeks as described above, then protrude the tongue maximally still allowing some air to escape around it. Then phonate the exercises as above. When releasing to a vowel, allow the tongue to spring back into the mouth preferably to a "dial-a-vowel" position. It may be noticed that the tongue thrust produces a temporary elevation of the larynx. The larynx should drop to its optimal position once the tongue has sprung back into the mouth for the vowel.

5. ONSETS

Jo Estill's work includes figures for practicing the onsets of vocal sound which are invaluable within the singing studio at all levels. (Estill, J. [1996]. *Primer of Basic Figures* [2nd ed.]. Santa Rosa, CA: Estill Voice

Training Systems.) Many teachers and singers are most grateful to her and her colleagues for their groundbreaking work in simplifying complex maneuvers and giving them such practical help by using everyday primal sound patterns to achieve various vocal configurations. Her work has been backed up with videolaryngostroboscopic evidence of vocal efficiency and health. All good systems are subject to change when they are put into the hands of practitioners; however, Estill's work on vocal onsets is so clear and so good that no changes are needed. I describe them below in my own words.

GLOTTAL ONSET

1. Close the vocal folds lightly by preparing to make a tiny cough but stopping short of exploding the air through the glottis. This closure should be effortless. Practice holding this vocal posture for a few seconds while noticing how it feels.
2. Move from this closed action directly into the spoken vowel /a/ or /i/.
3. Repeat step 1 but this time move straight into the sung vowel at a medium pitch. You will hear a tiny "click" at the onset of the glottal sound. Notice that breath is held back prior to this "click," but that it flows in order to phonate the vowel.
4. Practice on all vowels through your comfortable pitch range (medium).

BREATHY ONSET

1. Speak the breathy consonant /h/ before the spoken vowel /a/.
2. Speak/sing the breathy consonant /h/ before the sung vowel /a/, noticing that the airflow precedes the phonation.
3. Practice all vowels and at all comfortable pitches.

SIMULTANEOUS ONSET

1. Imagine the vowel and the pitch you wish to sing.
2. Start the sound with simultaneous coordination of breath and sound. It can help to achieve this by imitating the cry of a small kitten or the whimper of a puppy. Both these sounds tend to incorporate an efficient onset of breath and voice together.

NOTE: If abdominal support for the breath has been incorporated early in the tuition as part of the core components, there should be an automatic engagement of these muscles synchronized with the prephonation of the vowels. This can be checked by using the hands on the muscle junctions (see Chapter 4 on Breathing and Support).

THE USE OF VOCAL FRY/CREAK (LARYNGEAL MECHANISM 0)

Vocal fry often is seen by the speech and language therapist as a vocal abuse, but used judiciously it can greatly assist the development of an appropriate and efficient vocal fold closure for singers at the onset of the sound. I find it particularly useful in male voices, but it also proves very effective in female singers who have a tendency toward a breathy onset. A brief period of vocal fry/creak (which necessarily will be a very low pitch and volume) seems to help singers lower and relax their laryngeal setting and provide them with some awareness of the vocal fold closure. The closed quotient (CQ) is thought to "normalize," giving a clean onset with a good potential for focus in the sound. In a more developed singer, I would use a double octave leap from vocal fry to M1 or M2 as appropriate. This provides an excellent onset at the required pitch.

6. "DIAL-A-VOWEL"

RATIONALE

The everyday struggle of undergraduate students to cope with the seemingly simple task of making acceptable Italian vowels fired my curiosity about the habitual tongue settings of different languages. At a multidisciplinary voice conference I heard a presentation from a dialect coach from the world of theatre, which further aroused my curiosity when she explained how the gross posture of the tongue defined the recognizable linguistic characteristics of various dialects, and used this gross tongue posture as a template for working on the actual texts.

Awareness of the characteristics of the Italian language and experimentation with gross tongue posture led me to develop an exercise template which was promptly named "Dial-a-Vowel" for me by a perceptive student. This training system helps to "shortcut" the journey to Italian for students from other mother tongues. Surprisingly, I have also found it useful when teaching Italians who have been delighted to affirm that the Italian vowels really do "sing" themselves when honestly produced.

In this version I have used only the five pure Italian vowels, /i, e, a, o, and u/ for the sake of simplicity.

THE GROSS TONGUE SETTING

- Protrude the tongue to its absolute maximum.
- Allow it to spring back into the mouth and immediately say "mio Dio" noticing where the sides of the tongue touch the back upper molars on the /i/ part of the diphthong.

- With the tongue in this /i/ position, sing a supported /i/ vowel. While singing the vowel, slide the tongue minimally forward and back maintaining contact with the molars, until the sound resonates with the utmost clarity and comfort. This then will be the location point for the exercise. The blade and tip of the tongue should not be placed in any particular position in the mouth but relate naturally to the general position of the organ.

- The frontal jaw opening needs to be temporarily immobilized, thus forcing the tongue to take responsibility for the vowel formation on its own.

- Starting with the tongue in its location point, and the jaw slightly open, sing the 5 vowels legato on a comfortable middle pitch note—/i, e, a, o, u/. Notice that when the jaw is immobilized, the tongue makes a small but precise maneuver for each vowel. When the tongue is in a suitably high and back position, all vowels can be clearly articulated with the tongue still in contact with the upper molars. It is not suggested that this will be the ultimate singing position, but at this stage, the exercise is a means to attaining a more Italianate tongue setting and not a finished product.

Dial-a-Vowel

i - e - a - o - u - o - a - e - i

- Then sing a descending and ascending 5 note major scale staccato, starting on the 5th as follows: /i,e,a,o,u,o,a,e,i/. Again, immobilize the jaw so that the tongue will do the work, and notice the tongue excursion with the descent and ascent of pitch.

i - e - a - o - u - o - a - e - i

NOTE: On singers with a visible Adam's apple it is possible to see that the larynx itself lowers from /i/ through to /u/ and rises again back to /i/. In classical "bel canto" singing, there are different relative acoustic "sweet spots" for the different vowels. I recall talking to an acoustic scientist after a concert where the soprano had sung with such finesse it took the audience's breath away. He pointed out to me that she was "formant tuning" when she sang. She had been very well trained to seek this "sweet spot" resonance throughout her range. During the concert she was finding the "zone" instinctively as part of her artistry. All five of the pure Italian vowels respond to this exercise. The complex discrete changes in tongue shape between each vowel are guided in part by an automatic and subtle adjustment of the larynx itself for each vowel. Using the upper molars as a guide for location of the gross tongue posture ensures that the tongue itself must actively change position to give a clear vowel sound. This also prevents the base of the tongue from wrongly engaging during vowel formation.

■ The next stage of the exercise is for practicing each vowel. Sing the vowel /i/ for all five descending staccato notes then up the scale to the 9th and return as follows:

i - i - i - i - i

■ Then sing /i/ /e,e,e,e/ up and down the scale on /e/.

i - e - e - e - e

■ Then /i/,/e/, /a,a,a/ up and down the scale on /a/.

i - e - a - a - a

■ Then /i/, /e/, /a/, /o/, /o/ up and down the scale on /o/.

i - e - a - o - o

■ Finally /i/, /e/, /a/, /o/ /u/ and so forth

i - e - a - o - u

The tongue setting for each vowel should maintain its "dialed" setting for the ascending and descending scale and allow the singer to sing quickly and accurately without any effort. This lack of effort is the chief guideline for the students. When each vowel is in the "sweet spot" there is no mistaking that the scales "sing themselves."

- Once the template is learned and comfortable (i.e., the tongue maintains the integrity of the vowel), it is possible to open the jaw as required without loss of the "sweet spot" feeling.
- For the very high pitches, the tongue will come away from the teeth, but this will be a natural easing of the basic position and not a jamming down of the tongue root.

This exercise was developed to help students find an Italianate tongue posture and setting, but has proved extremely beneficial when singing in other languages. I believe the reason is that Western classical singing evolved out of the Italian language and the anticipated sound of a voice singing classically (with all its rich harmonics) is best found through the Italian template.

English is a language which encourages a different use of the jaw and tongue. This can create a bumpy line and muddy vowels, but the "dial-a-vowel" exercise set can be very helpful for this problem. Temporarily singing in English with an Italian accent, (after "dial-a-vowel" has been practiced) can be a way to experience clearer and more accurate vowels in the bel canto tradition of classical singing. Using this accent is only a temporary measure to raise students' kinesthetic awareness of tongue position.

7. VOWEL LEGATO

RATIONALE

This simple exercise is contained in the vocal manual of Manuel García and is a very useful way for the student to practice maintaining both vowel clarity and legato between two notes. The vowel sequence is not the usual /i, e, a, o, u/.

Once it has been mastered, I suggest that this exercise can be practiced with a specific emotion, either suggested by the teacher or chosen by the student.

Vowel Legato

The starting note in each voice type should be comfortably low so that the exercise remains below the singer's upper passagio. The dynamic should be a comfortable mezzoforte.

8. TONGUE RELEASE

RATIONALE

The classical "ideal" for singing is a low-larynx position which allows the resonating space to be longer (with the possibility of also being wider), thus increasing the acoustic parameters of the resonance.

The main **true** depressor of the larynx is the pair of sternothyroid strap muscles. These muscles need to be employed appropriately for the maintenance of an easy, comfortable low-larynx position. It is, however, possible to use other muscles to lower laryngeal position. In particular, muscles that attach to the base of the tongue and hyoid bone can be used incorrectly to depress the larynx in order to mimic the low-laryngeal position desirable for classical singing. This produces a dark, bottled sound with little vowel clarity or differentiation and severely reduced carrying power.

Often singers may contract or tense the floor of the mouth/tongue root as they inhale (imagining that they are creating extra space). The space that this creates is in the mouth instead of the oropharynx and laryngopharynx. This sets the mechanism badly for phonation, and I would recommend that teachers watch for this fault. Practicing inhaling without any contraction in this area, monitoring with the thumb and/or visual feedback via a mirror is advisable.

Singers who have been trained to seek both a low-larynx and low-tongue position often present with tongue-root tension (TRT) which can take a long time to correct. Persistence and courage are required for the many weeks/months it may take to tackle this problem but the rewards are considerable.

While doing the rolled "r" scale it is worthwhile checking for TRT and beginning a "weaning" process immediately. A singer's aural perception also has to be changed, as the personal feedback from singing with TRT is of a comfortingly dark sound, whereas when this tension is absent, there is much less for the singer's ear to indulge in. However, the listener gets a great deal more while the singer has to be convinced to "hear less." Here is a good case for recording the lessons on good equipment so that the singer's confidence can also grow by having this postlesson feedback. When the tongue root is engaged a "damping" of the upper harmonics occurs, and because of the inefficiency of bone-conducted sound within the singer's own head, this can sound preferable and pleasing to the singer. It is the equivalent of a child's comfort blanket, wrapped up in one's own sound, whereas the listener hears a dull, woolly quality.

For the general limbering up of the tongue I recommend:

BABBLING WITH GLIDES

Babbling (tongue sounds such as /d/l/t/k/g/) while phonating easily on ascending and descending glides.

TONGUE AEROBICS

This exercise should be done while maintaining good alignment of head and neck. The jaw will tend to protrude along with the tongue thrust so this also should be monitored.

TONGUE THRUST

1. Open the mouth and thrust tongue outward to its limit.
2. Retract tongue into a curled position (tip of tongue toward the uvula and at the same time close mouth).
3. Gradually build up speed of steps 1 and 2 and repeat until discomfort sets in.
4. Use babbling glides to release tension.

CHASE THE TOFFEE

1. Using the tip of the tongue and starting in the center of the gums above the upper teeth try to move a stubborn piece of imaginary toffee.
2. Follow this right around the mouth in front of the teeth, working each point for a few seconds.
3. Release tongue by doing the babbling glides.
4. Repeat with tongue inside teeth monitoring for tongue-root tension.
5. Repeat babbling glides.

TONGUE TWISTERS

This exercise should be done with full vocal connection to the support muscles and maintaining good alignment.

■ Repeat the following nonsense words (or make up your own) as quickly as possible on the notes of an ascending and descending scale arriving at the top and bottom notes of the scale on the final syllable.

MANALAVA—MA

BOGABILLA—BA

DOOROONARI—DOO

TOLODOLO—TO

RALLERINA—RA

KELLAGALLA—KE

THEEGADAGA—THEE

CHOOKOOCHILLA—CHOO

SHASSAFISHA—SHA

Tongue Twisters

Ma - na - la - va   ma - na - la - va   ma - na - la - va   ma - na - la - va

ma - na - la - va   ma - na - la - va   ma - na - la - va   ma

ma - na - la - va   ma - na - la - va   ma - na - la - va   ma - na - la - va

ma - na - la - va   ma - na - la - va   ma - na - la - va   ma

Stay in comfortable pitch range for all voice types.

Notice how little the jaw moves during the exercise and how precisely and quickly the tongue can make these syllables. Any drop in air pressure will cause the articulators to jam up and the flow of the exercise may be interrupted.

MONITOR FOR TONGUE-ROOT TENSION

Place thumb under chin and check that while singing the root of the tongue and the floor of the mouth are not tensing. If you want to experience the unwanted tension fully, pull the tongue back and push the jaw forward at the same time. It is surprising how often a singer will produce this problem if he or she is not made aware of what a free tongue and jaw feel like during phonation. This is basically a support issue: that is, if the breath is not under the control of the abdominal muscles the tongue root and jaw may assume an inappropriate vocal control function.

SCALES WITH CURLED TONGUE

Another problem of the tongue being incorrectly tense during phonation is when a student has been asked to place the tip of the tongue behind the front bottom teeth throughout singing. In order to keep this position one can grip with the tongue blade in a way which is inappropriate. The sound quality may be "gritty" and this problem can be corrected by having the student sing scales up and down with the tip of the tongue curled toward the uvula. This can be in the position of the English "r" (e.g., rabbit), and a scale can be sung on this semivowel. Generally, I follow this curled tongue scale with a thrust tongue scale to balance it, then finally a scale with the tongue in the correct position for the vowel. If the sound is still not clear, further scales can be added on such syllables as /ra-tha/. The sound quality should then be clear.

THRUST "TH" FOLLOWED BY VOWEL

A very useful exercise for the student with TRT is to sing a five-note scale beginning with the tongue thrust out of the mouth to its extremity making a voiced TH at the same time. As the singer makes the required vowel, the tongue springs back into the mouth cavity and should be free of TRT. All vowels should be practiced in this way.

Tongue Thrust

thrust tongue—TH   i
          TH   e
          TH   a
          TH   o
          TH   u

All voices stay in comfortable mid-range.

thrust tongue—TH   i
          TH   e
          TH   a
          TH   o
          TH   u

REPLACING FIRST CONSONANT OR VOWEL IN A SONG OR ARIA WITH THRUST "TH"

Following on from the previous exercise, sing an aria antiche and replace the first sound of each phrase with the thrust tongue voiced *TH*. For example, *TH*aro mio ben, *TH*redi mi al men, *TH*ensa di te, *TH*anguishe il cor, and so forth. After a few minutes of the above, try the song with the correct text but retaining the sensations of singing without TRT present. Monitor manually if necessary.

THE ULTIMATE RELEASE FOR BACKED TONGUE—
"THE ANTI-GAG TONGUE PULL"

There is another exercise that I use consistently for recalcitrant tongue root problems which I learned from an American colleague, but which I feel must be taught personally and with great caution. For this exercise to be safe and effective the student must have already established technical security of airflow, support, posture, and alignment. When I am teaching this technique, I monitor the student closely, and initially do not permit home practice. When I am confident that it is correct, I advise that it should be used in practice for no more than 3 minutes per day.

Raising the chin and tipping the head back as far as possible (to look at the ceiling), thrust the tongue out maximally and hold with a handkerchief or piece of gauze.

Gently tug while phonating on an ugly /æ/ vowel (a as in "cat"), using a twangy metallic sound. I suggest a chromatic scale over a short range, that is, a major third. This can be taken right through the singer's full range and should become easy to achieve as the tongue root is prevented from depressing and locking down onto the hyoid bone. The larynx itself will become elevated during this part of the exercise. Once the singer has experienced this tongue-root-free sound, he will be able to reproduce it with the head/neck in normal alignment. They may still need to use the ugly /æ/ vowel before moving on to clear Italian vowels with the larynx in its lower classical setting. If required, use the "pre-yawn" impulse (without engaging the tongue root) to settle the larynx into its lower optimum position.

The root of the tongue not only has muscular connections but also seems to be very sensitive to a singer's emotional state. Because of this, the TRT can be a recurring problem even in the well-trained professional singer when he or she is emotionally stretched (e.g., away from home and family, unhappy, etc.) This ultimate tongue root release exercise can be a "3-minute miracle," which can be used by professionals at the highest level as a quick check prior to a performance.

9. EFFORT LEVELS

RATIONALE

Singers have to develop into vocal athletes over time. At every stage of a singer's development, however, he or she will be making an effort in various areas of their instrument. The relationship between these effort levels should be monitored throughout the singer's development so that voice and body can be kept in balance. This is often an area that is not adequately addressed either by singers or teachers.

At regular intervals during a singer's development, I might ask the following questions:

- Where is effort "felt"?
- At what level is that effort?
- What sort of effort is it?

Although the issue of effort levels is contained in some of the singing pedagogy literature it has not been much discussed. Jo Estill raised awareness of effort levels and codified them in a way that is very useful to singing teachers.

I have found it useful to define the "what and where" with students by using a simple analog scale. For example, when a singer is straining for top notes (using pressed phonation) I will ask them, on a scale of 1 to 10, what the effort is at the larynx. They might reply, "8." I might then suggest to them that they reduce this to number 4 or 5 without changing anything else. The lightening of the vocal loading at the level of the larynx is often quite a breakthrough for singers who have perhaps had the wrong idea about singing high notes, especially in operatic repertoire. They have engaged in "bellowing and blasting" in order to make what they think is an operatic sound. The puffy cheeks exercise is a valuable shortcut toward balancing effort levels.

With support issues, I will ask similarly, what level (1 to 10) are you feeling in your torso? They may answer "oh, about 4" and I will then suggest that they change that number to an 8 without changing anything else. Using more activity in the abdominal support without increasing the vocal effort usually results in a better balanced tone and easier singing.

As singers become accustomed to monitoring effort in this way, they can then be encouraged to use the idea of voice/body ratio of effort, that is, "What is the ratio of effort, body to voice?" They may answer "4 in the body and 8 in the voice" so I might suggest reversing the numbers, that is, 8 in the body and 4 in the voice. This can then be adjusted and refined according to the teacher's ear. As the singers progress, they can readily self-monitor and this concept can go with them throughout their professional life.

The ultimate criterion in using this comparative scale of effort levels is that singing becomes balanced and easy. It may take time for the muscles in the torso to become strong enough to achieve a balanced tone. It may also take time for the vocal fold closure to become efficient. Some students make very fast progress toward a good balance of effort levels and need little intervention; however, raising their awareness is crucial in terms of the prevention of problems at a later stage. Remember, the puffy cheeks exercise can hasten this process.

Sometimes singers report a "finding of the zone" state where they do not need to worry about their voice production at all during an entire recital, concert, or opera. This is the whole purpose of having a good vocal technique, where the voice obeys the imagination for artistic and dramatic purposes and vocal technique itself is only a means to an end.

STACCATO EXERCISES

In order to find an ideal effort level for the upper ranges in all voice types I have found it beneficial to use a staccato exercise:

1. Using an easy vowel, sing an ascending and descending arpeggio to the 10th.
2. After the arpeggio has been practiced, elongate the top note while not changing the effort level of that note.
3. Sing the exercise on each of the five cardinal Italian vowels.

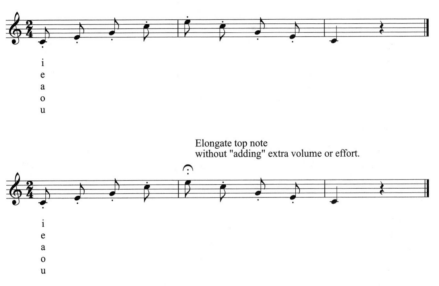

Effort levels: Staccato arpeggio

i
e
a
o
u

Elongate top note
without "adding" extra volume or effort.

i
e
a
o
u

Pitch range for all voices: starting on a comfortable low note
and rising in semitones to access the top of the upper register.

NOTE: The top notes may feel ridiculously easy and light to the singer, but usually contain all the power necessary to sing them well. If more power is needed it may be added from the support muscles rather than at the level of the vocal folds themselves. This "trick" can woo singers away from their bad vocal habits of overpressing in order to make their sound bigger, that is, if they believe you! Here it is useful to be recording the session and play the tape back immediately so that their doubts can be allayed. Often the unforced sound (the light sound) is louder than their pressed version, but the singers find this very hard to believe at first. I explain that the increase in resonance which occurs when the vocal tract walls are not inappropriately compressed is responsible. During pressed phonation the resonating surfaces can be inappropriately engaged, thus acting as dampers.

THE YODEL EXERCISE

This exercise can be used for a number of purposes, but mainly I find it invaluable in helping female singers access a very easy phonatory effort level in the middle register. After the core components are established and the vowel positions are comfortably established try the following:

1. Yodel (starting in low chest register). Do not "sing" the upper notes but just allow the pitches to "happen."

Yodel Exercise (female voices)

2. Repeat yodel and add a repeated /i/ vowel descending and ascending through a five note major scale.

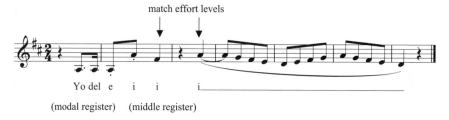

3. Repeat above and add scale up to the 9th and down again.

Extended range

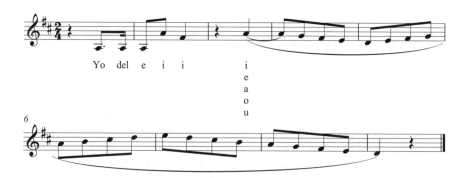

Pitch range : The Yodel must start in a comfortable modal register in all voices.

4. Use other vowels following the yodel.

10. THE SOFT PALATE

RATIONALE

For classical singing a high-domed soft palate greatly improves the resonance capability of the sound. This should not be confused with making larger spaces in the mouth (it is further back in the oropharynx). Over the years I have used various exercises to help singers find the high-palate position relevant to a classical sound. I find that the simplest way to bring about the elevation required is part of the "larynx lowering" instructions which I use (see Figure 7–1).

PRE-YAWN EXERCISE:

- Stand in alignment with head and neck well-positioned.
- Place thumb and index finger either side of larynx.
- Place tongue in an /i/ position in the mouth.
- Inhale as though about to yawn.
- *Stop there!* Do not complete the yawn.
- Notice that the larynx has dropped and the soft palate has lifted.
- Remove fingers and practice five times.

NOTE: In a complete yawn the tongue root is depressed and the soft palate lowered. Although in a full yawn the larynx is also lowered this maneuver relies on a poorly set oral capsule and should be avoided for singing.

USE OF THE "PUFFY CHEEKS" EXERCISE

The puffy cheeks exercise gives the singer an immediate ability to access the feeling of a high palate. The use of this exercise can shortcut the process considerably. (See above for full description of the exercise.)

EXERCISES FOR CLOSING THE VELAR PORT

To achieve this, Jo Estill has some suggestions such as sucking hard on the thumbnail and noticing the elevation which accompanies that act. She also suggests the use of a hummed /ŋ/ (ng) made on the very back of the tongue, followed by an energetic consonant /g/ and vowel. The consonant /g/ is employed quite firmly from the /ŋ/ position to kick the palate into activity on the vowel. I like to add a "sob" to the hummed /ŋ/ as this also has the effect of energizing the torso to support the sound. So (h) /ŋgi/, (h) /ŋga/, (h) /ŋgo/, and so forth, with the instruction that the student also notice the springing up of the palate as one makes the vowel. This exercise should be used in the midvoice range.

It is interesting to note that while the soft palate is in this elevated position, the larynx itself tends to keep its lowered position quite easily. There appears to be a natural demand for good airflow in this palate/larynx setting and, conversely, the setting is more easily maintained when the supported air is available. The most common fault in maintaining this classical setting is overuse of the jaw. The vowel /a/ is often the greatest culprit as students often think that they are making "space" by jamming their jaw open in a forward manner (position 2), rather than allowing it to drop open (position 1). During the student's development process, this jamming action can have the effect of losing the elevation of the palate which often coincides with an unwanted raising of the larynx. As soon as this position is lost, the tone loses its warmth and roundness and the remainder of the phrase will also probably be compromised.

Inappropriate muscle tensions in the jaw, tongue root, and pharynx can cause the soft palate to be pulled down. Manual therapy is very effective in releasing these tensions so that the singer can experience what their voice "could" do if freed up. The singing teacher must work in collaboration with the therapist, and often the questions of postural alignment and supported airflow must also be addressed. Only then will the palate be able to sustain its domed setting naturally and easily.

11. REGISTER TRANSITIONS

RATIONALE

In classical singing it is generally expected and desired that a singer disguise his or her register transition so that there is a matching of tonal qualities and vibrato across the range.

FEMALE (MODAL TO MIDDLE) AND COUNTERTENOR (MODAL TO HEAD) REGISTERS

Recognition and practice of the two registers:

1. Using modal (or speaking voice) talk or read a passage recognizing the register. If the speaking voice is husky or not focused, address this problem first by adding an instruction such as, "Use a more nagging tone" or "Use an Australian or American accent." Then take that phonation model into normal speech.

2. Using the same phonation, intone the same passage (like a vicar), recognizing the register and the lack of effort at the level of the voice. Use waistband muscles to support the continuous airflow required.

3. Starting on the lowest comfortable pitch, sing a 5-note major scale on each of the 5 Italian vowels /i, e, a, o, u/ in this register without allowing the voice to change, noting how much support is required at the upper extremity.

4. The 4×4 exercise: Commencing on the lowest comfortable pitch in modal register, sing an ascending major scale, with the first 4 notes in modal voice and the next 4 in middle/head voice. At this stage relish the differences in timbre between the two qualities and note the support level. The lower 4 notes should be sung in a light unpressured way and will give the singer the sensation of being "placed" high and forward. The 4 higher notes appear to relax from that position so that they feel a little deeper in the throat.

5. Extend step 4 by using scales on the next 3 or 4 semitones. Still use the same 4×4 pattern, which brings the note of transition higher by a semitone with each scale. The musculature will be worked in a way which will give choice of registers more flexibility when singing the music.

6. Extend steps 4 and 5 using different vowels.

Register Transition

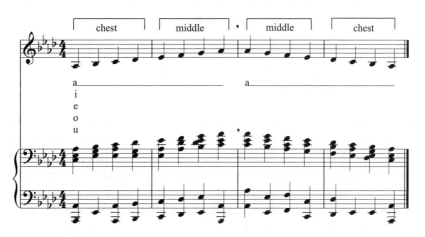

Sopranos starting note A♭3 (then A3, B♭3, B3, C4)
Mezzos starting note G3 (then A♭3, A3, B♭3, B3)
Contraltos (and countertenors) starting note G♭3 (then G3, A♭3, A3, B♭3)

Integration and Disguise of Register "Breaks" (i.e., Voix Mixte)

7. Settle the larynx in a comfortably low position (using a "pre-yawn" inspiration).

8. Repeat steps 4 to 6 in the lower laryngeal setting, monitoring that support is engaged.

9. Sing an ascending and descending chromatic scale on each vowel, commencing on the lowest comfortable pitch in modal register, and allowing the voice to change register wherever it will. You will notice that the place of change on the ascending scale will probably be different from that on the descending scale.

Chromatic scale, allowing register change to take place automatically

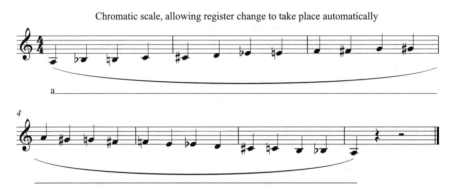

10. Finally, practice singing a sustained note, sliding from modal to head register and back again, disguising the changeover and maintaining the clarity of the vowel. It is important to notice how much the support muscles (waistband in particular) are needed for this maneuver. Repeat on other appropriate pitches.

BASSES, BARITONES, AND TENORS REGISTER TRANSITION EXERCISES

Chest to head: Using a rolled "r" scale through the upper register transition assists the singer to trust the cricothyroid tilt to manage this area of the voice. The singer's jaw needs to be free of tension, not jutting forward and not jamming open. I have found that when a singer's support is fully engaged and the jaw and tongue root are free, that this upper register tends to "change itself." By practicing the rolled "r" scale the tilting of the thyroid onto the cricoid cartilage manages the transition from thick to thinner folds. Thus, the only thing left to deal with is the singer's own aural perception of the sound being suddenly "different." Using good quality recording and immediate playback in the studio can help resolve this problem.

For singers who habitually try to use the thick edge of the vocal folds inappropriately in the upper reaches of the voice, the best exercise is a chromatic scale of 5 semitones up and back on the French /y/ sound.

■ Starting below the passagio using French /y/ sing a five semitone chromatic scale up and down.

Upper Passagio in men's voices

French /y/ chromatic scale

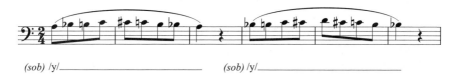

(sob) /y/_____ *(sob)* /y/_____

- Rise in semitone steps to the top of the singer's comfortable range.
- Alternate one scale on /y/ with the five cardinal Italian vowels in turn (/i, e, a, o, u/).

Extending French /y/ to vowels

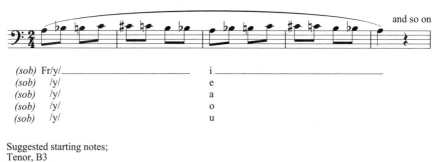

and so on

(sob) Fr/y/_____	i _____
(sob) /y/	e
(sob) /y/	a
(sob) /y/	o
(sob) /y/	u

Suggested starting notes;
Tenor, B3
Baritone, A3
Bass, G3

- Sing the scale on each of the five vowels.

Focused Vowels directly

Repeat previous exercise, omitting French /y/ and going directly to the vowel.
Use sob (or giggle) to prevent constriction.

(sob) i _____
ē
a
o
u

HEAD REGISTER TO FALSETTO

Falsetto is used mostly in the lower male voices for effect only. As a vocal register, it can be used, however, to help access the thin edge of the vocal folds. I was able to observe Cornelius Reid in a master class, who advocated its incorporation into standard vocal strengthening exercises. For example, I have used the following exercise with some tenors who were having trouble with the extreme top of their voices.

1. Using a standard "yodel" allow the flip into falsetto.
2. Using this falsetto vocal sound add support.
3. Using supported falsetto gradually increase the intensity until the thin edge of the vocal folds are fully approximating and the singer is in full head voice. (This could be thought of as a version of the messa di voce starting in falsetto then moving into head register and back again into falsetto.) In my experience it is best used with proper abdominal support.

"Messa di voce" in upper register

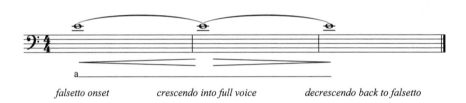

falsetto onset   crescendo into full voice   decrescendo back to falsetto

12. EXERCISES TO REDUCE JAW DEPENDENCY IN THE UPPER PASSAGGIO

One of the most common problems in dealing with the transition through the upper passaggio is the singer's dependency on the jaw opening, that is, in opening the jaw to accommodate the higher pitches. Singers who have inadequate abdominal support find themselves relying on the jaw to define the pitch. Without the appropriate engagement of the abdominal muscles, airflow may be inadequate, and the jaw ends up not just dropping open, but jamming open usually in its frontal position. I have developed the following exercise to correct this fault.

1. Sing a rising five-note major scale on the vowel /a/, beginning with the jaw open and starting 3 tones lower than the normal register pivot note. Sing the first 4 notes with the jaw open and then on note 5, close the jaw up and back about halfway. (This is effectively the opposite of what the singer has been used to.)

Soprano

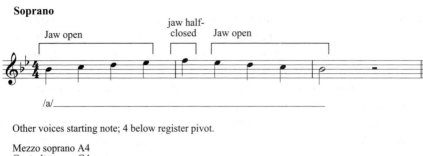

/a/_____

Other voices starting note; 4 below register pivot.

Mezzo soprano A4
Contralto   G4
Tenor   Bb3
Baritone   A3
Bass   F#3

2. Repeat, starting one semitone higher and closing the jaw on note 5.

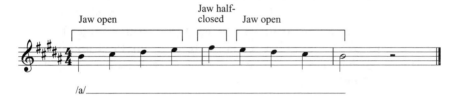

/a/_____

3. Repeat, starting one semitone higher and closing the jaw on note 4.

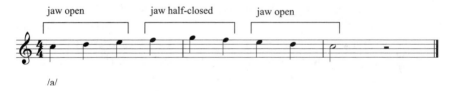

/a/

4. Repeat, starting one semitone higher and closing the jaw on note 4 and so on.

/a/_____

Repeat for two more semitones, reducing the jaw on the 3rd note.

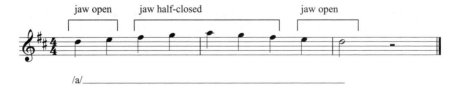

/a/_____

5. Sing the scales again but this time do not close the jaw; instead feel how loose the hinge feels (fingers can be used to monitor the temporomandibular joint, where no bulging should occur). The student also should pay attention to how much support is demanded by the voice when the jaw is loose, compared to when it is jammed.

6. For further affirmation, try the exercise on a rolled "r" which has a closed jaw position, and notice the workload, which automatically goes to the lower abdominal/pubic synthesis (LAPS). Then repeat step 5.

The next exercise set is useful for the upper passaggio in both male and female voices, and follows naturally from the previous exercise. I believe that it is very important not to have the tone "spread" in this area of the voice. Although the rolled "r" exercises can produce a perfect phonatory transition from thick vocal folds to thin vocal folds, it can be difficult for students to achieve this on vowels. Although many pedagogues use placement ideas to achieve focus, as a young singer, I personally had some bad experiences resulting from this method, and prefer to use physiologically based exercises to achieving this focus. Ironically, the end product feels "forward in placement."

1. Using a French /y/ sing a chromatic 5-note ascending and descending scale through the passaggio. Physiologically this vowel should produce a high-tongue/low-larynx setup which is advantageous in this area of the voice. It is likely that this vowel will produce the thin edge of the vocal folds rather than the thick edge as the tongue and lip position encourages laryngeal tilt.. Check with the thumb under the chin to make sure there is no tongue root contraction which would prevent effective tilting of the thyroid cartilage.

2. Sing the French /y/ scale, immediately followed by Italian /i/ matching the tongue and larynx tilt position as closely as possible.

Soprano

(sob) Fr/y/————————————————————————

3. Repeat with Italian vowels in turn, /e, a, o, u/

(sob) Fr/y/————————————————— i ————————————————
     /y/   e
     /y/   a
     /y/   o
     /y/   u

Table A–1. Table Showing Modification of Vowels for Upper Passagio Management.

Tongue setting	/i/	/e/	/a/	/o/	/u/
Larynx setting	French /y/	/a/	/o/	/u/	/u/

VOWEL MODIFICATION EXERCISE

Once a singer can negotiate the upper passaggio easily (and it should be easy!), there can be a final finessing of the sung vowel for the highest tones. I have noticed that my "dial-a-vowel" exercise produces a visible change in the vertical position of the larynx on most singers. I believe that there is subtle laryngeal setting for each of the 5 Italian vowels. I suggest that the singer think of the vowel one notch deeper than the one they are singing, that is, if they are singing /a/, they imagine they are going to sing /o/; this has the effect of keeping the throat slightly deeper. Then I suggest that while maintaining that throat sensation, they allow their tongue to sing the true vowel, namely /o/ in the throat, and /a/ in the mouth. For the /i/ vowel, I use the suggestion of the French /y/, the /e/ becomes /a/, the /a/, /o/, the /o/, /u/, and the /u/ remains itself because the larynx is already at its maximum depth.

Further reading should include *The Science of the Singing Voice*, by Johann Sundberg (1987, Northern Illinois University Press), and *Dynamics of the Singing Voice*, by Meribeth Bunch (1997, Springer-Verlag).

13. JAW TENSION

RATIONALE

In vocal literature, both pedagogical and scientific, there has been a plethora of instruction to singers to "open the jaw," "drop the jaw maximally," and "make space" with the jaw. The big problem with this sort of instruction is that many students translate it as a frontal opening which can easily turn into a "jamming open." Because of its muscular attachments the jaw has the capability of opening in two basic ways:

- Position 1. The jaw is allowed to fall open basically under the effects of gravity. In this opening the jaw opens down and slightly back and the muscles are minimally involved. The jaw feels loose.
- Position 2. The jaw displaces forward and down at the temporomandibular joint. This gives a large frontal opening of the jaw

which engages and tenses the muscles involved in opening (pterygoids) and also the floor of the mouth (geniohyoid and genioglossus particularly). The tension involved in this type 2 opening is counterproductive in classical singing. It has a detrimental effect on resonance as well as laryngeal and tongue position (see Figure 3–2).

Inappropriate tension in the jaw during singing can stem from a number of sources:

- General life tension (check for nocturnal teeth grinding, etc.)
- Inadequate or unsupported airflow
- TMJ dysfunction
- Malocclusions
- Misinformation during training (e.g., instructions to open the mouth as far as possible on certain vowels)
- Poor head-neck postural alignment
- Tongue tension
- Floor of mouth tension
- Articulatory deviations

In addition, confusion exists between the concept of phonetically "open vowels" and physiologically "open-mouth" vowels. Teachers and singers are not always clear about what is being sought. In classical singing the frontal opening of the jaw, which coincides with the jaw jutting and jamming forward and down from its hinge, is a vocal fault rather than a desired phonetic position for a sung vowel and can cause problems:

1. The space within the resonators can be compromised causing the tone to "white out."
2. The ability of the larynx to move freely in the neck can be restricted.
3. Open vowels will not match in quality with closed vowels.
4. The excursion of the jaw down and up slows the articulators giving the text a "chewed" sound.
5. Pitch scooping can occur.
6. Transition through the upper passaggio can be difficult and the top notes can sound blatant.
7. The jaw and tongue may not have independence of movement. This can result in the pitch changes becoming visible on the jaw. Also, the natural vibrato can be seen on the jaw and floor of mouth.
8. If the jaw is tight and jamming open, the in-breath may also be compromised with the head position distorted on inhalation.
9. As pitch rises, a jammed jaw may cause the head position and postural alignment to change, affecting resonance and articulation.

DEALING WITH JAW TENSION

1. Address head-neck postural alignment as previously discussed (see Chapter 3).
2. Appropriate airflow and abdominal support needs to be established. Accent Method is particularly valuable for this purpose (see Chapter 4).
3. Manual therapy to directly alleviate tension problems: This can be done by the student and teacher together, but if the problem is recalcitrant it is well worth getting help from a manual therapist, physiotherapist, or osteopath.
4. Exercises and maneuvers to be used in the studio:

   ■ Sing a sustained vowel on a midpitch and waggle the jaw up and down loosely.
   ■ Using the heel of the hands pull down on the masseter muscles lowering the jaw to position 1 opening (repeat 5 times).
   ■ Place thumbnail under upper incisors with knuckle braced onto the chin. Gently open the jaw with the knuckle preventing forward swing and sing glides on closed vowels followed by rolled "rrs."
   ■ Repeat glides and rolled "rrs" without thumb bracing, but keeping the jaw in position 1.
   ■ Sing scales up to the 9th on all vowels pausing on the top note and waggling the jaw up and down loosely. Monitoring the TMJ may be helpful.
   ■ Activate the "collar connection" by using a sob or giggle primal sound onset, then monitor the looseness of the jaw. *NOTE:* I have found that once the collar connection is engaged, it is much easier for the singer to loosen the jaw without a feeling of loss of control of their instrument.

Additional exercises are contained in Chapter 7 on articulation and can be used as necessary. For students who have significant jaw problems referral to a speech and language therapist is advised.

ENCOURAGING TONGUE AND JAW INDEPENDENCE

To discourage overuse of the jaw and encourage active use of the tongue:

1. Sing Italian arie antiche with pencil held lightly between the teeth.
2. Sing Italian arie antiche like a ventriloquist.
3. Sing Italian arie antiche with fingers monitoring in the groove between the pterygoid and masseter, but not using jaw opening at this stage.

4. Once the sensations of space at the back of the oropharynx are "in" then sing Italian arie antiche with loosely movable jaw while maintaining the same vocal posture. (*NOTE:* Considerable demands will automatically be made on airflow and support.)

Appendix 2

CORE CAPABILITIES FOR TEACHERS AND SINGERS

Marilyn McCarthy

These dictionaries of Core Capabilities have been developed in an attempt to identify and describe those things that make the difference between good and excellent performance for singers and their teachers. Capabilities are defined as *the abilities that enable people to act skillfully and in congruence with inner qualities and values in a situation and context*. This work will be continually improved and should be treated as a working document. The definitions remain the same for teachers and singers, but the behavioral descriptions differ.

The information in these dictionaries has been gathered, synthesized, and distilled from many sources. Although the definitions are identical for singers and teachers, the example behaviors change to reflect their differing roles and responsibilities. Please note that the behaviors represent examples only, and are not intended to be a full description.

Acknowledgments and thanks to Janice Chapman and John Chapman who spent countless hours discriminating and discussing capabilities and behaviors; the singers/teachers from the studio who contributed generously; and especially to the Department of Primary Industries and Resources South Australia (PIRSA) who encouraged me in 2001 to develop a Capabilities Dictionary which is now used to describe jobs, recruit, and conduct performance management conversations across the organization. This dictionary has influenced the development of the framework used here.

CORE CAPABILITIES FOR SINGERS

Capabilities—Definition	Behavioral Description
Personal Soundness	
Self-Awareness Conscious of self as a physical, mental, emotional, and spiritual being; aware of how beliefs, attitudes, feeling states, and ways of acting affect others in different situations.	*Reflects on own behavior; explores and understands how cultural and personal values and attitudes shape decisions; articulates own world-view and respects the different views of others; sensitive and responsive to the impact of self on others.*
Ongoing Learner Actively seeking to understand personal and professional strengths and weaknesses; employing a range of approaches to improve and develop abilities.	*Open to the input of others and responsive to feedback about self and performance; interested in new ideas and approaches; actively tests limitations; engages coaches/mentors for new areas of development; takes risks in extending abilities and applying knowledge/skills to new settings; adapts own learning style to different situations; learns from experience; takes advice from others and evaluates for usefulness.*
Emotional Intelligence Demonstrating awareness of feelings and how they affect performance; using emotional energy as resources to enhance performance.	*Broadens and deepens the range and access to emotional resources; changes emotional states which negatively impact on life and performance; develops awareness of, and skills in expressing emotional resources in vocal expression; willing to engage with, and express the emotional quality of the music; aware of the link between body/feelings and voice quality.*
Resilience Demonstrating ego-strength to maintain presence in challenging situations; calling on inner resources to recover from setbacks, maintaining equilibrium and performance under pressure.	*Maintains a strong sense of self in difficult/varied situations; maintains optimistic orientation; picks up after setbacks; sees setbacks as due to manageable circumstances rather than personal flaws; develops and uses strategies to deal with criticism from self, management, media, and audience; develops and draws on positive/supportive qualities and emotional strengths to act as buffer.*

Risk-Taking Knowing when and how to take risks that enhance personal growth and career development.	*Demonstrates adventurous and daring attitude in going beyond comfort zone; aware of the costs and benefits in taking risks; confronts limiting beliefs and self-image; takes considered risks that extend development and professional experience; knows when to actively avoid risks which may be damaging to self or career.*
Self-confidence; Self-assurance Self-assured, holding deep belief in own potential and musical ability, and in ability to learn and deal with new situations.	*Unshakable confidence in musical ability; projects an air of being at ease which generates confidence in audience; consciously supports and encourages self to develop confidence; monitors and actively builds belief in ability to achieve and to overcome obstacles; assertive in setting boundaries and limits.*
Courage Acting bravely and purposefully in the face of uncertainty and fear.	*Recognizes fear or uncertainty in self; once chosen, acts decisively; learns and employs strategies to deal with fear; employs positive qualities and emotions to act as buffer.*
Drive/Determination Pursuing goals with enthusiasm and focus; maintaining energy and intention in the face of obstacles.	*Draws on passion to sustain drive; single-minded in concentrating over long periods; demonstrates capacity for hard work; keeps eye on the vision to sustain energy and focus; shows drive and strength of will and resolve, even when faint-hearted; persistent in following through to a conclusion; continually strives for highest potential; makes personal sacrifices to achieve career success/satisfaction.*
Self-direction/Self-control Demonstrating an inner locus of control in decision-making over time, under pressure, and in a variety of situations.	*Demonstrates an attitude of self-sufficiency; uses initiative to identify opportunities and anticipate problems; seeks the relevant perspectives and takes responsibility for choices and decision; takes ownership and responsibility for decisions and the repercussions.*

311

Capabilities—Definition

Behavioral Description

Mastery

Artistry
Using presence, skill. and communication to awaken, shape, and transform the experience of the audience.

Studies and applies understanding of the musical and cultural style to the music; generates confidence in the audience; captures the imagination and feelings of the audience; excites a range of responses in the audience which engage the imagination; moves people on a range of levels; transports the audience from the mundane into other realms and possibilities.

Musicality
Demonstrating a unique quality of sound, intuiting and conveying the style and intent of the composer; conveying the essence of the music.

Engages the audience with the affective nature of the music; shows insight into the expressive intention of the composer; steps aside from personal issues, external demands, and judgments to enter the music and the moment fully; demonstrates an unerring memory for the music; interprets and renders the composers intentions with integrity.

Performance Skills
Accessing a range of personal qualities and dramatic skills to communicate the roles and styles required for a performance.

Remains engaged with the character; enters the drama and the moment fully; rises to the occasion and thrives in the public arena; demonstrates sensitivity to others and ability to work collaboratively to enhance the whole.

Professional and Technical Expertise

Vocal Technical Expertise
Demonstrating the vocal technical knowledge and the specific skills relevant to the task of singing.

Understands how the voice works and how to produce it consistently in different circumstances; demonstrates masterful grasp of principles and technical frameworks that underpin voice production; sustains vocal technique when touring, under personal pressure, and in difficult circumstances; demonstrates excellent grasp of languages and how to sing them; shows high levels of dedication and hard work in learning and refining new material and new roles.

Physical Awareness/Fitness Demonstrating body awareness and fitness that sustains high performance.	*Demonstrates educated awareness of and connection with the body as an instrument in the act of singing; sensitive to the pressures of performance on the body; rests when appropriate; maintains a fitness program that supports high performance.*
Industry Knowledge Keeping up to date with major issues and trends in the industry; understanding the implications for the industry and for the career.	*Develops and maintains networks with key stakeholders and associations, and uses information to assist in decision-making; reads widely to maintain awareness of changes in the industry.*
Career-focused Maintaining dedicated focus of activity to achieve goals.	*Places high priority on career; enlists the support of primary partners; develops and communicates long-term vision; makes flexible goals and plans; when required, makes tough decisions to achieve goals; seeks professional assistance from others to support direction.*
Communication	
Presentation Skills Preparing and presenting self, information, and ideas to individuals or groups in an articulate, appropriate, and confident manner.	*Highly professional in making presentations and auditioning; adapts presentation to make impact in particular situations; conveys ideas clearly and in a way which is relevant and able to be understood by the audience.*
Building and Maintaining Relationships Developing and maintaining constructive collaborative working relationships.	*Develops rapport with wide range of people; authentic and open in dealing with colleagues; recognizes and acknowledges the contributions of others; engages in collaborating with others for mutual benefit; actively develops support networks; takes time to know and link with key players in different facets of the industry.*

Capabilities—Definition	Behavioral Description
Conceptual/Thinking Skills	
Creativity/Innovation Using imagination and inventiveness to develop or bring forth new artistic or intellectual approaches; introducing new ways and changes to established processes or procedures.	*Uses imagination to explore and develop new roles and approaches to the work; takes artistic and intellectual risks; trusts intuition and inspiration; supports self in the process; invents and tests novel ideas and approaches for their value; demonstrates sensitivity to the cultural and musical implications of innovation; manages the repercussions of change.*
Intuition Direct knowing or sensing something not obvious or evident using only rational processes; perceptive insight; an impression.	*Recognizes and uses "gut feel" as instincts or "knowings" to make decisions; reads the atmosphere in a situation and senses emerging issues; discriminates between intuitive hunches and perceptions and personal projections; protects intuition by knowing when to disclose and when to hold back; when disclosing, backs intuition with logical or reasonable information.*
Researching and Analyzing Investigating and gathering information from formal and informal sources about a range of issues and topics; using critical thinking to assess information, perceive implications, and make sound judgments.	*Researches issues pertinent to musical and artistic roles; seeks expertise from specialized fields when appropriate; applies information to own musical and artistic performance.*

CORE CAPABILITIES FOR TEACHERS

Capabilities—Definition	Behavioral Description
Personal Soundness	
Self-awareness Conscious of self as a physical, mental, emotional, and spiritual being; aware of how beliefs, attitudes, feeling states, and ways of acting affect others in different situations.	Questions and actively reflects on behavior; checks out the impact of self on others; examines and develops comfort with own life story and relationship with voice; is clear about personal preferences and issues and does not project them into the teaching-learning partnership; aware of how cultural and personal values and attitudes shape biases and views of self and others; clarifies and articulates own world-view and respects the different views of others; aware of own learning style and how this impacts on the teaching-learning partnership.
Ongoing Learner Actively seeking to understand personal and professional strengths and weaknesses; employing a range of approaches to improve and develop abilities.	Actively seeks feedback about self and performance; interested in new ideas and approaches; engages coaches/mentors for new areas of development; takes risks in extending abilities and applying knowledge/skills to teaching individuals and groups.
Emotional Intelligence Demonstrating awareness of feelings and how they affect learning and performance; using emotional energy as resources to enhance performance and guide actions.	Recognizes and controls own emotions; reads and responds appropriately to the emotional climate in situations; understands the nature and role of feelings in voice production; raises awareness and encourages ownership of feelings in students; educates and develops the capacity to utilize feelings as resources for artistic and musical expression; comfortable with intimate personal exchange which is relevant to the teaching-learning partnership; knows how to listen deeply and respond to strong feelings; introduces positive thinking to shift mood; monitors own feelings in the situation and declares skillfully and appropriately to enhance learning; employs playfulness in exchanges; can pace self through stress and challenging situations; is optimistic in outlook.

Capabilities—Definition	Behavioral Description
Flexibility Adapting approach to meet the needs of a variety of people and situations.	*Recognizes when mindsets are stuck and changes approach; shifts roles easily to respond appropriately to the same person/people in different situations, for example, as teacher; friend; professional colleague; identifies student's learning preference, for example, kinesthetic, visual, auditory and adapts teaching style to meet varied learning needs; remains present to each situation and is able to respond to the unexpected.*
Motivation Fostering, enhancing, and inspiring energy and commitment that impel toward a course of action.	*Leads, guides, and enthuses others; expresses excitement and passion about own work; recognizes and utilizes the energy and passion of the student; recognizes and rewards achievement; enhances and works with the motivating energies of students; maintains a focus on empowerment and develops confidence in developing self-direction.*
Mastery	
Artistry Using presence, skill, and communication to awaken, shape, and transform the experience of the audience.	*Uses own experience and artistry to engage the Inner Singer and Creative Artist in expressing the essence of the music/role; is skilful in using metaphor and visual imagery to enhance artistic expression; engages the singer's imagination in appreciating and interpreting the music/role; provides feedback which is objective and which mirrors the impact of the singer's performance on self.*
Musicality Understanding and demonstrating a unique quality of sound, intuiting and conveying the style and intent of the composer; the essence of the music.	*Demonstrates sound understanding of musical intent and cultural styles; builds musical development on a sound vocal technique; coaches skilfully; encourages students to express the heart and essence of the music; demonstrates how to sing languages; appreciates and critically examines composer's intentions; provides perceptive, behavioral, and well-targeted feedback to students about musicality.*

© Marilyn McCarthy 2005

Performance Skills
Accessing a range of personal qualities and dramatic skills to communicate the roles and styles required for a performance.

Assists singer to maintain connection with emotional intent; encourages singers to develop skills by seeking appropriate courses and coaching; draws on own performing skills and shares these with student; builds confidence in student; attends student performances to evaluate the progress and identify areas needing further development.

Professional/Technical Expertise

Vocal Technical Expertise
Demonstrating the vocal technical knowledge and the specific skills relevant to the task of singing.

Demonstrates thorough knowledge about the relationship between the physical, mental, emotional, and spiritual resources, and vocal performance; applies a wide range of skills and approaches to bring about secure vocal function and development; models for the student; demonstrates sound knowledge in the physiology of voice; explains in a way which is easily understood by the listener.

Holistic Approach
Working with the whole person and the relationship between the physical, mental, emotional, and spiritual dimensions to develop singing.

Appreciates how the person is greater than the sum of the parts and looks to bring that out; understands when it is appropriate to engage and address different levels (the Inner Singer, the Creative Artist, the Master Technician, etc,) and when to facilitate integrative processes; uses a range of communication skills including empathy and deep listening to convey understanding; willing to be authentic with the student while maintaining objectivity and expertise; maintains the long view of the person and their potential while working with issues in the present moment; recognizes when out of their depth and acknowledges/refers.

Consulting Skills
Using specialist knowledge and expertise to identify issues and problems and develop jointly satisfying solutions.

Clarifies norms and roles, and facilitates agreement about purposes and goals for the consultation; quick to grasp and assess situations and provide objective feedback; provides information and advice which empowers the singer's decision- making processes; remains engaged at a personal level while maintaining objectivity and clear thinking; works together with client/singer to develop mutually agreeable solutions.

Capabilities—Definition	Behavioral Description
Integrity/Ethical Behavior Behaving according to the values and ethical principles of the field; honoring trust and demonstrating high levels of confidentiality.	*Continually clarifies and evolves agreements about norms guiding the partnership; respects personal and professional boundaries; creates an environment in which singers feel safe to participate; maintains strict confidentiality; honours contracts and agreements.*
Theory into Practice Translating, communicating, and demonstrating theory in a way which makes sense and can be easily adopted into practice by the learner.	*Clearly articulates core principles, coherent concepts, and frameworks at relevant times in the learning process; takes small and measured steps; uses relevant metaphor to stimulate imagination; continually checks directions and understanding with students; coaches and demonstrates to connect theory with bodylmind, feelings and intuition; develops objectivity and self-assessment skills in the student.*
Industry Knowledge Keeping up to date and understanding the implications of major trends and developments for the industry and for the careers of singers.	*Builds and utilizes networks for referral and to gain information and contacts which enhance prospects for students; reads widely to maintain awareness of issues and trends.*
Communication	
Communicating Communicating effectively with others; exchanging information and ideas in ways which facilitates shared understanding.	*Communicates love of music and singing; listens carefully and deeply, clarifies content and communicates understanding of the other's viewpoint; checks out perceptions and experience of the student; uses a range of approaches to present views, for example, visual, kinesthetic, conceptual, and factual information.*

Facilitating Change
Leading people through the change process toward learning, resolution, and growth.

Demonstrates thorough knowledge of adult learning principles and diverse learning styles; astute in judging readiness for change; picks the right time and situation; monitors and works with the individual's learning style; engages whole person (body, mind, feelings, and soul) in the change process; stimulates the imagination to extend student; skilled in providing accurate, behavioral feedback which enables recognition of the need for change; deals with barriers to change; knows when to challenge and when to support; courageous in confronting stuckness; reinforces positive steps in the change process; invites honest response.

Developmental Approach
Holding an overview of the stage of development in the change process and continuing to foster growth.

Holds an overview of the stage of development in the change process; sees and communicates long-term possibilities while maintaining focus on developing microskills appropriate to the level; identifies a pathway for change which is appropriate for the stage of development; breaks the learning down into achievable bits; recognizes right moment to introduce new directions; maintains an orientation toward empowering student.

Relationship-Building and Maintaining

Relationship-Building and Maintaining
Developing and maintaining constructive collaborative working relationships with others.

Uses high-level empathic skills to develop rapport and trust with students; willing to build authentic communication by sharing from own experience; demonstrates deep respect for the student; clarifies boundaries, roles, and responsibilities in the relationship; knows when to raise relationship issues, when to disclose own issues affecting the relationship, and when to stand aside and maintain a focus on the work; sensitive in addressing personal/political issues that affect the singer's potential opportunities (e.g., race, gender, weight).

Conceptual—Thinking Skills

Capabilities—Definition	Behavioral Description
Creativity/Innovation Using imagination and inventiveness to develop or bring forth new artistic or intellectual approaches; introducing new ways and changes to evolve established processes or procedures.	*Takes artistic and intellectual risks; shows excitement and energy in exploring the new; sees connections, patterns, and possibilities between unlikely elements; trusts intuition and inspiration; supports self in the process; recognizes when old ways don't work; uses creative ways to find new solutions.*
Intuition Direct knowing or sensing something not obvious or evident using only rational processes; perceptive insight; an impression.	*Recognizes and uses "gut feel" as instincts or "knowing" to make decisions; reads the atmosphere in a situation and senses emerging issues; knows when to disclose intuition and when to hold back; tests intuition for validity/acceptability in complex situations; backs intuition with logical or reasonable information; discriminates between intuitive hunches and perceptions and personal projections.*
Researching and Analyzing Investigating and gathering information from a range of sources; using critical thinking to assess and examine issues.	*Actively uses networks to gather and source information; reviews a range of literature and other media; uses critical thinking and analysis to select relevant information; makes sound decisions based on assessment of critical factors and desired outcomes.*
Problem-Solving Identifying and describing problems; illuminating the elements and devising strategies for resolution.	*Employs rational and lateral thinking to seek the source of the problem; carefully examines all contributing factors; remembers information about singer that may impact on problem; makes sense of immediate problem in terms of a wider conceptual scheme; develops and tests solutions with students to enhance successful outcomes thinking.*

BIBLIOGRAPHY

Cripe, E. J., & Mansfield, R. S. (2002). *The value-added employee.* London, UK: Butterworth-Heinemann.

Goleman, D. (1995). *Emotional intelligence. Why it can matter more than IQ.* London, UK: Bloomsbury.

Goleman, D. (1998). *Working with emotional intelligence.* London, UK: Bantam Books.

Mindell, A. (1995). *Metaskills: The spiritual art of therapy.* Portland, OR: Lao Tse Press.

Mindell, A. (1992). *Leader as martial artist.* Portland OR: Lao Tse Press.

Mindell, A. (1995). *Sitting in the fire.* Portland OR: Lao Tse Press.

Seligman, M. E. P. (2002). *Authentic happiness.* Sydney, Australia: Random House.

ADDITIONAL RESOURCES

31 core competencies explained. Available from: http://www.workforce.com

The Consortium for Research on Emotional Intelligence in Organisations. *The emotional competence framework.* Available from: http://www.eiconsortium .org

Appendix 3

PRIORITIES IN DEVELOPING THE YOUNG ADULT CLASSICAL SINGER AT MUSIC COLLEGE

Janice Chapman

The conservatoire model for the teaching of the young adult classical singer has evolved and been in use for 200 or more years. The main "first study" module of the 3- or 4-year degree courses remains the 1-hour (or in some cases 90-minute) weekly one-to-one lesson with a singing teacher. This is essential to the development of the potential solo artist and is the preferred way of teaching across all musical instruments including voice.

Young instrumentalists normally enter music colleges with grade 8 distinctions in their chosen field. Singers come with a wide variety of talent, achievement, and potential, but they have one thing in common—their instrument and their technique are largely undeveloped. Although much singing may have been enjoyed during their school years, it is generally accepted that serious singing lessons begin only after puberty has allowed the vocal instrument to reach a stable condition.

When singers audition for college places, they usually are within the 18 to 21 age range, and they only have a 1 in 10 chance of succeeding, as the competition is fierce. They will have in their "bag of goodies" some of the following attributes:

- A good voice
- Instinct for sining
- Musicality
- Acceptable level of musicianship skills (A levels, grade 8, etc.)
- Intelligences, including aspects of IQ and EQ
- Languages (and/or a good ear for language)
- Love of the vocal arts
- An ability to work very hard and to concentrate
- Innate communication skills
- A body type that is compatible with the voice type
- Kinesthetic awareness.

In my opinion, the traditional mode of teaching often falls down when it fails to take into account the need to develop the student's instrument. The mere copying of a demonstrated sound often sends confusing and mixed messages to students who may be unable to understand how to adjust their vocal function to match the model. Imagery is the common parlance, and this can be highly effective, especially when the nuts and bolts of the mechanism are fully understood by the teacher. The fundamental framework underpinning the approach is detailed theoretical understanding of the vocal function, anatomy, and physiology. Then the craft of teaching can include imagery and be highly effective. The danger comes when imagery is used without being founded on factual knowledge. For example, when a singing teacher suggests to a student that they "need more space" they might use an image of "swallowing a hot potato." Unfortunately, this leads to tongue root and pharyngeal constriction which actually can close rather than open space. From endoscopic evidence it is clear that the space the singer is trying to open is not in the mouth itself but farther back and down in the oro- and laryngopharynx.

WHAT ARE THE PRIORITIES FOR SINGERS IN THE FIRST YEAR OF MUSIC COLLEGE? A QUESTION OF TIMING

- An awareness of the body as the instrument
- A sound vocal technique based on anatomical and kinesthetic experiential understanding, leading to the incremental building of a viable instrument

■ Stamina, which builds over the entire 4 years of a course—there is a muscular coordination and strength aspect, requiring appropriate exercises, and repetitions of these, to create good habits. Repertoire selection must also be graded for development value for each student

Figure A3-1 shows my pedagogical model with the core components at the center. I think that this is where singers should begin their vocal development.

SUGGESTED IDEAL CURRICULUM (STARING WITH THE CORE)

In the first year, useful classes addressing core capabilities include:

■ Singing lessons: 45 minutes twice weekly (primal sound access, technique-building)

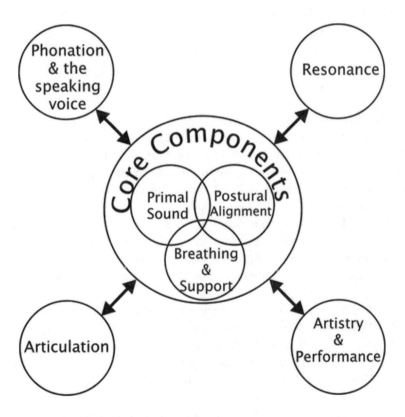

Figure A3–1. Pedagogical model.

- Instruction in vocal anatomy, physiology, and function, including vocal health
- Alexander technique, Feldenkrais, Pilates, dance, T'ai Chi, movement skills, and so forth.
- Musical skill development: aural, keyboard, history of music, harmoy, and so forth.
- Personal performance development. Work helping their centering, concentration, confidence, and so forth, which can include group workshops, acting exercises, and so forth.
- Languages: basic Italian and English only at this stage
- Continuous assessment.

INAPPROPRIATE OR SOMETIMES EVEN COUNTERPRODUCTIVE DURING THE FIRST YEAR, BUT VALUABLE AT A LATER STAGE

- Masses of repertoire
- Lots of coaching on style and finesse
- Classes in German, French, Spanish, Russian, and Czech
- Examinations.

WHY?

- Changing things in the body takes time. Muscles are "stupid" and respond to low-impact repetitive exercises.
- Singers' way of learning is best served by an incremental approach. Overloading the brain and creating pressure to achieve on multiple levels distract from the core tasks of instrument-building.
- The Italian language was the basis on which Western classical singing evolved via "bel canto," and it is widely accepted as being the most singer-friendly. Generally speaking, German, Russian, French, Spanish, and Czech present more problems technically at the outset.
- The achievement of a viable working technique allows natural expression of musical and stylistic artistry to evolve, which is the desirable end product. Without a technique, artistry is always compromised. This is why coaching for artistry comes at a later stage.
- The constant need for students to prepare new and finessed repertoire for exams detracts from vocal progress. Continuous assessment of progress by the Singing Teacher and Head of Department is a better way at this stage.

ARE WE MEETING THE STUDENTS' NEEDS?

- Yes and no . . .
- Most students receive singing lessons weekly; however, the teaching they encounter can be very variable, as the teachers themselves have a variety of backgrounds and skills and different approaches to teaching.
- All colleges provide movement-type classes.
- Very few colleges introduce lectures in vocal anatomy, physiology, function, health, and acoustics.
- All colleges provide for languages, musical skills, performance skills, and so forth.

WHO ARE THE TEACHERS?

- Performer/Teacher: Active professional singers who combine performing and teaching
- Retired Singers: Professionals who take up teaching at the end of their performance career (this is the largest group)
- Coach/Teacher: Generally a pianist by training who has had experience being a vocal repertoire coach and has subsequently taken on the role of singing teacher, but who has never been a singer themselves
- Nonperformer/Teacher: Trained to be a singer but turned to teaching as a professional pathway choice. This includes the young career teachers, who may have trained as singer/teachers, possibly acting as an apprentice to a senior teacher
- Experienced Teachers from the private sector: Freelance or coming from the secondary school system, these are teachers who have achieved a good reputation before being invited to join the staff at a conservatoire.

STRENGTHS AND WEAKNESSES OF THE EXISTING SYSTEM

- Each of these kinds of staff brings different skills and values to a department. Drawing on the various talents of the staff and using them in creative and sensitive ways will serve the best interests of the students. Colleges permit students to change teachers during their training, and this can be at the instigation of either the student or the teacher. It can be a question of timing, that is, the right sort of skills and the right sort of teacher in the right order.

- Where there are compatible pedagogical philosophies within a department, innovations in this area may include open studio policy with the possibility of team teaching.
- In many professions ongoing education and development to ensure that practitioners are up to date is a requirement. In cultivation of best practice, colleges may be strengthened by expecting evidence of professional development from their staff.
- Being a great performer does not automatically translate to being a fine teacher. Teaching represents a shift of profession and requires additional training.
- Being a fine pianist and musician with experience of operatic or other vocal repertoire (but with no personal singing experience), does not automatically enable a teacher to create a vocal technique, especially for a first-year student.
- Without performing experience, a trained teacher may not have understanding of the demands made on singers when put into a performing environment.

PROFESSIONAL DEVELOPMENT OPPORTUNITIES AT PRESENT

The British Voice Association (BVA) has been running courses and seminars for over 20 years, which include training in the Estill Model, Accent Method, Vocal Profile Analysis, Foundations of the Singing Voice with the City Literary Institute, London, and many more. Meribeth Bunch-Dayme ran a series of courses on vocal anatomy and physiology. The Association of Teachers of Singing more recently has included scientific and academic presentations at is conferences and seminars and runs a regular residential summer program of teacher training. The BVA has mounted a very successful and ongoing incursion into the institutions with its "Road Show," but to date, although students are very enthusiastic, it is rare for members of the vocal staff to attend.

CONTINUING PROFESSIONAL DEVELOPMENT— REASONS WHY THIS MATTERS

Pedagogy based on physiology/anatomy/function/acoustics, and provable scientific information is essential in the 21st century. In the past, singing teaching was transmitted through intuitive, experiential, and experimental methodology based on subjective sensations, often using unrealistic imagery. But prior to the development of fiberoptics and endoscopy, this was all that was available. Now, when reality-based imagery is used, it changes and enhances the singers' learning potential, and the haphazardness is reduced.

Attendance at the various courses, seminars, and conferences by members of vocal faculties from within the tertiary system has been disappointing and sparse. It should be pointed out that students have access to current information via the Internet, are doing their own research, and are demanding more from teachers. Student-led education is the modern paradigm, and teachers need to catch up and keep up.

HOPES AND SOME SUGGESTIONS FOR THE FUTURE

- Enquiry and review procedures. At present there are no requirements for teachers of singing to attain certification or accreditation. We need to move toward the national accreditation of singing teachers, especially those teaching at an elite tertiary level.
- Questionnaires to former students. Where are they now, and how successful has the system been in the past? What is their opinion on how it could improve?
- College managements need to set and implement new benchmarks for the recruitment and in-service training of their vocal staff. All new staff could be offered a mandatory training package in fundamentals of the singing voice.
- Present remuneration levels are unrealistic. There should be parity with the "going rate" for quality singing lessons in the private sector compared with those in the tertiary sector. (Often, private teaching is at double the hourly rate.) Could continuing professional development be linked to pay incentives?

IN CONCLUSION

- Putting the student's needs centrally to the course structure means we should consider the first year as a voice and technique-building period. This could be designated a "foundation course" for the special requirements of the singing voice. Colleges and conservatoires would possibly need to agree to a common strategy. At the end of the foundation year, singers could be put into B.Mus 1 or accelerated to B.Mus 2 according to their development and their needs.
- Teachers of singing need in-service training, and an attitude toward continuing professional development, which encourages them to embrace new and exciting information suitable for the 21st century while retaining the heritage of artistry on which the profession relies.

Acknowledgments

This plenary lecture was given at the "Choice for Voice" Conference, British Voice Association at the Royal Academy of Music, London, 15 July 2010.

Declaration of Interest

The author reported no conflict of interest. The author alone was responsible for the content and writing of the paper.

Source

INDEX

Exercises *(continued)*
  soft palate, 297–298
  staccato, 295
  tenors transition exercises,
    300–301
  tidal movement practice, 274–275
  tongue aerobics, 289
  tongue/jaw independence
    encouragement, 307–308
  tongue release, 288–289
  tongue-root tension monitoring,
    291
  tongue thrust, 290
  tongue twisters, 290–291
  ultimate release for backed tongue:
    anti-gag tongue pull, 293
  vocal fry use, 284
  vowel legato, 287–288
  vowel modification, 305
  yodel, 296

F

Feldenkrais, Moshe, 23
Feldenkrais method, 34, 36
  body alignment, 44

G

Gould, Wilbur (Jim), 191
Gym programs
  cautions, 68
  free out-breath for resistance
    activities, 68

H

Harris, Sara and Dinah, 50
Hearing
  in an enclosure, 236, 238
  brain and singing, 239–241
  in the head, 238–239
  language and singing, 241–244
  of oneself, 235–236
    singer's formant, 237
  pitch, singing/speaking voice,
    234–235
Henrich, Nathalie, 70

Holistic aspects. *See also* Primal
  sound
  case studies
    Barry, inexperienced overbooked
      baritone, 6–7
    Valerie, soprano student, seeking
      to add classical to variety of
      other styles, 12
  Discover Your Voice (Brown), 4
  My Story: Janice Chapman, 4–6
  overview, 3–4
  "Patterns of Breath Support in
    Projection of the Singing
    Voice" (Thorpe et al.), 6
  "Primal Singing—Making
    Connections" (Chapman), 4
  singer as walking musical
    instrument, 4
  singing and need to survive, 4
Howard, David, 71

I

Incremental aspects
  developing functional components
    before combining, 10
  efficient learning of skills platform,
    11
  muscle memory timing, 11
  as natural reinforcement process, 11

L

Lamperti, Francesco (1813–1892)
  lutte vocale (appoggio), 42
Lieberman, Jacob, 33–35

M

Manual therapy, 34
Massage therapy, 36
The Mechanism and the Technic
  (William Vennard/Carl
  Fischer), 262
Models
  linear, first form, 12
  nucleus/satellite, 13–14
  rationale for using, 13–14